The Wars of the Maccabees

The Wars of the Maccabees

The Jewish Struggle for Freedom, 167–37 BC

John D. Grainger

First published in Great Britain in 2012 by
Pen & Sword Books Ltd
47 Church Street
Barnsley
South Yorkshire
S70 2AS

Copyright © John D. Grainger 2012

ISBN 978-1-84884-475-9

The right of John D. Grainger to be identified as Author of this Work has been asserted by him in accordance with the Copyright, Designs and Patents Act 1988.

A CIP catalogue record for this book is available from the British Library.

All rights reserved. No part of this book may be reproduced or transmitted in any form or by any means, electronic or mechanical including photocopying, recording or by any information storage and retrieval system, without permission from the Publisher in writing.

Typeset in 11pt Ehrhardt by
Mac Style, Beverley, E. Yorkshire

Printed and bound in the UK by CPI Group (UK) Ltd, Croydon, CR0 4YY

Pen & Sword Books Ltd incorporates the Imprints of Pen & Sword Aviation, Pen & Sword Family History, Pen & Sword Maritime, Pen & Sword Military, Pen & Sword Discovery, Wharncliffe Local History, Wharncliffe True Crime, Wharncliffe Transport, Pen & Sword Select, Pen & Sword Military Classics, Leo Cooper, The Praetorian Press, Remember When, Seaforth Publishing and Frontline Publishing.

For a complete list of Pen & Sword titles please contact
PEN & SWORD BOOKS LIMITED
47 Church Street, Barnsley, South Yorkshire, S70 2AS, England
E-mail: enquiries@pen-and-sword.co.uk
Website: www.pen-and-sword.co.uk

Contents

List of Illustrations vii
List of Maps viii
Maps ix
Genealogical Tables xiii
Abbreviations xvi
Introduction xvii

Chapter 1: The Dispute 1

Chapter 2: Terrorism and Guerrilla War 9

Chapter 3: Victories 17

Chapter 4: The Beginnings of Imperialism 27

Chapter 5: Defeat 39

Chapter 6: Achieving Independence 51

Chapter 7: The Defence of Independence 67

Chapter 8: Early Conquests 77

Chapter 9: The Samarian War 85

Chapter 10: Internal Upheavals and the Ptolemaic War 93

Chapter 11: Gadora and Gaza 101

Chapter 12: War in the East 109

Chapter 13: The First Civil War 113

Chapter 14: The Second Eastern War 119

Chapter 15: A War for Damascus 131

Chapter 16: The Second Civil War 135

Chapter 17: The First Roman War 143

Chapter 18: The Second Roman War 149

Chapter 19: The Parthian War – and Herod 157

Chapter 20: Conclusion: a Belligerent Dynasty 165

Notes 167
Bibliography 181
Index 185

List of Illustrations

All photographs are copyright of the author

Competing religions
1. Petra – the High Place
2. Panias – the Cave
3. Philadelphia – Temple of Zeus

Hellenization
4. Caesarea – the Cardo
5. Caesarea – the Palace
6. Caesarea – the Bathing Pool

Battles
7. Lachish and the way to Beth Zur
8. Marisa – the elephant
9. Hazor
10. Hamath Tiberias
11. Skythopolis
12. Sepphoris – the Nehovot Valley

Jewish expansion
13. Iraq el-Amir
14. The Yarmuk valley
15. Korazim – the Synagogue
16. Korazim – the Synagogue
17. Korazim – Olive Press
18. Umm er-Rasas – Mosaic of Gadora
19. Gamla

Maps

List of Maps
1. Judaea: land, neighbours and cities ix
2. Judah Maccabee's wars x
3. The Trans-Jordan lands xi
4. Alexander Iannai's Kingdom; Pompey's Reduction xii

Map 1: Judaea: land, neighbours and cities.

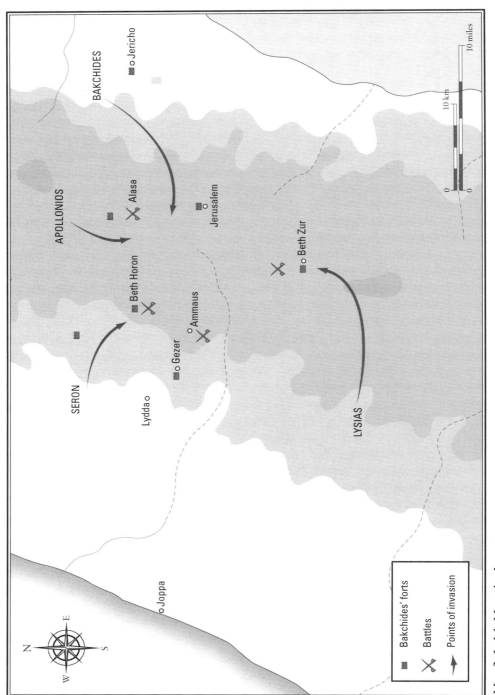

Map 2: Judah Maccabee's wars.

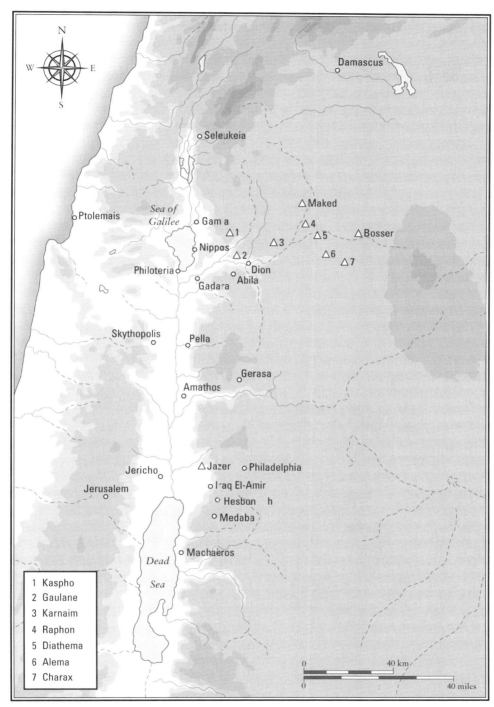

Map 3: The Trans-Jordan lands.

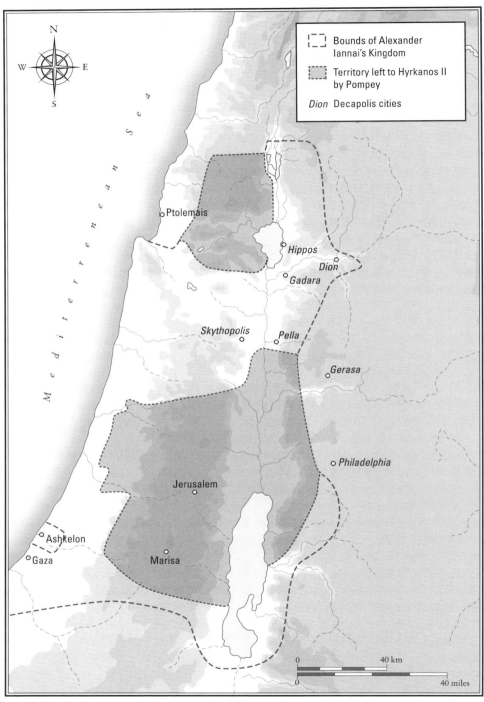

Map 4: Alexander Iannai's Kingdom; Pompey's Reduction.

Genealogical Tables

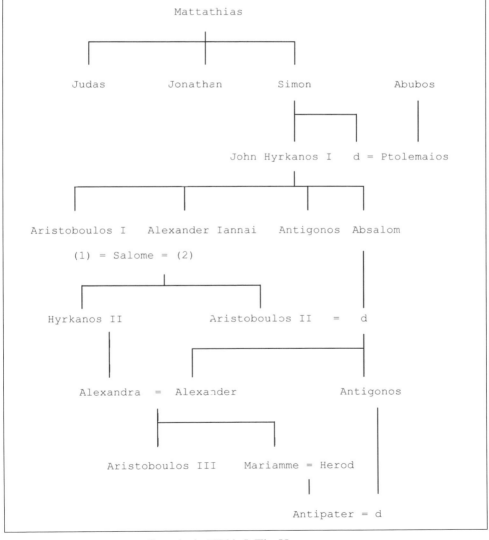

Genealogical Table I: The Hasmoneans.

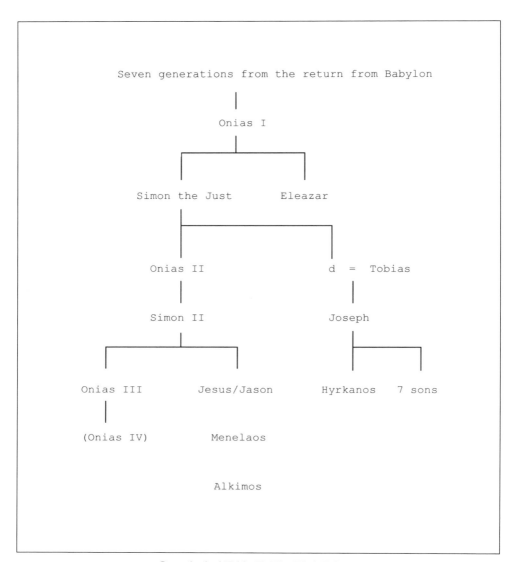

Genealogical Table II: The High Priests.

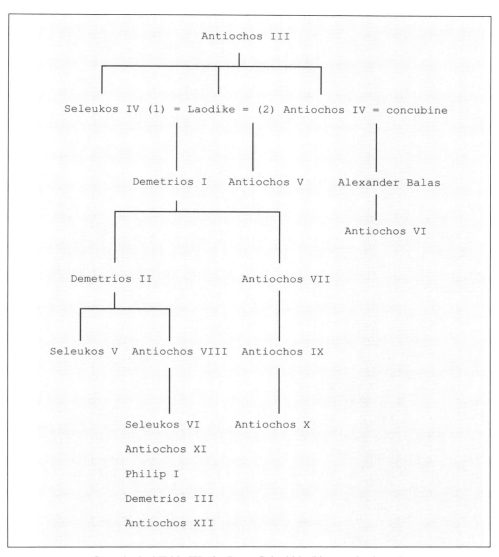

Genealogical Table III: the Later Seleukids (kings only shown).

Abbreviations

App. – Appian
Arav. – R. Arav, *Hellenistic Palestine, Settlement Patterns and City Planning, 337–31 BCE*, British Archaeological Reports, International Series 485, Oxford 1989
Bar-Kochva, *Judas* – B. Bar-Kochva, *Judas Maccabaeus*, Cambridge 1989
Eshel – H. Eshel, *The Dead Sea Scrolls and the Hasmonaean State*, Jerusalem 2008
Grainger, *Syrian Wars* – J.D. Grainger, *The Syrian Wars*, Leiden 2010
Hengel – M. Hengel, *Judaism and Hellenism*, trans. J. Bowden, London 1974
HTR – *Harvard Theological Review*
IEJ – *Israel Exploration Journal*
JJS – *Journal of Jewish Studies*
Jos. *AJ* – Josephus, Jewish *Antiquities*
Jos. *BJ* – Josephus, *Jewish War*
I Mac. – First Book of Maccabees
II Mac. – Second Book of Maccabees
New EAEHL – *New Encyclopedia of Archaeological Excavations in the Holy Land*
PEQ – *Palestine Exploration Quarterly*
Plöger – O. Plöger, 'Die Feldzüge der Seleukiden gegen den Makkabäer Judas', *Zeitschrift fur Deutsche Palästina – Verein*, 74, 1958, 158–188
REJ – *Revue des Etudes Juives*
Schürer – E. Schürer, *The History of the Jews in the age of Jesus Christ*, rev ed., 3 vols, Edinburgh, 1973–1980
SCI – *Scripta Classica Israelitica*
Shatzman, *Armies* – I. Shatzman, *The Armies of the Hasmoneans and Herod*, Tubingen, 1991

Introduction

This is an account of the wars conducted by and against the Maccabean family of rulers in Palestine in the second and first centuries BC. They ruled varying amounts of that country between the rebellion led by Mattathias in 167 and the end of the direct family line in 37. (Note: all dates unless otherwise indicated are BC). The final date overlaps with the beginning of the rule of Herod, who claimed to inherit the Maccabean kingdom.

The Maccabees were a family from the town of Modiin on the edge of the Judaean plateau, about twenty-five kilometres west of Jerusalem. They emerged as the leaders of the Jewish rebellion in the 160s BC against the Seleukid king, and ruled as high priests and then kings of the Jews, once the rebellion had succeeded. They are also called Hasmonaeans, from the name of an ancestor; 'Maccabee' is a term derived from the Hebrew word for hammer applied to the first of their military men, Judas, either from a peculiarity in the shape of his head, or, by extension, because of his policies.[1]

The crisis that produced the Jewish revolt set a pattern that recurred throughout the history of the Maccabean state. In the end it resulted in the destruction of their people in yet another revolt, this time against the Romans. The original revolt took place in the context of a continuing dispute within the Jewish community in Judaea, and it began a series of wars aimed at first at securing the independence of the Jews in Judaea against the Seleukid kings, and later at conquering an empire. The wars of the Maccabees were thus both foreign and civil, and this entanglement had emerged already during the earliest disputes.

This is a time and place that has been researched for centuries in enormous detail, for it is the time of the emergence of a new Judaism, the background to the origin of Christianity, and the Jewish attitudes developed in the Maccabean time led directly to the great revolts against Roman rule between AD 66 and 135. It is an area and time that, to be considered fully and in detail, requires volumes. Here, however, I am looking at only one aspect, literally the wars of the Maccabees.

Needless to say I will need to stray at times from the military history into other areas. In particular it will be necessary to stop every now and again to consider the source material that relates to the wars. Essentially this consists of works by the historian Josephus, and two books of the biblical Apocrypha, I and II Maccabees. None of these is wholly reliable as a historical account, despite apparently relating a clear story – hence the need to stop and regroup every so often.

The sheer quantity of secondary discussion is overwhelming, though much of it is not relevant for a military history. I am not here concerned overmuch with the religious dimension of the events – though, of course, the origin of the wars was in part a religious crisis, at least for the Jews. This, in turn, means that my account stresses the political and military aspects of the period.

By sidelining the religious element it is possible to see the politicking rather more clearly, and this requires a distinctly sceptical approach to the source material. Far too many of the modern accounts accept the basic premises of the ancient sources, and, since the sources are exclusively Jewish, those modern accounts tend to be justifications for Jewish actions. Most even accept or ignore the all-too obvious distortions and inaccuracies in the sources. The result is that modern accounts are too often only retellings of the accounts in Josephus and the Maccabees books. (The documents found in the Judean desert – the 'Dead Sea Scrolls' – are of very little assistance.[2]) But retelling of ancient sources is not the task of the historian, who needs to look more closely at those sources, to take account of other points of view, to detect bias, and to detect lies and distortions. This I hope to have, at least, partly accomplished.

The Jewish state that emerged from the wars discussed here was an anomaly in its world. Few if any new states emerged in the ancient world by rebellion and of those that did only Judaea lasted more than a short generation. It was an anomaly also in its origin, as a religious revolt. However, once established – by 128 BC – it rapidly became just another minor state, perhaps more aggressive than most. Its particular, initial political conditions that were largely the result of its origin, rendered it particularly unstable.

Chapter 1

The Dispute

The problem that developed into the Jewish revolt in Palestine began with an argument over the tenure of the office of high priest of the temple in Jerusalem. This had been hereditary in the same family since the beginning of the Persian period, in the sixth century BC, though it would seem that the king had the right of confirmation in return for a tribute of, apparently, twenty talents. (The power of confirmation was thus with the Great King of Persia, then Alexander of Macedon, then the Ptolemaic kings, and finally with the Seleukid kings from 200 BC onwards; there is no sign earlier than the 170s that this caused any problem.) The high priest was the religious chief of the temple but he was also the effective head of the community of the Jews in Judaea, and was the man who was consulted by kings and their officials when necessary. This, in effect, made Judaea a tributary autonomous state within the overall kingdom.[1]

The ruling kingdom had been that of the Ptolemies in Egypt during the third century BC, but then the whole of Palestine had been conquered by the Seleukid king Antiochos III, a conquest confirmed by a peace treaty in 195, which was ratified by the marriage between Ptolemy V and Antiochos' daughter Kleopatra in that year.[2] Antiochos formally confirmed the status of Judaea as an autonomous community,[3] and his son Seleukos IV, who succeeded in 187, continued that arrangement.

During the period of early Seleukid rule, however, tension developed within Jewish society in Judaea over the acceptance of the customs and practices of Greek culture and society. Judaea was virtually surrounded by communities that were Greek or had become hellenized. These communities had developed relatively slowly during the time of the Ptolemaic rule, but the greater openness of the Seleukid kingdom seems to have encouraged a greater Hellenic consciousness. The Seleukid kings had long been known for their encouragement of urban development, founding new cities, and helping the growth of existing ones. Their Ptolemaic rivals had been less encouraging, so after the Seleukid conquest of Palestine, the confidence of the Greek and Macedonian and hellenized inhabitants of the region grew.[4]

On their remote highlands the Jews had received such influences later than those peoples near the coast or in the lowlands north of Judaea, or even in the lands beyond the Jordan. In all these areas Ptolemaic and Seleukid kings had established new cities or had encouraged older settlements to become self-governing ones, moulding them into cities of Greek type. To anyone outside, Judaea looked to be a prime candidate for hellenization. Jerusalem, the only urban centre in the highland area, could be organized as a Greek city, with Judaea around it as its *chora*, its territory.

This was a project of a group of men in Judaea, especially in Jerusalem. However, this would cause the high priesthood to suffer a loss of prestige and power – unless it was the high priest himself who took the lead. The high priest in office in Seleukos IV's reign, Onias III, resisted such a development. He is described by II Maccabees as 'a zealot for the laws' – that is, the particular Jewish law, the Torah.[5] He was, no doubt, supported in this by the council of elders, which was also given the Greek name of *gerousia*, though how firm that support was is unknown. Indeed, as will have been seen by the language in this paragraph, much of this is not at all certain.

The new Seleukid king, Antiochos IV, was approached in 174 by a group of men from Jerusalem asking that they be allowed to organize themselves as 'the Antiochenes in Jerusalem', to be able to establish a gymnasium and a corps of ephebes – young men receiving a Greek education – and to be separated from the authority of the high priest. In order for this to take place it was necessary that Onias III be replaced, since any high priest who was 'a zealot for the laws' would certainly oppose the reduction in his power that these innovations implied. Onias' brother Jesus – or Jason as he preferred to be known, in Greek – was appointed to replace Onias, who was thus deposed. Jesus/Jason also promised an increased tribute, which his enemies, needless to say, described as a bribe.[6] Jason was thus installed, and the 'Antiochenes' established themselves and their gymnasium.

The gymnasium was important, for it was a central institution of any Greek city, combining education, sports and religion. To be able to participate in events at the gymnasium it was necessary for a man to have had a Greek education – hence the corps of ephebes – to speak Greek, and to be able to converse intelligently on such Greek subjects as philosophy and music. All this was done in part to honour Greek gods. Here was an obvious area of dispute. The fact that there were enough men in Jerusalem in 174 to be able to do all this and qualify as 'Antiochenes' must mean that there had been some Greek immigration and settlement, but also that a fair number of Jews had received a Greek education. For the present, this group was essentially a private, if very obvious, organization within the predominantly Jewish town, but it consisted of the wealthier parts of the population, and, of course, had the general support of the high priest.

It is possible that the ultimate intention of the 'Antiochenes in Jerusalem' was to gain control of the city and convert it into a fully organized Greek *polis* (city-state); they may also have been content with what they had already gained. The problem was that the means they had to use to gain their ends began the process of destabilizing Judaean society. Having a high priest at its head meant that Judaea was a theocratic community, so that wider aims could not be realized without much disruption. For perhaps three years the gymnasium operated, and became popular even with some of the priests of the temple, beneath, and close to which, it had been established.[7]

This suggests that the regime of Jesus/Jason maintained an interesting and difficult balance between Jewish beliefs and practices and the incoming Greek ideas and practices. So we can distinguish three groups in Jerusalem at the time – and probably only there, and not as yet in the countryside. These were: in the political centre, so to speak, the party of Jason; to one side there were the traditionalist Jews; and on the other there was a group keen to expand Greek influence further, whom it is customary to call the 'hellenizers'.[8] It was this third group that took the next step. Impatient with the slow progress of the hellenization they wished for, they adopted Jason's tactics, but went one stage beyond. A delegation went to King Antiochos and persuaded him to replace Jason as high priest with a man called Menelaos. A larger tribute was promised, described as a bribe, of course, this time with perhaps more justification, and so the change was ordered.[9] (The repeated mention of money in these negotiations leads to the assumption that the king was 'bribed', and such was the accusation at the time. But a fee was always paid by a new high priest; given that they were asking for an exceptional favour, an increased tribute is to be expected.) It was also, of course, a demonstration of the authority of the king – Antiochos IV was a usurper and such demonstrations were necessary for him. At the same time the old practice of confirming the accession of a new high priest had now become actively replacing one with another. This all took place without protest in Judaea, so far as can be seen, but in terms of the government of Judaea it was actually a *coup d'état*.

Jason, like Onias III, fled from Judaea to escape his enemies. Onias had gone to Antioch, where he had sought sanctuary in the grove of Apollo at Daphne,[10] a move that makes it clear he was personally in fear. At the same time his presence near Antioch suggests that his prospects of persuading Antiochos IV to reinstate him were not negligible. Jason, on the other hand, took refuge across the Jordan in Ammanitis,[11] in all probability with Hyrkanos, the head of the Jewish Tobiad family, who had established a temple of Jewish type at Iraq el-Amir, twenty kilometres east of the Jordan. Hyrkanos was a hellenizer, related to the high priestly clan, very rich, and locally powerful.[12]

The existence of three living high priests is indicative of the divisions in Jewish society. But it may also be a sign, perhaps, of the king's contempt. Until the reign of Antiochos IV, the succession of high priests had been orderly. Now it was confused, and Menelaos was not even a member of the high priestly family, though he was certainly a priest. Antiochos' attitude meant that the incumbent high priest could not feel safe, for it might seem that some other pretender could bend the king's ear and persuade him to appoint a new man, just as Menelaos himself had. The deposed Onias and Jason would be prime candidates to replace him. This must be the explanation for the next move by Menelaos' faction. They went one stage further than before, by organizing the murder of the deposed Onias III, enticing him out of the sanctuary at Daphne to do so.[13]

It must be emphasized that all these changes produced no obvious opposition by anyone in Jerusalem, though it was not, as the sequel of it showed, wholly or universally accepted. The extremists – the Menelaos group – had, abetted by the king, seized control from the moderates, the Jason group. As hellenizers, the Menelaos faction disregarded local customs and prejudices, finding them unpalatable. The higher tribute Menelaos had promised the king came from the temple treasury, and would have to be replaced from taxation. He profaned some of the temple furniture, at least according to his opponents.[14] That is, having seized power, the hellenizers were implementing their programme. The description is from accounts written by his and their political enemies – but this does not necessarily mean that the change was unacceptable to everyone.

The situation in Jerusalem, at least according to II Maccabees, was uneasy. Menelaos organized an armed guard, said to be 3,000 strong, who were attacked in a riot. Their numbers and arms did not avail them against a disorganized crowd armed with blocks of wood, stones, and handfuls of ashes, which strongly suggests that the number and power of the guard is much exaggerated.[15] The story is probably distorted, but it reflects the problem Menelaos and his people had in imposing their will on a population that they had not carried with them in their changes. These were exactly the conditions for a counter-coup. The ex-high priest Onias had been eliminated – possibly another cause for local anger – but Jason, representing a more moderate strand among the hellenizers, was close by, just across the Jordan with Hyrkanos the Tobiad. At such a place, he was clearly another target.

Jason may well have realized that he must either flee and hide or return to Jerusalem and resume his office. Apollo and Antioch and the proximity of the king had not saved Onias. Indeed, Onias' murder was attributed to a notorious thug called Andronikos, who was also responsible for killing the king's stepson Antiochos the young king (but then acting on Antiochos' orders). So, for Jason, hiding with Hyrkanos across the Jordan was not a safe option. He returned to Jerusalem and resumed the office of high priest. Menelaos escaped into the citadel.[16]

Jason clearly had substantial support within the city, and he must have calculated that his counter-coup could be made acceptable to the king, probably by another hefty payment of tribute, particularly since the king had now become involved in that most expensive of royal activities, a war. A new contribution from the temple treasury in Jerusalem would no doubt be most welcome.

This war is what is now termed the Sixth Syrian War.[17] It was initiated by the regents for the child king Ptolemy VI of Egypt largely for reasons of internal Egyptian politics, for the reconquest of Palestine and Syria was a potentially unifying cause. They also expected to receive a welcome in Palestine, where it was only a generation since the Ptolemaic king had ruled there, and some at least of the inhabitants were nostalgic for this. (The Tobiads in Ammanitis had gained their wealth as Ptolemaic tax-officials; such people might well be pleased at a Ptolemaic return.) The general situation was thus somewhat delicate, but the Ptolemaic preparations were so clumsy and incompetent that Antiochos was fully warned and given plenty of time to prepare his response. He brought his army into coastal Palestine to await the attack, being careful to stay well within his own territory so as to avoid any charge of preventive or provocative aggression.[18] He thus had considerable forces close to Jerusalem in 171–170, but apparently did not intervene.

Either he did not want to be distracted from the bigger problem with Egypt, or he did not see the Jerusalem problem as worth his attention. He was able to invade Egypt and gain control of Pelusion, the fortress that gave access from the Sinai desert road into the Delta. The incompetent regents were swiftly removed, but Antiochos found it difficult to find anyone in Egypt with whom it was possible to make an enduring peace.

The war lasted two years. At the end of the first campaign, in 169, Antiochos returned to Syria with his army, leaving a garrison at Pelusion to guarantee his ability to reinvade Egypt if necessary. It was while he was in Egypt on this first campaign that Jason returned to Jerusalem and deposed Menelaos. This was reported to Antiochos while he was in Egypt and he interpreted Jason's action as a rebellion, and as a rebellion in support of Ptolemy at that – exactly the situation he must have feared all along. (Jason's connection with the Tobiads was no doubt an element in this interpretation.)

Menelaos had been Antiochos' (latest) appointee as high priest, no matter what sums of money had been paid or promised. To overthrow the authority of one of the king's officials, as Jason had done, was clearly rebellion. Perhaps Jason did not see it that way, for he had been Antiochos' appointee also, but he and his supporters seem to have been a majority of the Jerusalemites – the Menelaos regime had collapsed very easily. When Antiochos returned from Egypt, therefore, he believed he had to deal with a rebel regime in a fortified city on the flank of his line of march. The rebels may have been friendly with the enemy regime in Egypt, but even if not, the fact of a rebellion against him left an opening that could be exploited by whatever authority eventually emerged in control in Egypt. From Antiochos' point of view it had to be dealt with quickly, before the Ptolemaic regime could recover and exploit the situation.

He took his army up into the hills, seized Jerusalem, and looted the temple treasures. Needless to say, he was opposed, and an unknown number of people in the city were killed. The first book of Maccabees characteristically lists in detail the items taken from the temple, but recounts the violence against the people in a brief phrase. Josephus is more specific, saying that the king 'killed many of those who were in opposition', which means Jason's supporters.[19] The vagueness of both in reckoning casualties suggests that exaggeration is at work.

Menelaos was then reinstated as high priest,[20] while Jason fled across the Jordan once more, where the Nabataean king Aretas held him prisoner for a time, perhaps until he could see the result of the crisis, then he was allowed to go on to Egypt. It seems that Hyrkanos the Tobiad died at about this time, no doubt as a result of this crisis.[21] Antiochos' invasion of Egypt next year seems to have persuaded Jason to move on further, and he is said to have taken refuge in Sparta, where he died.[22]

The restored regime of Menelaos was now subjected to a closer royal supervision, for the king left one of his men, Philip the Phrygian, in the city.[23] These measures ensured that Jerusalem remained quiet during Antiochos' second Egyptian expedition in 168, when at last, and with Roman help, he succeeded in extracting a viable peace agreement from a more or less stable Ptolemaic government. When

C. Popillius Laenas, the Roman envoy, drew his circle in the sand and bade Antiochos make his decision on making peace with Egypt there and then, he was in effect guaranteeing that the Ptolemaic government would accept the cession of Palestine and Phoenicia to the Seleukid king, which the deposed regents had challenged.[24] Since this peace was to be in the names of the kings (not a group of regents or usurpers who could be overthrown at any moment, and whose undertakings could therefore be repudiated) that agreement would hold until one of the signatory kings died. Antiochos was therefore free to attend to other problems, in particular he could march off to the east without fearing a Ptolemaic attack while he was away.

In Jerusalem, following the restoration of Menelaos and the final elimination of the threats from both Onias and Jason – and Hyrkanos – the most determined hellenizers were once again in control. But the repeated changes of regime and the king's reaction had now stimulated strong opposition. Quite likely it was only the irruption of the royal army into Judaea that had alerted the people outside the city to what was really happening. The response was the development of a more extreme Jewish group, entirely opposed to the hellenizers, a group that emerged from the original traditionalists who had followed Onias III. And the violence that had been introduced by Jason and the king stimulated violence in return. In 167 a new administrator, Apollonios, was appointed by the king. He is described as a 'high revenue official' by I Maccabees, or as 'the general of the Mysians' by II Maccabees – the former seems the more likely. Whatever his precise post, he had the authority to collect taxes and to deploy troops, so perhaps the confusion and discussion as to his post is unnecessary.[25] Philip the Phrygian was presumably replaced by Apollonios. Both men, in fact, took functions and authority from the high priest, just as had the Antiochenes

Whatever Apollonios' precise governmental task was, he faced opposition. The spoliation of the temple, and the use of the temple treasures by the recent high priests to secure their appointments, will have severely reduced the available cash in circulation. The violation of the temple had surely angered many in Jerusalem beyond the traditionalists. The king identified the opposition – he was obviously informed by Apollonios, and perhaps also by Menelaos – with the practitioners of the traditional Jewish religion. Apollonios faced violent resistance, and to face it down he dismantled the city walls and built a powerful fortress, called the Akra, probably on the hill of Ophel south of the temple, the original site of the early city.[26] This activity probably took a year, but the city remained badly disturbed. Many left the city, no doubt staying with relatives in the countryside.[27] Having secured his position militarily, and having identified the source of opposition as the devotees of the temple and the law under the old Jewish religion, the king gave orders that the temple be converted to the worship of Zeus Olympios, and that the old cult be replaced by the worship of Greek gods[28] – or so we are told by Maccabees, followed by Josephus.

But this was not how Hellenistic kings worked. The procedure would be to respond to local concerns or requests, and in this case the matter would have gone first to Antioch, just as had the proposals to change the person of the high priest. The initiative must have come from the 'Antiochenes in Jerusalem', and the king will have agreed when assured that this was what the local population wanted. He was not unfamiliar with the situation in Jerusalem, as past events had shown, and those in power in the city clearly wanted changes. Being in power they were presumed to be able to carry out the scheme. Casting the blame on the king was the work of later interpreters of these events.

The change to the temple,[29] of course, pushed the hellenizers to an extreme, further perhaps than they had ever intended to go, and at the same time it outraged the traditionalists, who dubbed the situation the 'abomination of desolation', a well-chosen phrase that successfully obscures what was actually done. No doubt many of the middling sort, the followers of the dead Jason, were just as angry. The basis of Menelaos' support was thus narrowed drastically.

This is where the issue spread decisively into the countryside. Until this point it seems that Jerusalem had been the focus of events, and there is no sign that the country people had been seriously affected. It could be said that Menelaos had finally triumphed, and that Jerusalem had developed into the semblance of a Greek city, though there is no indication that it was formerly constituted as such. But the violence of Jason, of Menelaos, of the king, and of Apollonios, began to affect the people outside at last, for refugees who fled the city to get away from the urban violence brought news of it. The order to replace the Jewish cult by the worship of the Greek gods now reached right into the lives of these country people, and often they did not like it. This is where the Maccabees came in.

Chapter 2

Terrorism and Guerrilla War

The Maccabee family was headed by Mattathias, who had five sons. Mattathias was a priest, and when the enforcers of Menelaos and Apollonios, acting in the name of King Antiochus, fanned out through the Judaean countryside to compel the abandonment of the old rites and the adoption of the new,[1] he was one who objected. He was not alone in this, but he was in a distinct minority. There was considerable resentment, as one would expect, at the enforced changes, though there was also an acceptance of them by many people, a fact usually glossed over or ignored in Jewish histories. As was to be expected, the population of Jerusalem, the Antiochenes in the city and others, were not reluctant to accept the change, and it is clear that a similar acceptance was generated in other parts of Judaea, where, as I Maccabees admits, 'people thronged to their side in large numbers'.[2] But this attitude was by no means universal, and therein lay the future difficulty.

The changes are said to have been imposed on Judaea by royal decree, and indeed I Maccabees quotes the decree in a paraphrase that is clearly a distortion.[3] This was later interpreted as a royal attempt to unify religious practice throughout the kingdom, but this is clearly nonsense, an attempt to shift the blame for the coming disaster onto royal shoulders, who were the clear enemy when the work was written. There is no other indication anywhere that Antiochos IV had such an aim, and indeed it would be very strange if he had, for the hellenic religion was inclusive, not, as was Judaism, the reverse. In reality this attempt at 'religious reform' was the next stage in the programme of the Antiochenes in Jerusalem, so the blame, if any is to be allocated, for the 'persecution' that followed is to be laid on the reforming Jews and their Greek fellows in the city. Therefore, since the new practices were resisted by the traditionalists within Judaea, the latter were equally responsible for the violence. The traditionalists were driven to rebel by the force that was being applied to them.

Mattathias was a locally influential man in Modiin. As a priest he regularly visited Jerusalem, so he clearly understood the disputes, and the rival positions adopted in the city. There is no indication that he was seriously concerned during the years of conflict in the city over the high priesthood between 174 and 167. He did, however, become involved once the Menelaos party decided to enforce the reformed religious practices on the general population outside the city. Mattathias was just the sort of man the reformers wished to recruit to their cause, for he and his like could influence the rest of the population. The enforcers were sent out to check on progress, to persuade, and later to enforce the changes. At that point Mattathias' anger broke through.

The story is related in I Maccabees in such a way as to seem to justify Mattathias' actions, but the details look reasonably authentic. A 'royal officer' came to Modiin to oversee the regular sacrifice, conducted according to Greek rites. This was probably not the first visit. The majority of the local population had participated in the past without resentment, and clearly did so on this occasion. Only Mattathias and his sons refused, or so it was said. (An alternative account in II Maccabees claimed that he and nine others hid out in the desert,[4] which may have been a way of avoiding participation. Assuming, without any warrant, that five of the men were his sons, we have no indication of who the other three were, but nine men is hardly a large part of the local population.) He had apparently kept clear of the sacrifices before, but on the crucial occasion he was present when a local man stepped forward to perform the prescribed sacrifice on an altar especially constituted for the sacrifices: it was not one that had been used previously for the traditional sacrifices. (The use of the altar in the Jerusalem temple for such sacrifices, whether or not a cult image was installed, was the 'abomination of desolation' to the author of I Maccabees.[5])

The event so far indicated no conflict, indeed there was a careful avoidance of offence by the hellenizers, and of resistance by the traditionalists. The 'royal officer' was alone, without even a bodyguard. He was probably an administrator, or perhaps one of Menelaos' men. Being on his own he clearly expected no trouble, a reasonable assumption since this was not the first sacrifice at the site. The altar was so located as to avoid what Mattathias would call 'pollution'. Yet it was obviously an event that caused some uneasiness, and, as a local leader, Mattathias would know this. Indeed it is reported, in a pair of contrasting short speeches composed by the author of I Maccabees, that the officer pointed out that Mattathias' influence would be helpful and, if he chose to exercise it in the hellenizers' direction, he would be suitably rewarded.

This offer, if it was made (and it may well have been made, though the account in I Maccabees cannot be assumed to be wholly correct), is portrayed as insulting, though the officer must have thought he was speaking to a receptive man. Mattathias is reported as replying with some scorn and insisting on the enforcement of the Jewish law. He refused to participate in the new forms of worship. So far, nothing had been done that anyone on either side of the argument could object to. Mattathias and the official were having a relatively straightforward conversation, and it seems highly unlikely that participation in the actual sacrifice was compulsory. So Mattathias' next action was deliberately incendiary. He killed both the man who had come forward to sacrifice on the new altar and the royal officer who was supervising. For good measure he also destroyed the altar.[6]

The event is portrayed by I Maccabees as spontaneous, though this is unlikely – Mattathias was clearly armed, for instance. If it was planned, however, it was unsuccessful. After the murders Mattathias went through the town of Modiin, shouting that the people who shared his views should 'Follow me'. No one did, apart from his sons. Instead the town turned hostile, and the six men took to the hills.[7]

Mattathias' action was thus not well received by his neighbours, who unanimously refused to accept his action, and clearly denied his leadership, either through fear or from distaste – or both. Some will have liked the new religious regime; probably the majority were indifferent. The assumption by the royal officer that Mattathias was influential may have been correct if he had joined the hellenizers, but his influence obviously failed when it ran against the general opinion. That is, his influence was rejected because he was now advocating a policy that was unpopular.

The family was outlawed, both because of the murders and because of their rejection of royal and high priestly authority, but they were not the only ones. Soon he had friends with him. And elsewhere there were other rejectionists who fled to other wilderness places. (We cannot assume that Mattathias' action was the first violent rejection; he is prominent only because his sons became the leaders of the later revolt.) For a time the Menelaos party tried persuasion, but, like Mattathias, they were willing to use violence. Waiting until the Sabbath, their forces cut down one group (or more).[8] Mattathias, for all his insistence on the law, was sensible enough to see that operating it in full rigour only invited such attacks.[9] The rigorous observance of the Sabbath was quietly abandoned.

This conflict was one within the Judaean community. There is no sign of royal involvement other than that the king's name was invoked, regularly, to influence outlaws to submit, and that some of the forces occupying the Akra in Jerusalem were employed by Menelaos against his enemies. He had the support of Apollonios, and probably also the governor of the whole region, Koele Syria. As a result the king was assigned the ultimate responsibility for the policy being imposed, though it was essentially an internal Jewish matter. It was also one in which the use of violence on both sides steadily increased. This had to involve the king eventually for, as ruler, he was naturally concerned with the internal peace of his kingdom.

II Maccabees has several stories of people who resisted the reformers and are said to have died for it.[10] How far these are true is impossible to verify. In written form they are sixty years later than the events they claim to describe. The charged atmosphere of the time, and the lack of interest on either side in writing things down at the time they happened, meant that it is likely that the plain truth had largely vanished, so exaggeration is at least likely, and invention even more so. (This also applies, of course, to the story of Mattathias' killings at the altar, though it has to be said it has a ring of accuracy about it.)

There was certainly plenty of violence. Mattathias' murders at the altar were only the start; the Menelaist attack on the desert-dwelling recalcitrants was their reaction. The violence entrenched the divisions within the Jewish community in Judaea, so that now there were, on one side, the hellenizers, the followers of Menelaos and the king; on the other were the traditionalists, who split into those who resisted in the full rigour of the law, and suffered for it, and those who, like Mattathias' group, modified the law in order to resist the more effectively. Then there was a bigger group, probably the majority, who kept their heads down, and went along with whoever was in power locally; they were the ones who suffered most.

This middle group were the people whom both sides had to control. Mattathias, his sons, his followers, and a group called the Hasidim who came over to join him from the strict observers,[11] now carried out a campaign to 'persuade' this neutral majority to obey them. Given the violent atmosphere in which it had developed it is clear that this was a terrorist campaign. Both I and II Maccabees report this: 'they turned their wrath on the guilty men and renegades; those who escaped their fierce attacks took refuge with the Gentiles';[12] Mattathias 'came on the towns and villages without mercy and burnt them'.[13] This is an aspect of these events that is not generally emphasized, for the propaganda of the Maccabees, instancing the defilement of the temple and so on as their motivation, has been widely accepted. Yet this was, it must be said, a terrorist campaign of a thoroughly brutal sort, one that appears to have been waged at the expense of the lives of the ordinary people of Judaea – other Jews, in other words.

The terrorists were numerous enough, and secret enough, to move about the country destroying altars they did not like, killing Jews who worshipped at those altars, forcibly circumcising Jewish boys who had not undergone the operation: circumcision had been one of the practices obnoxious to the Gentiles and is said to have been forbidden by the king. Any who could not accept the terrorists' authority were driven from their homes. This was a relatively easy campaign, for their opponents, peaceable farmers and villagers for the most part, were scarcely prepared to combat it. When Mattathias died, a year or so after his original murders at the altar, naming his son, Judah, as his successor as leader, a large part of the Judaean countryside appears to have been more or less under their control – that is, they had no organized opponents, and the neutral people had been terrorized into doing as they were told.

The hellenizers in Jerusalem clearly could not cope with this, and help was brought in by Apollonios. He was able to call up and lead a force of soldiers collected from Samaria, and as such he is identified by some as the governor of that region. Even so, he was still a relatively minor functionary, subject to the governor of Koele Syria and then to the king. He was also hemmed in by other officials, each with his share of the administration, which he guarded jealously. Apollonios is said to have commanded 'a large army', but the author of I Maccabees does not really know much about the fight that took place and his definition of Apollonios' force as 'large' is only a guess, or a later assumption.[14]

For this first battle between Maccabean forces and the Seleukid army some assumptions are reasonable. Judah's army was strongly motivated by religious and political feelings, but it was not composed of professional soldiers. Judah himself was clearly, as this and later fights would show, an intelligent and inspirational commander of guerrilla forces. His opponent, Apollonios, was a Seleukid administrator who may have come from Macedon (or that may have been merely his family's origin). He had gone through the military training followed by all Greek and Macedonian youths. If he really was governor of Samaria, he will have had occasion to command soldiers in action, since governors were expected to keep order, and low-level disorder was a constant problem. (If his post was 'commander of the

Mysians' he was a professional soldier.) His troops will have included some Seleukid professional soldiers, but probably not many. Samaria had a garrison, but it was not a large place, and Apollonios could only take part of its forces away. His force was composed of the militia of the city, men liable to emergency service, citizens of the *polis*. They, like him, had some training, and they were probably more or less fit, but they cannot in any way be regarded as skilled and experienced soldiers. Above all, their commander was not particularly proficient, and they themselves had no strong motivation.[15]

The site of the battle can only be guessed. Judah and his people had taken refuge in the Gophna Hills in the north of Judaea, not far from Modiin, so Apollonios probably headed directly for that area. From Samaria he brought his army due south to the main road which headed for Jerusalem along the watershed of the Judaean Hills. The Gophna Hills were a little to the west of the road. The Seleukid soldiers had to climb up from the lowland to the plateau by a series of ever higher ridges before reaching the comparative level route along the top.

It is worth considering what Apollonios' aim was in this campaign. He had been called in by Menelaos and his followers who ruled Judaea, but whose control was threatened by Mattathias' and Judah's campaign of terrorism. Judah's authority extended only so far as his forces reached, and was liable to melt away when any of Menelaos' forces arrived at a particular place. Judah did not, it seems, yet control any of the Judaean urban centres, not even his home town of Modiin. So Apollonios' purpose was to eliminate Judah and his band of terrorists. His march was thus not directed at Jerusalem, which remained in Menelaos' control, but at the Gophna Hills, and at Judah and his army, who had taken refuge there. Judah's aim, by contrast, was simply to survive, and if defeated, to escape with as many of his men as possible.

Apollonios was a known quantity, and perhaps a judgment had been made of his capabilities, while Judah presumably had some idea also of the capabilities of Apollonios' men. On the other hand, Apollonios will have known little of Judah or his forces, neither their numbers nor their capabilities. Previously they had done no more than upset altars, murder political opponents, and circumcise boys. Apollonios knew they were untrained, and he did not realize – how could he? – that he was faced by a man, Judah, who had elements of military genius in his character.

As it happens, 'battle' is scarcely the best label for the meeting of these two forces. Apollonios, like all commanders in Hellenistic armies, fought in the ranks. His army was more accustomed to being in a regular formation than Judah's, but on rough ground it would not be possible to maintain a phalanx, and Judah is very likely to have deliberately chosen to fight on ground unsuitable for a phalanx. (The precise location is not known, though guesses have been made – somewhere in the Gophna Hills is the only guess worth consideration.) Both forces will have been in loose formations, which, when they closed to fight, were probably little more than mobs. Apollonios was killed, at which point his troops, probably reluctant from the start, fled. It seems probable that Judah had deliberately targeted Apollonios: a direct attack on the enemy commander was to become his standard tactic. I Maccabees claimed that many of Apollonios' men died, but knew nothing of numbers. No doubt Judah had difficulty in maintaining control of his forces. Any of Apollonios' men who were reasonably fleet of foot would get away without difficulty, as would any man who kept his head and looked alert. Apollonios' men were fairly well armed, and wore some protective armour. They were also more proficient in individual combat than the Jews, due to their earlier training. On the whole, it seems likely that most of Apollonios' people survived.[16]

Judah appropriated Apollonios' sword, and used it thereafter. It was clearly a talisman; a symbol of his first victory, and a sign in his and his followers' eyes that he was favoured by their god. The defeated forces also left a good deal of spoil behind, including weapons. There is no reason to believe that the Jewish force was armed with little more than 'farmers' tools', as has been assumed.[17] Weaponry was by no means uncommon amongst ancient populations, but the Greeks and Macedonians no doubt had the better weapons, and Apollonios' sword was probably better than most. So the enemy's weapons armed the Jews, making Judah's men even more dangerous, both as soldiers and as terrorists.

The defeat of Apollonios did not mean much in terms of power and authority. Judah and his people were still largely confined to the Gophna Hills except when they went out on terrorist raids. But they now faced the difficulty that the Seleukid authorities in Palestine were alerted and were compelled to make a new effort. Undoubtedly Judah understood this and prepared for another attack. In the lowlands an officer called Seron, an ambitious professional soldier, was given the job of eliminating Judah and his people.

Seron's precise position in the Seleukid administration has caused some confusion. He was of roughly the same rank as Apollonios, though more on the military side. I Maccabees calls him 'commander of the army of Aram' (that is, Syria), and Josephus promotes him to be governor of Koele Syria. The first is vague but describes precisely what he was; the second is an interpretation of the first, and wrong.[18] His base was somewhere near the coast, probably at Ptolemais-Ake, the provincial capital. He is described by I Maccabees as anxious to make his reputation, which sounds authentic enough, but he was not conducting the expedition on a whim. Apollonios had been able to make his attack on his own authority, but Seron was not a semi-independent governor, and was instructed by the governor of Koele Syria. That is, the concern within the Seleukid administration about the situation in Judaea had moved up a notch, from local (Apollonios) to provincial governor. There is no indication that anything more than a report of what had happened had yet gone to Antioch. Indeed Antioch, both the city and the royal headquarters there, was at this time fully preoccupied with preparations for King Antiochos' great celebration parade in Daphne, which took place in the summer of 166, and this will have involved some of the forces normally stationed in Palestine.

There was therefore not much in the way of armed forces available for Seron. Apart from those who went to Antioch for the parade, others had to remain in the garrisons. Seron had the use of what was left, plus those he could gather from the Greek and Macedonian population in the same way as Apollonios – no doubt some of those who had been in Apollonios' army were in Seron's. This indicates the fairly low level of concern in the Seleukid administration over what was happening in Judaea. The author of I Maccabees refers to the enlistment of 'sinners', which appears to mean the hellenizers in Judaea. If they did join Seron's force they must have moved out of Judaea and joined him somewhere in the coastal plain before he began his march into the hills, and Josephus does interpret them as being fugitives. However, this expression may also refer to Greeks in general, for whom the religious Jews had no respect, and so to those recruited for the campaign from the coastal cities. It would not be surprising, of course, if Seron had both.[19]

Seron's aim is suggested in part by the participation of the hellenizers, and by the statement in I Maccabees that he was intent on revenge.[20] This presumably refers to the defeat and death of Apollonios. Given the presence of the hellenizers, it was also a reply to the terrorizing activities mounted by Judah's people. Seron's aim in strategic terms is also suggested by the route he took. Apollonios, from Samaria, had automatically marched due south along the main road. Seron could have followed that route, and might have emphasized his revenge aim by doing so. But instead he came up from the coastal lowlands, by the Beth Horon route, and this indicates that he was aiming at more than avenging Apollonios' death.

The Beth Horon route climbed from Lydda in the plain, through Modiin to intersect the main road to Jerusalem seven or eight kilometres north of the city, just south of modern Ramallah. On the plateau it crossed south of the Gophna Hills, so that by occupying that route, Seron could hope to cut Judah's raiders off from the main part of Judaea. This would provide some protection for the rest of the population, who might then come out more decisively in support of the high priest. Seron could then move north to attack Judah's army in its hideouts.

The problem, as surely Seron appreciated, was to get through the Beth Horon route. This was in two sections, at first a fairly gentle climb in a reasonably wide valley, where his army could march in a reasonably compact and disciplined formation, and then the ascent from Lower Beth Horon village to Upper Beth Horon, which was a much steeper climb of 225 metres (730 feet) in less than two miles (2.8 kilometres). This climb lay along a narrow valley said to be too narrow for two camels to march side-by-side; the road bent and twisted, with steep walls and drops on either side, overlooked by the hills. If he had any experience of the country, Seron knew of this route, and as a professional soldier in the Seleukid army he knew of the difficulties of moving an army along such a way – and he knew of the solution to those difficulties.

The way to traverse such a route safely was to move slowly, with great caution, and send out parties to seize the flanking hilltops before the main army and its impedimenta even attempted the narrows. Unfortunately, this required highly professional, specially trained forces, and large numbers of men, which were not available to him. His total force was smaller than that Judah commanded. Judah is said to have had about 6,000 men,[21] which may be only a little exaggerated. So Seron could not detach a whole series of parties to seize the hilltops or to go on scouting missions, for if he did he would soon have no army left. Instead he simply had to move with great caution, keeping his forces together and hoping to intimidate by apparent strength. Seron surely sent out some patrols, particularly ahead along the road, even if he could not utilize the whole variety of recommended methods for hill fighting.

Judah did not have his whole force with him for the fight; instead he selected a smaller group, presumably the best and most disciplined fighters. It seems that he was taken by surprise by Seron's route of march, and had to move fast to reach his ambush point in time. His men are supposed to have complained that they were both hungry and tired, and they were certainly rendered fearful by the sight of the size of the approaching enemy force. But no ambush can be conducted by a large force in hills, since it has to be kept secret and hidden until the attack is launched, and a small force could move faster than one of several thousands. It may also be that Judah feared defeat and took only a small force so that if his forces were destroyed others could continue the work.

In the event Seron's numbers and precautions did not avail. The site of the clash is not recorded, but it was somewhere along the Beth Horon Ascent, between the lower and upper villages, presumably some way along it, and probably the fighting was spread over a good distance. The result was another defeat for the hellenizers and their Seleukid allies. This time, having stopped the advance of Seron's forces by the ambush of the head of the column and the tail of the Seleukid army being forced to retreat, Judah was able to organize a pursuit along the valley as far as the plain (where, if they reorganized, the Greeks could defend themselves more easily). Seron was killed early on. Probably, like Apollonios, he had been in the front of the advance and so was picked off. I Maccabees claims 800 of Seron's men were killed, and implies, reasonably enough, that most of the killing took place during the pursuit. The number is, of course, not reliable, and is no guide to the size of either army, but it is unusual in being reasonable, even believable.[22]

The conduct of the battle by Judah indicates that he now commanded an army that was rather more than a bunch of refugees using terror tactics against their internal enemies. He was able to move his force to an ambush point quickly; able to select a particular set of men, who, even if they were hungry and tired – and scared – were able to launch a surprise attack, having kept silent and hidden until the decisive moment; able to conduct a pursuit that effectively destroyed the enemy army; and able to halt the pursuit when more dangerous territory was reached and so preserve his force for the main battle. In other words, the Maccabean army had developed a significant degree of skill and professionalism, though it remained small and could only be used for such operations as ambushes (and terrorism). It was still not large or skilled enough to be able to face a large and professional force, or to control much territory beyond its base.

Chapter 3

Victories

The two battles against Apollonios' and Seron's armies took place during 166. In Antioch the king, having had his great parade, now organized an expedition into the eastern territories and set off during 165. In the west he was already friendly with the main powers in Asia Minor, and since 168 he had had a binding peace with the Ptolemaic king, and this made it possible to go to the east.[1] Rome's interest in his affairs was shown by the visit of Ti. Sempronius Gracchus, who toured the eastern Mediterranean in 166–165, but Gracchus went home to report that there was nothing for Rome to worry about: Antiochos was going to the east.

Antiochos made his son joint king (Antiochos V) at the age of nine, and left him in Antioch under the regency of Lysias,[2] a member of a family long conspicuously loyal to the Seleukids: they had retreated from Asia Minor when that area ceased to be under Seleukid rule, abandoning substantial local power there. During 165, Antiochos marched with his main army to the east, to Babylonia, Persia, and on.[3]

Amid all this the defeats of two minor Seleukid forces in Judaea were probably annoying, but scarcely serious; they did not deflect him from his main purpose. With the king in the east the matter of Judaea was thus left for Lysias to deal with. However, all these preparations in Antioch had provided Judah with a respite from attacks lasting for several months. The time was spent in developing his own army – for it was obvious that another attack was to be expected – and in continuing the internal campaign against Menelaos and the hellenizers. From accounts of the next campaign, which took place in the summer of 165, it is clear that Judah extended the area under his control after the Beth Horon victory. He was able to call an assembly at Mizpah on the Jerusalem Road, halfway between the Gophna Hills and the city, implying that he held control of territory almost as far as Jerusalem itself, and that he could flaunt his power within ten kilometres of the city without fear of being attacked. He obviously had control of the people of the Beth Horon road, though perhaps not at the lower end, which was accessible from the plain. Whether he had control of any territory south of Jerusalem is not known, but at least he would be able to send his gangs into that region, so forcing his enemies to send some of their forces there as protection – or as rival tyrants.

With a larger territory at his command, and so a larger population, Judah could recruit a larger army, and gather more supplies. At the assembly at Mizpah the army was reorganized, regiments and companies being set up and officers appointed as 'commanders of thousands, commanders of hundreds, commanders of fifties, and commanders of tens'.[4] This systematization had clearly not been needed earlier, and so the implication is that a much larger army now existed. This does not necessarily contradict the reference (in II Maccabees[5]) to his earlier army of 6,000 men. Judah now apprehended that a much bigger attack from the lowlands was approaching, and a much tougher and more flexible armed structure was needed. At Beth Horon he had commanded himself, as he had against Apollonios; now he would be a general, giving orders to officers who would be in direct command of their men.

At Antioch, Lysias had been left 'half' of the Seleukid army, while Antiochos marched east with the other 'half'.[6] Exactly what was meant in terms of numbers by this curious division is not known, but it seems most likely that the author of I Maccabees was simply guessing. The Seleukid army consisted of a full-time professional force, which thirty years before had been about 35,000 strong. In the parade at Daphne in 166 there were about 66,000 soldiers, an unknown number of whom were from the reserve. Antiochos IV had marched east with the main Seleukid field army, probably at least 30,000 strong; Lysias at Antioch had a lesser force at his disposal, most of his men disposed in garrisons and at the borders. Both armies could be brought up to greater strength in emergencies by calling out the reserves.[7]

Lysias certainly had a substantial force at his command, and he had been given a general instruction to use it to deal with Judaea. He appointed a new governor in Koele Syria, Ptolemaios son of Dorymenes, and a new commander of the Judaean expeditionary force, Nikanor, son of Patroklos, who was presumably Seron's replacement. Another commander, Gorgias, was probably subordinate to Nikanor,[8] though later he was governor of Idumaea (and so a subordinate of Ptolemaios), and this may have been his post at the time of Nikanor's expedition. I Maccabees gives Lysias the credit for these appointments, but such major offices would have had to be checked with the king first, and indeed Antiochos may well have instigated the appointments himself before he went to the east.

This time there could be no possibility that the Seleukid attack could approach unexpectedly, as with Seron. The Seleukid army was too large, the new appointments too public. Yet the Seleukid commanders were not without guile and resource. Nikanor brought his army to the edge of the hills and formed an entrenched camp near Ammaus, just next to modern Latrun, but down on the lower land. He had to wait for other forces to join him, including some from North Syria. He is credited with an army of 40,000 foot and 7,000 horses, which is an obvious exaggeration. If Nikanor had a quarter of that number, it would still be inflated.[9] His main force was gathered from the cities of the coastal plain, from Gaza north to Ptolemais-Ake, partly garrison troops, partly mobilized reserves. The soldiers he was waiting for, from North Syria, may well have been the professional force that had been left with Lysias.

From Ammaus Nikanor had the choice of advancing along the Beth Horon route, as Seron had tried, or the parallel valley to the south, the Wadi Ali, which is the modern main road to Jerusalem. His aim may have been to relieve the pressure on the Antiochenes in Jerusalem or to destroy Judah's forces first, using the same strategy as Seron had attempted. His base camp gave him the option of making either aim his priority.

This helps to explain Judah's rival camp at Mizpah. From there he also had two options: either to head north-west to defend his basic territory in the Gophna Hills if Nikanor chose the Beth Horon approach, or south-west to confront an attack along the Wadi Ali if Nikanor headed for Jerusalem. But, like any competent politician, Judah used the camp for more than one purpose. Apart from organizing his army into sections, he also instituted a selection process, sending home 'the builders of houses, the betrothed, the planters of vineyards, and the faint-hearted'.[10] This is a curious grouping. The first three are fairly obvious as being economically and demographically useful. The 'faint-heated', though, would presumably include not just the neutrals, but also those whose loyalty lay with the opponents of the Maccabees. The common factor was that all of them were only partly committed, having other, more personally urgent matters on their minds. It would be dangerous to have them in the ranks in a fight, even if their presence increased the army's numbers.

The assembly was also put through a process of morale-building. The army's purpose was defined as a religious cause by a day of fasting, by a display of the Torahs, which had been 'defiled' by the 'Gentiles', and by Judah's exhortation. This all took place before the selection process, and no doubt the emphasis on the religious element helped to reveal those at the meeting who were less than enthusiastic. Finally, there was some trumpet blowing, which may have been elementary training in signalling by trumpet, and a speech by Judah, though the text as supplied in I Maccabees was a later composition by the author, and we cannot know what he said, other than that it was presumably a rousing address.[11]

This assembly-cum-muster became known to Nikanor at Ammaus. Judah could scarcely have kept it secret, even if he wished to, and perhaps he hoped it would deter any attack. So many of the men were dismissed to their homes that information was bound to reach Jerusalem, even if they did not go to Ammaus directly. Some men from the Akra garrison were with the Seleukid forces later, and they could have carried the news. For the first time, therefore, the Seleukid commanders knew that their opponents were collected in one accessible place, and would therefore be easy to attack. The possibility of a swift blow existed.

Gorgias, with a selected force of infantry and horse, was sent to mount this attack. He is said to have had 5,000 foot and 1,000 horse, but these figures must be reduced substantially, by perhaps three quarters.[12] He used, it seems, the Beth Horon route that Seron had tried, gambling presumably that his sudden swift march would preempt any attempt at an ambush, particularly since the Maccabean army had been gathered in one place in the camp at Mizpah. He certainly had time to get to the narrows of the pass before Judah's force could reach it, for Judah would need to receive the news of his march before his force could set out to intercept. Gorgias was guided by men from the Akra garrison, presumably those who had brought the news of the Mizpah assembly.

The news went both ways, for Judah was informed of Gorgias' march in time to move out of his camp and begin his own move. Gorgias began during the day, probably in the morning, and there was clearly time for Judah's scouts – no doubt positioned in the hills above the Seleukid camp – to bring the news to Mizpah. Judah could have tried to ambush Gorgias, but he must have realized that he had started out early enough to get to Beth Horon first, the only reasonable ambush point. Alternatively, Judah could have stood and fought at Mizpah, but this was clearly courting defeat against a professional army in the open plateau, on relatively level ground. Gorgias' forces could use their normal tactics of assault there, with a phalanx flanked by horsemen. This was a formation Judah's men could not withstand. But Gorgias was bringing only a detachment of the Seleukid force. The main army was still near Ammaus under Nikanor, in its entrenched camp. So a third possibility existed for Judah. He could do the unexpected, a reverse-Gorgias march, making an attack on the enemy base.[13]

Judah's force marched by a route somewhat to the south of that used by Gorgias, along the plateau-top. So for a time these armies were each approaching the other's camp on different routes. Gorgias' force arrived at its target first, during the night, only to find the camp abandoned. Gorgias assumed that the enemy had received word of his approach – as it had – but concluded that the men had therefore fled. There was, no doubt, plenty of evidence that the assembly at Mizpah had been held there, but in the dark it will not have been clear where the men had gone. Indeed, by sending off those men Judah did not wish to keep, indications of movement in all directions may well have been left. Gorgias, presumably after a rest and food, and so no doubt in the morning, sent out parties in search of the enemy, which rendered him essentially immobile for some time.[14]

Judah's approach to Nikanor's camp was by contrast unexpected and undetected. He marched through the night, probably reaching a point fairly close to the enemy camp, but still undetected in the darkness. The distance is about twenty-seven kilometres, which could be covered in perhaps five or six hours. The army came to a position above the Ammaus camp. In the morning they were seen, and when he realized this Judah at once ordered the advance to attack, mainly downhill. The Seleukids had cavalry patrols out during the night, so they were not wholly unprepared, and it was these that had detected Judah's force. As soon as the Maccabean army was sighted the alarm was sounded, but by that time the attackers were going in. The Seleukid force was caught just coming awake, some men in the camp, some outside it, altogether a classic surprise attack. It was, of course, the only way an entrenched camp could be captured by a relatively small force, particularly since it is probable that the Seleukid army outnumbered its opponents. Those who got out of the camp to face the attack had to move uphill and so faced the Jewish attack on the slope, clearly at a disadvantage. The defeat of this force pushed them into flight down to the plain, and those in the camp were panicked.[15]

The defeated force scattered, some to Gezer, where there was a Seleukid fort, others to Ashdod or to Iamnia further on; still others fled southwards to, or perhaps simply towards, Idumaea. If Gorgias was already governor of that area, many of these places were in his region, and so the fugitives may have been heading instinctively for their homes. The differing destinations also suggest that by taking the camp Judah's forces had pushed the enemy army out in several directions. A pursuit was organized, but did not last long. The clear danger was that by pursuing in several directions the Jewish force would itself disintegrate. Judah successfully recalled his men.[16] No doubt they were weary, but the main reason for the recall was that Gorgias' force would soon return to the plain. If he found the Maccabean army scattered he would be able to reverse the result of the dawn fight.

From Mizpah Gorgias could not see what had happened at the main camp, but he soon must have realized that there was no Jewish force near him, and that his surprise attack had failed. It may well have occurred to him that the absence of the Jewish force meant that the same tactic as he had used had been tried on Nikanor. Once the full daylight was available, the trail made by Judah's army would be visible. So Gorgias was probably alerted not long after dawn. Then smoke was seen, for Judah's men set fire to Nikanor's camp – or perhaps the breakfast fires simply spread. Gorgias recalled his patrols, if he had not already done so, and set out to march back towards the burning camp.

Judah, with a weary army composed of men who had to eat – they had fasted the day before and marched all night and then fought a battle – gathered his men in the plain, and waited for Gorgias. The latter, however, was not going to tangle with an alert and victorious army. He shied away, marching on past Judah's force towards the coast, or, more likely, to Gezer – though I Maccabees claims that his forces 'panicked' and that they 'fled'.[17] This also suggests that Gorgias' force was much smaller than the 5,000 infantry and 1,000 horse claimed in I Maccabees. Judah's army was perhaps 3,000 men, scarcely diminished by the battle, so Gorgias will have had less than that, maybe only half. Further, these men were also very weary and hungry, having been marching – they had marched more than fifty kilometres – and searching since the previous morning.

Judah, when he saw Gorgias avoiding battle, allowed his men to loot Nikanor's camp. Since this had already been burnt it is likely that the pickings were rather less than the author of I Maccabees imagines: 'gold in plenty and silver and blue and marine purple and great wealth'.[18] The words used here by the author were purely conventional, even invented. Missing is any reference to the collection of weapons discarded by the fleeing soldiers, which is something that Judah at least would have insisted on.

The Maccabean army, despite its victories, was still not capable of any aggression into the lowlands, nor of gaining control of a fortified or well-defended town. Further, the tactics it used were merely ambushes and surprise attacks, so Judah was clear that his force was not capable of a stand-up battle with a trained enemy army of equal size. The men were still poorly armed. They were relying on home-made weapons and on scavenging from the enemy. Judah's victories had been largely due to the assumption on his enemy's part that they were partly armed bandits, an assumption that was not far off the mark, but one that led to over-confidence on the part of both Apollonios' and Seron's armies. These forces may also have been unenthusiastic about their task. But the defeat of the competent Seleukid force led by experienced commanders at Ammaus meant that Seleukid over-confidence was unlikely to continue. Further, the Seleukid government had by now invested too much in attempting the suppression of the rebellion to give up. The Judaean problem had now gone from being a problem for the governor of Koele Syria to one for the government in Antioch.

The regent Lysias, by his very position, was vulnerable to enemies at home in the event of defeat. Lysias had appointed Ptolemaios son of Dorymenes, as governor in Ptolemais-Ake, and his and Nikanor's failure inevitably reflected back on the regent. His response was to blame Ptolemaios son of Dorymenes, who was dismissed. His replacement was another Ptolemaios, called Makron.[19] This new appointment required the agreement of the king, who was still in the east, so the process took time. The battle at Ammaus took place in the late summer of 165, so Ptolemaios Makron's appointment was probably not confirmed until well into the autumn.

Ptolemaios Makron is an interesting man. He was from a prominent family of Alexandria in Egypt and had ruled as governor in Cyprus for a dozen years during the regency for the infant children of Ptolemy V, operating in a very independent fashion. In the Sixth Syrian War, Antiochos IV had invaded Cyprus, and Ptolemaios Makron switched sides, together with a large proportion of the Ptolemaic army on the island. He and they had to leave when Cyprus was returned to Ptolemaic rule, at Roman insistence, in the peace treaty. Now he re-emerged as governor of Koele Syria. This career strongly suggests that his appointment might well have been at the king's initiative and not Lysias'.[20]

He came to Ptolemais-Ake with a new conciliatory policy, making contact with the Maccabean rebels and putting them in touch with Lysias. Two Maccabean delegates, Johanan and Absalom, went to Antioch. They and Lysias were able, according to a document presented in II Maccabees, to reach agreement on some issues, but on others Lysias did not have the authority to act. He did agree to send to the king for a decision on these issues, with his recommendations, and, meanwhile, he appointed envoys to continue discussions.[21]

A pair of Roman envoys lent their weight to the talks, asking that the rebels keep them informed.[22] They rather took the side of the rebels, but this was not necessarily a Roman policy designed to disrupt the Seleukid kingdom. It may rather have been a policy designed to bring about stability. Lysias was clearly thinking in terms of concessions to the rebels, and he and Ptolemaios Makron certainly took the view that this would bring advantages.[23]

The king, far off in Iran, refused to make the concessions that Lysias had recommended, and this message will have arrived at Antioch during the winter of 165–164. In the meantime, Menelaos and the hellenizers had made their own proposal as an alternative to that suggested by the Maccabees, that an amnesty be proclaimed, limited to a short period, in which concessions on ritual foods and the Torah were to be made. The king agreed to this, as a means, it was hoped, of drawing out of the rebel camp significant numbers of Jonah's supporters. The king's agreement was delivered to Menelaos in the form of a letter from the king to the *gerousia* (council of elders) in Jerusalem dated 15 Xandikos (10 March) 164. The time within which the amnesty operated was just fifteen days, until 30 Xandikos, clearly intended to force a concentration in the minds of those who might accept, and to prevent the leaders of the rebels from attempting a further negotiation of the terms.[24]

There is no sign that this ploy worked, insofar as it was aimed at weakening the rebel forces. The concessions were no doubt welcomed by the general Jewish population, but they will surely have realized that the amnesty and the revocation of the punitive royal measures were direct results of the military successes of the Maccabees. Menelaos may have hoped that his initiative in suggesting the amnesty would give him some popular credit, and perhaps it did, but it is unlikely that many people knew of the course of the negotiations. On the other hand, the Maccabean military resistance to the Seleukid armies was well known. This popular perception was quite correct: it was the resistance led by the Maccabees that had been most persuasive to the Seleukid rulers in Ptolemais-Ake and Antioch – and to the king. Menelaos would never have suggested making any concessions without the Maccabean victories.

The concessions made by the king were not enough to persuade the men fighting with the Maccabees to give up. The Maccabees would settle for nothing less than their full demands. They were, after all, the victors in all the fights. In particular, the hellenizers still controlled Jerusalem and the temple, where Zeus Olympios was worshipped. The Maccabean central demand now became the 'cleansing' of the temple, which in turn meant that the hellenizers in Jerusalem would have to relinquish control of the temple and the city, which would also mean that Menelaos cease to be high priest. The Maccabees were still intent on overthrowing the Judaean government.

By the summer of 164, therefore, it was clear to Lysias in Antioch that the concessions that Menelaos had persuaded him and the king to make had not extinguished the rebellion. The Maccabees were still in arms, stronger than ever. The regent brought his army south, a larger force than Seron or Nikanor had commanded; I Maccabees claims he had 60,000 foot and 5,000 horse,[25] hopelessly enlarged numbers; Lysias probably had something fewer than 20,000 men. Judah himself is credited in I Maccabees with 10,000, also probably an inflated figure.

Lysias decided to avoid a direct attack through the hills of the northern or western borders of Judaea and opted to move in from the south, along a road through Idumaea. Possibly this was on the recommendation of Gorgias, governing in the southern coastal plain, and well experienced in attacking through the Judaean hills. Lysias' exact route is not known, but since he got to Beth Zur, he will have approached along one of the valleys east of Gaza. The climb along any of these wadis was open and relatively gentle, the tracks and roads moving up by a series of shelves. He did not encounter any opposition until he reached Beth Zur, which lies on a ridge eight kilometres north of Hebron. Beth Zur had been the southern border post of Judaea under the Ptolemaic and Seleukid government, and had remained under Seleukid control all along. His army was partly in occupation of the fort and partly camped nearby, preparing to march on towards Jerusalem.[26]

Judah brought his army south to face the attack. He had a force larger than he had commanded at Ammaus a year before, but it was still much smaller than that of Lysias. His propaganda had no doubt emphasized his victories, and perhaps the ease with which they were won. The relaxation of the royal prohibitions could also encourage men to join what looked like the winning side. But Menelaos still controlled Jerusalem and its people, and he retained considerable support outside the city as well, even if it was suppressed by the Maccabean terror tactics. By bringing his army to the south Judah was very likely moving into territory in which he did not have much automatic support, and this time he found an enemy army fully prepared and alert, in a country in which an ambush was not possible, or where a night attack was unlikely to have any effect. He had to avoid a direct frontal collision if he was to avoid total destruction.

The impossibility of either ambush or open battle left Judah with only one resource: harassing raids. The Seleukid army had to march almost thirty more kilometres to reach Jerusalem, and the route was along the spine of the Judaean Hills. To delay that advance was going to be difficult, but a start was made while the Seleukid army was camped at Beth Zur by an attack on the Seleukid camp. The Jewish sources claimed that several thousand Seleukid soldiers were killed by the raid – indeed the wording of I Maccabees can be read as suggesting a stand-up face-to-face battle. It is claimed in I Maccabees that 5,000 died, and this is repeated by Josephus; II Maccabees more than doubles the figure.[27] Neither can be accepted, any more than can the notion of a full battle. What took place was a Maccabean raid, likely enough at dawn, on the Seleukid camp. The results were no doubt infinitesimal, though enough to convince any Seleukid sceptics that the Maccabean forces really did need to be taken seriously.

And yet Lysias ordered his army to retreat. He took it back the way it had come, and 'rode off to Antioch'.[28] This gave a colourable cover to the Maccabean claim to have driven off the invader, though, in fact, the Seleukid army withdrew in good order, unharassed by the Maccabean army.[29] Lysias retired, rather than retreated, convinced, as the next campaign would show, that he had located the Maccabees' weak southern border, and, as I Maccabees acknowledges, determined to return with a larger army, which he set about recruiting as soon as he got back to Antioch.[30] However, the army was not to be used only for another attack on Judaea.

I Maccabees' narrow view of events ignored the real reasons for Lysias' actions. He had withdrawn from Beth Zur because he had received news that King Antiochos IV was dead. (As a further indication of the narrow view of Maccabean historians, II Maccabees ascribes the king's death – described in wholly imaginary and repellently gloating terms – to divine punishment for his enmity to the Maccabean cause.[31]) Lysias' power base rested on Antiochos' support and so had instantly crumbled with the king's death. He had to secure the control of the person of the ten-year-old Antiochos V, who was in Antioch. When he got there, Lysias had to remove challengers to his authority in the court and the city, and had to recruit an enlarged army. It happened that Antiochos had appointed another regent, Philippos, probably to consolidate his work in the east and command the army there. Philippos was likely to be a challenger to Lysias' position when he returned to the west. The death of Antiochos IV had pushed the problem of Judaea to the bottom of the list of Lysias' concerns.

Judah and the Maccabean cause had gained another respite because of the enemy's wider concerns. The confrontation at Beth Zur had ended late in 164 (Antiochos died in November), so it was reasonable to assume that Lysias would be pinned down at Antioch for several months at least. Judah could therefore set about implementing his own aims. One result of the death of the king was that Menelaos and the hellenizers were made as uncertain as Lysias. The hellenization of Jerusalem had relied to a large extent on the support and encouragement of the king, and it was not certain that the new regime would continue that policy. The uncertainty in Antioch was thus mirrored by a similar uncertainty in Jerusalem. Of this Judah could take advantage.

As Lysias marched away, and as the news of the king's death spread, Judah turned his own forces northwards to march to Jerusalem. The city was unfortified, the condition in which it had been left by Apollonios four years before, with the exception of the Akra, the new fort that overlooked the temple from the south. The demoralized condition to which the hellenizers had been reduced by their defeats and by the death of the king, meant it was not difficult for Judah and his army to occupy the city, pushing their dejected opponents into the Akra, and so to reconsecrate the temple, reviving the traditional Judaic rites.

The interpretation put upon these events by the Maccabees, and reflected in the words of the Maccabees' books and in Josephus, was that the small Maccabean army had been assisted in its fight against the mighty Seleukid force by the Jewish god. Therefore that god's temple was now rightfully 'cleansed'. This was, of course, a dangerous delusion, though it was not the first (or last) time such an interpretation was made of military events. It was dangerous because it ignored alternative explanations – the effect of the death of the king and Seleukid indifference. Future attacks would therefore be combated by the same small army, on the assumption of divine assistance.

For the present, however, Judah and the Maccabees appeared to have triumphed, and their cause was assumed to be 'right' and justified by results – though not by the hellenizers in the Akra, or by any Seleukids who took any interest. Both of these were irreconcilable, and one reason for their attitude was the knowledge of just how the Maccabees had gained their power. Menelaos, for one, was familiar with the court at Antioch and will have appreciated the real reason for Lysias' retirement from Beth Zur. And he knew that the Maccabees' control of the countryside was based on brutality, murder, and terror. Behind the citadel walls, Menelaos the high priest and his people had no inclination to give themselves up to such enemies.

Chapter 4

The Beginnings of Imperialism

Throughout their accounts of the early years of the crisis in Judaea, both books of Maccabees refer back repeatedly to the past history of the Jewish people. It is a staple of the speeches put into Judah's mouth that the problem facing the army was one that had been faced and overcome in the past by earlier heroes and armies. The names of places are regularly rendered as they had been in the past – so 'Philistia',[1] 'Aram',[2] 'Israel'[3] are all employed – and Judah is even made to refer to the passage of the Red Sea before the battle of Ammaus,[4] and before his 'victory' at Beth Zur he is said to have called up the memory of Saul and his son Jonathan.[5] Whether Judah really said such things is not known – for the speeches are clearly much later compositions and on several occasions no speech could possibly have been delivered – but these references may well have been in the minds of the soldiers. These were men fighting for a religious cause, and they had been brought up on the words and stories of Jewish history. That is the essential basis for understanding what happened next.

After the victory celebrations over the taking of Jerusalem, and presumably somewhat euphoric, the Maccabean leaders thought of the future. To expect the temple to remain in their hands once their small army had left the city was unrealistic, and the news that Lysias was increasing his forces, and that the Seleukid army in the east was returning westwards, were good indications that Judaea would not be free from royal attention for very long, whoever emerged in control of Antioch. It was therefore necessary to look to Judaea's defences.

The threatening, and still garrisoned, Akra was separated from the temple by a rapidly built wall, which was eventually to encircle the temple itself, converting it into a rival fortress.[6] How effective this would be was obviously uncertain. The population of the city had been reasonably content with the worship as organized by the hellenizers until Judah's army arrived, and it is unlikely that all the citizens were happy with the new regime. Beth Zur was taken over and strengthened,[7] so Lysias' strategy was expected to be repeated. The presence of Gorgias as governor of Idumaea was a standing threat, even if all he did was to maintain control over the route Lysias had used in his approach. None of this was likely to be effective against a major Seleukid attack.

From the start Judah's main problem had been military manpower. Seizing Jerusalem did not help much. The news of the 'victory' at Beth Zur and the seizure of Jerusalem will have convinced some waverers and neutrals that he was the man to join, but Judaea would never be able to produce an army large enough to dispute directly with even a large fraction of the Seleukid forces. Judah's main advantage, militarily, was that his troops were strongly motivated. He needed more men like that.

The deliberate recollection of the past by the Maccabees in their rhetoric of rebellion and self-justification also drew attention to the past political history of the Jews in Palestine, when Jewish kings had ruled the whole land 'from Dan to Beersheba',[8] as far as the Mediterranean coast, and east over the Jordan. These regions therefore became aspirations for the rebel regime, and Judah set about staking Maccabean claims. This is the ideological background for a series of expeditions Judah now launched.

The evacuation of persecuted Jews later became the justification for all these campaigns. A letter is quoted in I Maccabees, claiming that Jews in Galaaditis were being persecuted and had taken refuge in a place called Diathema.[9] Another message, from Galilee, claimed persecution of Tyre, Sidon, Ptolemais, and 'all heathen Galilee'.[10] This was the reason given for these expeditions. However, neither 'letter' is dated, and the strong suspicion must exist that they were later inventions designed to supply justification for the expeditions.

The expeditions certainly took place, at least some of them, but the way they were conducted, and their targets, suggest that the rescue of persecuted Jewish populations was not their original purpose. The letter and the reports of persecution were thus probably *post-facto* inventions. This is not to say that the scattered Jewish groups outside Judaea were unaffected by what was happening inside that land. The Maccabean rebellion surely had repercussions among them, and they could well be subject to suspicion and investigation at least. Given the unpleasant methods used by the Maccabean persecutors inside Judaea, this would not to be surprising, and to the local authorities such suspicion was justified as a precaution. Within Judaea those suspicions could conveniently be exaggerated for propaganda purposes. I shall here, therefore, assume that the Maccabean justification is largely false and invented later, and that the expeditions went out as a mixture of raids and conquests. In one case at least the raid was stimulated by the activities of anti-Maccabean Jews.[11] It is worth noting that there are other justifications claimed for Judah's work, in particular that old enemies needed to be punished and new enemies deterred. These are more convincing as reasons for the expeditions than the letters.

It is not certain if these expeditions were successive or simultaneous. Nor is it altogether clear exactly where some of them went. A raid is mentioned against 'Akrabattene', for example, which has been located both to the north of Judaea and south of Idumaea. This raid is mentioned along with one into Idumaea, so this seems to be the likeliest direction for it, in which case Judah's forces reached as far as the southern end of the Dead Sea.[12] A raid against the 'sons of Baian' is often thought to have been across the Jordan, but the wording of I Maccabees makes a distinction between these Baianites and a separate expedition that did involve crossing that river. The Baianites are described as a group who interfered with travel 'with their traps and roadblocks and continually ambushing the Israelites', which rather suggests a group not far from Judaea who lived in part by brigandage.[13]

These two expeditions, against the Idumaeans and the Baianites, would seem therefore to have been directed at peoples who had roused Maccabean ire in the recent past, by ambushes, or, in the Idumaean case, by supporting the Seleukids. Lysias' expedition had come through Idumaea, and some of the fugitives from the Ammaus fight headed for Idumaea for refuge; Gorgias was the governor of Idumaea. This Maccabean campaign can best be seen as partly a deterrent and partly revenge.

Idumaea was a region that included the cities of Iamnia and Ashdod. This expedition is described in much, but contradictory, detail in II Maccabees. A continual guerrilla-type war is implied in the south between Maccabees and Idumaeans, who were joined by fugitives from Jerusalem fleeing from Maccabean authority, all organized it seems by Gorgias, and based in 'strategic fortresses'.[14] Judah organized the campaign to combat this threat, and is credited with capturing 'the Idumaean fortresses', and killing 20,000 of the enemy. 'Fortresses' must mean forts at the most, for there was nothing bigger than that in the area other than the cities; the death toll is, as usual, wildly exaggerated. The only realistic detail describes a siege of two towers that were held by '9,000' of the enemy. The Maccabean force was commanded by Judah's brother Simon and by a man called Josephus, and included 'Zacchaeus and his men'. The besieged bribed Simon's men to get out. This was later denounced by Judah, who executed the 'traitors'. The whole story abounds with contradictions, but presumably reflects in some way the capture of Idumaean forts.[15] The fortification of Beth Zur and the raid against the Idumaeans was part of the same policy of the defence of the south and control of the road from Idumaea towards Jerusalem. But the raids were also directed against anti-Maccabean Jewish fugitives in the region.

Across the Jordan the governor (*strategos*) was Timotheos. In II Maccabees he is named along with three others, Apollonios son of Genaios, Hieronymos, and Demophon, all of them said to be *strategoi*.[16] Timotheos is firmly located east of the Jordan, but the other three could be governors of any in the regions around Judaea. These men were of the same rank and had the same responsibilities, as Apollonios in Samaria and as Gorgias in Idumaea. That is, they all ruled fairly restricted regions on behalf of the Seleukid king, being responsible to the king through the governor of Koele Syria, by now Ptolemaios Makron. Timotheos was encountered first in relation to the people of Ammanitis and then in Galaaditis, east of the Sea of Galilee. (The other men cannot be located.)

The retirement of Lysias from Beth Zur did not end the pressure on Judaea, as the activity of Gorgias shows. The other neighbouring governors were no doubt mobilized to maintain it. In Ammanitis Timotheos is said to have collected a mercenary army and was threatening to invade Judaea.[17] Judah took his army – said to number 8,000 men, a plausible number for once – into Ammanitis, the country around Rabboth Ammon, now the city of Philadelphia. The fighting centred on Jazera, which is said to have been captured.[18] Numbers are as usual exaggerated, as are battle descriptions, but some names emerge – Chaereas (described as Timotheos' brother) and Apollophanes, who were officers under Timotheos. The death of Timotheos is described, though he was alive again a little later – one of those contradictions that saps belief in the whole series of events. This does fit to a degree with a section of II Maccabees, a short account that is clearly displaced chronologically, in which it is claimed that Timotheos' force lost 20,000 men in the battle with Judah. But this version also claims that Chaereas, not Timotheos, commanded, though Timotheos is said to have died. After the battle the Jews, as is to be expected, but as is usually ignored in other accounts, collected weaponry from the battlefield.[19]

There is another aspect of this expedition that is worth attention. The place Judah captured, Jazera, is not far from Iraq el-Amir, where the Tobiad Hyrkanos had built a temple for Jewish worship. Hyrkanos was the man who had given refuge to the deposed high priest Jason, and so Hyrkanos may be presumed to be a moderate hellenizer – his temple-cum-palace strongly suggests a sympathy for hellenism. It was from there that Jason launched his attempt to recover the high priesthood, with the aid of a thousand men, who were presumably at least in part supplied by Hyrkanos. Josephus reports that after Jason's defeat, Hyrkanos committed suicide, to forestall a worse fate at the hands of Antiochos IV,[20] but it is now generally reckoned he lived on until perhaps 168, dying in the aftermath of the king's raid into Judaea.

If Hyrkanos could supply Jason with a force of a thousand men, it is obvious that there was a considerable Jewish community living in the area. This is presupposed by Hyrkanos' temple, which was presumably designed for the same sort of worship, sacrifice, and so on, as in Jerusalem. These Jews were probably sympathizers with the hellenizing party, certainly of the moderate sort.[21] Hyrkanos' suicide will not have destroyed that community, but will certainly have weakened it. These were, of course, enemies of the Maccabees, just as there were those fugitives who were operating with Gorgias, and those in Judaea who had been terrorized into conformity. It seems therefore more than coincidental that Judah's first trans-Jordanian expedition should be aimed exactly at the region of this Jewish anti-Maccabean group. Hyrkanos may have incurred the enmity of Antiochos IV, but the rebellion in Judaea will have aligned his people (after his death) with the Seleukid governor Timotheos, and so Timotheos came out of Philadelphia to protect them.

Judah was thus attempting by this expedition to eliminate yet another source of Jewish opposition. Judah's force met that of Timotheos at Jazera, and they are said to have fought 'many battles', until Judah captured Jazera. Josephus improves on this by claiming that Jazera was burnt and the wives and children were taken prisoner.

The aim of the Maccabean army cannot have been to take Jazera, which was of no importance, nor attack Philadelphia, which was a well-fortified Greek city. The 'many battles' between the forces, each of which were only a few thousand strong at most, may perhaps be reduced to a number of serious skirmishes. The capture of Jazera may well have happened, but as a feat of arms it is scarcely notable. (It was certainly not a city, as Josephus claims, and may not even have been burnt, for this is not mentioned in I Maccabees.)

This first Maccabean expedition across the Jordan needs a better explanation than a possible threat from Timotheos and his small army. The existence of the Tobiad community provides a better reason. None of the Jewish sources claim that this was a 'rescue' expedition, but make the point that the inhabitants of Jazera were treated in the same way as other conquered places – the men were all killed and the women and children enslaved. The expedition was therefore a combination of a raid for loot, an imperialist attempt at expansion, and the purging of a rival political centre.

The Tobiad massacre, note, was perpetrated by Judah and his army. It is further evidence of the Maccabean methods of 'persuasion'. This was a force buoyed up by religious zeal, which had recently cleansed and purified its recovered temple, which was in the habit of referring to its internal enemies as 'sinners', and which had shown no compunction about killing hellenizers inside Judaea, overthrowing their altars, and forcibly circumcising Jewish boys who had not had the operation. The Tobiads certainly fell into that category, and they received the same treatment.

Timotheos was also the organizer of the defence when Judah led his army into Galaaditis. This was the country called Gilead by the Jews, the land north of Ammanitis. The name Galaaditis implies that it was a sub-province with its own *strategos*. (The '-itis' ending is a mark of such a sub-province, as in Ammanitis.) This should have had its own governor, but Timotheos is said to have been in charge.

Galaaditis was the first area Judah is said to have invaded in order to rescue oppressed Jewish communities. The letter quoted in I Maccabees reported that they were being threatened, and had gathered themselves into a fort at Diathema, and that Timotheos was in command of the forces operating against them. The letter also claims that their fellow Jews 'in the region of Tobias' had been massacred and their wives and children taken captive. ('Tobias' in this case was another regional name, not referring to the Tobiad family, which was based further south.) At the same time refugees from the north reported suffering persecution in Galilee by people – defined only as 'heathens' – from Ptolemais, Sidon, Tyre, and Galilee. In response Judah took his own army into Galaaditis and sent his brother Simon with a smaller force – 3,000 men, it is said – into Galilee.[22]

Judah's campaign in the east is described in confusing terms in I and II Maccabees and in Josephus. There may be a common origin to all these accounts, but reconstructing it is very difficult.[23] None of the sources really knows what happened. All three have a set of different place names, to such an extent that identifying most of them is very difficult, and tends towards guesswork.[24] The common elements are an assertion that Judah regularly captured a series of places and in each case massacred the inhabitants. In I Maccabees and Josephus two fights against Timotheos' army are described, but these are not independent sources, Josephus being very dependent upon I Maccabees for this section. The gathered Jews at Diathema are reported as being under siege by Timotheos' forces, which siege was relieved by Judah's arrival. A second encounter between Judah's and Timotheos' forces, at Raphon or Romphon, resulted, of course, in a defeat for Timotheos. On the return of the army to Judaea, shepherding the Jews from Galaaditis, the 'city' of

Ephron was captured and its inhabitants massacred. This is the only incident and place name common to all three accounts.[25]

It is impossible to accept much of this. An army that had never captured, or even attacked, a fortified place is now described as assaulting and capturing a whole series of 'cities'. The route the army is said to have taken is impossible to follow, unless one source is taken as correct and the others discarded. Above all, the motives ascribed to Timotheos are simply unbelievable.

He is said to have laid siege to Diathema (which cannot be securely located), into which the Jews from the surrounding towns had fled. But Judah is later described as collecting together 'all the Israelites in Gilead' to take them into Judaea. So the people in Diathema may be Jews, but they were certainly not all the Jews from the towns of Galaaditis.

None of these places, except perhaps one, can be accepted as 'cities'. The exception is Raphon/Romphon, which is usually assumed to be the later Raphanaea, which was certainly a city – that is, a *polis* – in the Roman period, though it is unlikely to have been of that rank at this time. None of the other places is heard of again. But there were cities in the area, though they never feature in the account – Gerasa, Gadara, Hippos, Abila, Dion, Pella were fortified places capable of defying an army, and are never mentioned. The named places in the Jewish accounts were thus only villages. They may have had some sort of encircling walls, but none of them were fortified in any real sense. Judah's campaign therefore kept well clear of cities and he attacked only villages.

The campaign, in fact, is best seen as a search for the army of Timotheos, which had blocked Judah's invasion of Ammanitis earlier. Judah gained information from some Nabataean Arabs, supposedly about Jews being held captive in various towns. He is said to have captured or occupied these places, but no Jews are ever said to have been rescued. Timotheos' army, besieging Diathema, was driven off. This is the place where Jews are said to have been gathered, according to the letter they supposedly sent, but there is no reference to them being rescued. Timotheos' army was finally located at Raphon, where it was defeated (again), and pursued into Karnaim, where the refugees took refuge in a temple of Atargatis; the town was captured and the temple and its occupants burnt. By implication Timotheos was one of the casualties, but in II Maccabees he was captured and then released. (He had been 'killed' once already, of course.) Again, no rescue of Jews is referred to. In all this strange campaign, the purpose as stated in Maccabees was to come to the aid of persecuted Jews, but none was ever rescued. We may conclude that the rescue purpose was a later invented justification. Another reason must be sought.

It seems more likely that this was another attempt – the invasion of Ammanitis was the first – to extend Maccabean control over strategically important places east of the Jordan and so to block attacks from that direction. Beth Zur's new fortifications were intended to block access to Judaea from the south, a danger that Lysias' campaign had highlighted; in the west and north the defeat of the Seleukid armies of Apollonios and Seron and Nikanor had shown that defence in that region was possible using the natural geography and relatively small forces. An attack from the east was still possible, by a combination of local Seleukid forces and hellenizer-Jews from Hyrkanos' country, but by gaining control of the region east of the Jordan, and by destroying the local military power there, the approach from the east could also be blocked.

This campaign was being conducted in a region that forms a natural division between the area dominated by Damascus to the north and that dominated by Amman (the ancient Philadelphia), to the south. It is rough country, with difficult lava spreads impeding travel, and it overlooks the valley of the Yarmuk River, which is deeply entrenched and forms an eminently defensible line and region. Seizing this area meant that Judah could hope to prevent any Seleukid movement southwards that way. The Seleukid army must then approach along the coastal plain, and attack Judaea by way of routes where earlier attacks had already been foiled.

The campaign was particularly brutal, with repeated massacres of the local population, including the Jews of the Jazera region. Such an approach was an extension of the terror tactics already used in Judaea, an attempt to frighten the local population into either giving in or leaving. But the existence of the Greek cities – Gadara, Hippos, and so on – foiled any such intention, since all they needed to do was to shut their gates and mount a guard. Meanwhile, the continued existence of Timotheos' army prevented Judah's forces laying siege to any of the cities, since that would pin the Judaean forces down at one place and render them vulnerable. The repeated defeats of Timotheos' army indicate that it continued to exist. The continual destruction of villages would soon leave the area desolate, and the Jewish forces would then begin to suffer from a lack of supplies, and would need to leave.

This is all assuming, of course, that the accounts of the campaign in the Jewish sources are accurate. It is worth recalling that the preceding campaign against Lysias in the Beth Zur area had been proclaimed a victory, when it was not. Given that the justification for the campaign, to evacuate a threatened Jewish population, is clearly wrong, the claims of victories could also be wrong. The claims of the death of Timotheos are inaccurate, and his army was fought often, in the Jazera campaign and later in the north. It could well be that claims of Judaean victories were equally fallacious. The relish with which massacres are reported is very unpleasant, but it does fit with the terrorist campaigns that had already been used in Judaea, Idumaea, and Jazera, and perhaps these can be accepted, though possibly exaggerated.

After such a vicious campaign the local Jews surely became unpopular, if they were not so already, hence their evacuation from their homes. On the march back to Judaea another city, Skythopolis, lay on their route. The Jewish inhabitants there stated that they were in no danger, so Judah bypassed the city; it was also well fortified, so the story may well simply be an excuse for his not attacking it. At the same time the Jewish inhabitants of this Greek city showed no inclination to join the Maccabean cause, presumably because they tended towards the hellenizers' cause. Living as they did in a well-established Greek city, this would not be surprising.

The expedition that Simon took to Galilee at the same time had much the same experience. The Jews of Galilee were threatened by enemies, both by their neighbours and by the armed forces of the cities of Tyre, Sidon and Ptolemais-Ake, according to the letter. Simon, with 3,000 men, went north. Tyre and Sidon are not mentioned again, and Ptolemais only as the destination of the (Gentile) refugees who were displaced by Simon's attack.[26] Ptolemais was the provincial capital, with strong walls and a large garrison, the trained militia of the city. It could certainly have subdued any Jews in Galilee, if that was the official policy.

Again, it is better to change events around somewhat, and to ignore the supposed appeal. Simon actually took his forces north on a raid, partly for loot and partly to deter any attack. His activities stimulated enmity towards Jews in the area, so that Simon had to bring them back with him. He may have reached the gates of Ptolemais, but he could only have done so if he arrived totally unexpectedly, since his force was not strong enough to cope with what the governor in Ptolemais-Ake could field. (The purpose of I Maccabees was to glorify Simon, and one wonders if the raid actually took place; it may have been invented to show Simon, scarcely mentioned in the war otherwise, as active and enterprising as Judah.)

These four raids, against Idumaea, Ammanitis, Galaaditis, and Galilee, were partly defensive in purpose, aimed to pre-empt any attack that might be planned by destroying, or at least defeating, the surrounding armed forces. Where a fortification could be developed, as at Beth Zur, it was built or improved, but the main purpose was to drive enemies, and potential enemies, away. An unintended result was the development of enmity among the surrounding peoples towards the Maccabees, who must have been disliked already. This transferred itself into enmity towards local Jews, some of whom may well have welcomed the Judaean invaders. So those Jews who wished to go were evacuated back to Judaea. When these events were written up a generation and more later the evacuation became the presumed purpose of the whole exercise.

Loot was another major incentive, to deprive their enemies of resources and acquire those resources for the new Judaean government. Another raid was organized, by two commanders not of the Maccabee family, Josephus son of Zacharias, and Azarias. These two were left in Judaea, supposedly ordered by Judah not to try anything. Nevertheless, they set out on a raid into the lowlands, but were met outside Iamnia by Gorgias the Idumaean governor, and defeated.[27] They cannot have expected to capture any city, certainly not Iamnia, nor could they have held on to any place if they did capture it; the object was presumably loot. Since this was a Sabbath year in the highlands, perhaps they aimed to gather food as well.

The defeat of this expedition was followed by a new expedition by Judah to wipe out the memory by a new victory. The account, in II Maccabees, is another doctored version. Gorgias advanced after his victory into the Idumaean area south of Judaea, a region already damaged by Judah's earlier attacks. Judah captured Hebron, and broke down its fortifications. Then he headed west, marching through Marisa towards Ashdod. Gorgias, commanding an army of 3,000 infantry and 400 cavalry, plausible figures for once, met the Maccabean force before it reached Marisa. In the fight Gorgias escaped from a hand-to-hand combat (with the Tobiad Dositheos) thanks to the intervention of a Thracian cavalryman, and later Judah came to the relief of a hard-pressed section of his army. At the end Gorgias 'escaped' by way of

Marisa, but Judah withdrew to Adullam, which is ten kilometres northeast of Marisa in the direction of Judaea. I Maccabees also describes a raid into the territory of Ashdod, where the army destroyed altars and statues of gods, looted the area, and then went home. The overall implication is that Gorgias retired into his cities after fighting it out in the open.[28]

Taking into account the usual distortion of the Maccabean authors we may discount a good deal of the claimed successes. The capture of Hebron may be regarded with suspicion, as well as all the 'forts' in the area. It is not even certain that Hebron had much in the way of fortifications – a fairly flimsy wall designed to keep out the local Bedouin is perhaps what might be expected. This was not the modern city, which dates from the time of Herod, but Tell el-Rumeidah, across the valley, which was the site of the city in the Iron Age, though it had faded away since. What Judah captured was a more or less desolate site, certainly no more than a hamlet.[29] Marisa was probably unfortified. It was a town developed in the Ptolemaic period by settling a colony of Sidonians at the site. It is on a hill (now Beit Guvrin), and was probably defensible against local raids, but a substantial army would capture it easily. There is no sign of a wall, or of a citadel, unless there was one on the top of the mound.[30] Ashdod, which was fortified, was not even attacked. Josephus' rewriting of all this exaggerates supposed Maccabean achievements, but Judah was only campaigning against places that could not resist.

There is also a curious notice, which was also in II Maccabees, which seems a distraction or an expansion of these events. It is said that there was a conspiracy in Joppa to remove the Jews from the city. This is described in terms that emphasized both Jewish reasonableness and Gentile duplicity and cruelty. Judah is credited with a revenge attack in which the ships in the harbour, and the harbour itself, were burnt. He is said to have followed this with a similar attack on Iamnia, which was similarly successful.[31]

This may be explained in terms of the harbours of both of these places being open roadsteads and unfortified, but other sources do not mention the events in Joppa, and do not bring Judah anywhere near Iamnia. It seems best to take these supposed attacks as pure invention, later justification for the Jewish terrorist measures and expulsions at Joppa. At the same time this is a clue to the point of all this raiding, evacuation, and neighbouring enmity.

The purposes of all these expeditions is unlikely to be the 'rescue' of Jews under oppression. There are far too many contradictions in the stories for that to be accepted, though persecution may have been the result of the raids. A possible alternative would be strategic defence, especially in the trans-Jordan raids and in Idumaea. The attacks on the Idumaeans certainly look to be intended to deter local participation in the next Seleukid attack. Both Timotheos and Gorgias, as local governors, were attempting either to contain the Maccabees or to invade Judaea.

These raids cannot be said to have been successful. The attacks in Ammanitis and towards Iamnia and Ashdod were blocked by the forces commanded by Timotheos and Gorgias respectively. Simon's raid into Galilee, if it actually happened, was sudden and swift, but he was compelled to bring back some Jewish refugees, either because they had been attacked or because attacks on them were now expected. The raid into Galaaditis is the most difficult to evaluate. The problem is to sort out what its purpose was. The letter quoted in I Maccabees from the people blocked up in Diathema must be suspect, particularly since when the siege there was relieved, there is no mention of the rescue of Jews. The evacuation of Jews from Galaaditis, like that from Galilee, is best seen as the necessary consequence of Judah's raid rather than as the purpose of the raid in the first place.

So, using scepticism as to the motives ascribed by the Jewish sources, these raids are best seen as looting expeditions and pre-emptive defensive moves. It may be relevant that they took place in the second half of a sabbatical year, when the land in Judaea was left fallow. This would cause hunger in the year following, and the conflicts of the previous years – the Maccabees' terrorist attacks, in effect a civil war, and the Seleukid invasions – had surely disrupted Judaean agriculture. Even if the storehouses saw the people through the sabbatical year, the year after was bound to be difficult. On the other hand, there was no fallow year in the surrounding lands, whose agricultural system presumably included fallow fields in rotation rather than for the whole region. Raids to steal their food might seem a useful move. Overthrowing a few altars and burning a temple or two would be a pleasant extra; collecting loot from the victims would be regarded as normal military activity.

The claim, made repeatedly, that fortified towns were captured by the Maccabean forces must also be disbelieved. Either the towns – all too often called '*poleis*', cities – were not fortified and so were easy to take, or they were fortified and were not captured. I Maccabees, in particular, tends to apply the formula of capture-and-massacre all too easily. Any places that are known to have been seriously fortified – Iamnia, Ashdod, the Jerusalem Akra, the cities across the Jordan – could not be taken, and these examples strongly imply that the Maccabean army had no siege capability. Nor is this surprising. It was in origin a terrorist group, capable of ambushes and guerrilla raids. Few if any men in the army had any previous military training. Experience over the past years converted those who had survived into more or less competent soldiers, good in attack, capable of long disciplined marches, but conducting a siege is a very different proposition.

These explanations – looting, evacuation, deterrence – are reasonable explanations of most of this fighting, but the story of Joppa cannot be included, since in all likelihood it was an invention. So the question is, why invent it? Joppa, in fact, was always an important Jewish target. It was one of the few decent ports on the coast near Judaea, and was therefore the most convenient outlet to the sea for those living in the hills. Later it became the first place on the coast to be captured by Jonathan.

This seems to be the clue to its inclusion in the wars of Judah. The places that were attacked by Judah were all places that were later to be the targets for Maccabean conquest, and the stories of these raids were intended to emphasize the 'claim' of the Jews of Judaea to rule over the whole of Palestine and the nearby areas across the Jordan. The accounts of Judah's wars were written up much later than the events they purport to describe, and in part in the light of later developments: the conquests of the later Maccabean rulers were thus prefigured in the necessary work of rescue and punishment by the first of them. This renders all these stories dubious. That against Joppa is clearly an invention; Simon's raid is quite possibly also invented; the raids to the east and south can be accepted, though the accounts are clearly distorted.

The Jewish rebellion on the high plateau had begun as a religious complaint about hellenizing developments in Jerusalem, but had quickly expanded into imperial conquest. These raids by Judah and under his direction are the first signs of that ambition. The policy of frightfulness, evident at home and in Galaaditis, and the concentration on unifying all the Jews under their rule, prefigured the later development of Maccabean imperial policies. But there was one item that restricted Maccabean activities, even in the homeland, and that was the continued enmity of the Jews in the Akra, which was also the enduring symbol of Seleukid political authority there.

Chapter 5

Defeat

The raids instigated and conducted by Judah had uniformly failed to secure further territory beyond the hill plateau for the nascent Judaean state, except for Beth Zur, and independence would not be achieved while the Jerusalem Akra was controlled by the high priest, Menelaos, and the Seleukid government. It was also obvious that to attack that fortress would bring the full and unwelcome attention of Lysias and the Seleukid army.

Lysias, however, was fully preoccupied. Some of the troops that had been in the east with Antiochos IV had returned,[1] but Philippos and the rest had not yet arrived. Philippos may not yet have made his intentions clear, but Lysias was certainly uneasy. The governor of Koele Syria, Ptolemaios Makron, was one of the victims of the purge he felt it necessary to conduct to bolster his position,[2] and Ptolemaios had been an advocate of negotiations. The raids conducted by the Maccabees into the surrounding lands, generally unsuccessful though they had been, were also a source of irritation, and surely discredited Ptolemaios Makron''s policy of conciliation, just as Lysias was surely criticized for permitting them. Complaints to Ptolemais-Ake, to Damascus, to Antioch, were undoubtedly made, and Timotheos and Gorgias will have sent in their reports.

By seizing control of the temple in Jerusalem Judah gained control of all the city except the Akra to add to his control of the countryside, and this made him in the ruler. The people outside the city, the rural population, were habituated to look to Jerusalem as the source of political authority. In effect Judaea was a city-state, even if not formally a *polis*. But the Akra was a clear symbol of the limitation, even the illegitimacy, of Judah's power – he was still the leader of a rebellion against the legitimate high priest. For Judah the Akra was an eyesore, a threat, and a standing challenge to his authority. For Lysias it was the essential basis for the Seleukid claim to rule in Judaea. If the Akra fell to the Maccabee rebels their claim to be the legitimate rulers in Judaea, would be unchallenged. Its fall would be a major political defeat for Lysias, and might well so undermine his authority that he would be easy to overthrow.

The situation was precisely what the Seleukid city founders had intended as their method for keeping control of a city. All the cities – Antioch, Apamea, Seleukeia, and the rest – were given walls to protect them from enemies, but also citadels within which a royal garrison protected the king's interests as against the citizens.[3] The installation of the Akra in Jerusalem had brought the geography of the city into line with other Seleukid cities. The Akra was thus maintaining the king's interest as against that of the people of the city. So the Maccabean rebellion had actually brought Jerusalem closer to the normal Hellenistic city.

Both Judah and Lysias were under pressure of time. For Judah it was obvious that an attempt would be made to relieve the Akra siege; for Lysias the longer he was absent from Antioch the more opportunities his enemies would have to plot and perhaps seize power there. Lysias put off his expedition for some time, hoping that the Akra would hold out until the situation at Antioch was cleared up.

Judah's siege made no progress for a time. He was facing serious and active resistance, to such an extent that I Maccabees could even suggest that it was Judah's force that was besieged.[4] Judah tightened the blockade and began an active assault. I Maccabees claims he began using battering rams and artillery,[5] which may or may not be correct. Anyone in the Hellenistic world would know of such things as battering rams, so the author may have simply assumed they were in use. The Akra held out for another twenty years, so Maccabean siege technique was not very effective – though, to be sure, there were other factors operating to prevent the citadel being taken

At this point some of the besieged, including Menelaos the high priest, left the Akra and went to Antioch.[6] (The fact that they were able to leave the Akra implies that the siege was less than rigorous.) Their news, presumably of the progress of the siege, brought Lysias south, and he brought the young King Antiochos V with him. No doubt Lysias knew by now that he faced a rival in Philippos, who was moving west with the rest of the royal army, and his trump card in the face of Philippos' challenge was control of the king, who therefore had to go wherever Lysias went. The message from the Akra must have been urgent indeed to bring him away from Antioch at such a crucial time.

Lysias used the same approach march as in his first expedition, south along the coastal plain and round to take the route through Idumaea, and on to Beth Zur. This refortified post had to be taken by siege, which was a fairly quick process, though I Maccabees imagines raids and counter-raids, building and burning siege machines.[7] It may be that Judah indulged, as before, in raids on the Seleukid camp, but they would not stop this army. (Perhaps Maccabean propaganda about the first confrontation with Lysias had persuaded many that another raid would suffice to drive the Seleukid army away, again.)

Lysias' army was even more formidable than that in his earlier campaign. The figures provided by the Jewish sources are 100,000 infantry and 20,000 horse in I Maccabees, 110,000 foot, 5,300 horse, 22 elephants, plus chariots in II Maccabees. Josephus gives two totals, in one he copied those of I Maccabees, elsewhere he gives 50,000 infantry and 5,000 horse.[8] All are, as usual, much exaggerated, but in this case Lysias really had brought a large part of the Seleukid forces available in Syria, so perhaps half of Josephus' lower figures might be acceptable. On the number of war elephants that Lysias used a consensus that he had eight has been reached, but this is only based on an assumed copyist's error; it has no greater validity than any other figure.[9] These numbers only reflect the fact that the Seleukid army was about to overwhelm the Maccabean forces with little difficulty. Maccabean pride insisted that it was only by overwhelming numbers, perhaps the largest they could imagine, that Lysias could have succeeded.

Beth Zur was besieged until the garrison was on the verge of starvation.[10] It did not help that one of the men inside was an agent for the attackers, and kept them informed, at least until he was found out.[11] Once the place was taken Lysias moved on, and was faced by the full Maccabean army at Beth Zakaria, about eight kilometres further north. Judah had chosen a place that could be defended by the smaller force, a narrowish pass, but it was not ideal, as the sequel showed. His earlier successes constrained his response to the invasion, for as the ruler of Judaea (as he was now) it was his duty to protect the population, and therefore he had to meet the invader on the border of his territory. Beth Zur had been the border post, and once it fell Beth Zakaria was the next position on the road north towards Jerusalem which suited his army. He could no longer apply his well-tried methods.

The Judaean army was, of course, outnumbered, and was faced by an experienced commander who could organize his army and adapt it to the situation. To get through the pass Lysias divided his force into several units, each consisting of one elephant, 1,000 infantry, and 500 cavalry. Each unit could operate to some extent independently,[12] with skirmishers going ahead. I Maccabees claims that 600 of these were killed, so there certainly was a fight – but Maccabean casualties are not reported,[13] and since they were defeated they were probably much greater than those in Lysias' force. One incident only in the actual battle is reported, in ecstatic terms: the attempt by Judah's brother Eleazar to kill an elephant and so disrupt the Seleukid advance. He succeeded in reaching and stabbing the elephant, though not necessarily in killing it; he was himself then killed, supposedly when the elephant fell on him.[14]

This isolated incident, portrayed as a triumph, is used to disguise the fact that when the armies actually clashed the Maccabean army was wholly defeated. (All the Jewish sources hide this defeat, even claiming the reverse.[15]) Lysias and his army were therefore then able to march on to Jerusalem, relieve the Akra siege, and blockade the temple area. Judah and his surviving soldiers fled to the Gophna Hills.[16]

At Jerusalem the temple fortifications were, according to I Maccabees, bombarded by all the devices of Hellenistic siege warfare – battering rams, artillery, fire arrows, scorpions. Yet at the same time it makes the point that there was only a minimal garrison inside the temple area, and there was little or no food for them, the supplies having been consumed by the refugees brought in from Galaaditis and Galilee. So, despite the claim that the siege lasted 'many days' these contradictions suggest that Lysias did not actually need to spend long on the siege – in contrast to the lengthy Maccabean siege of the Akra – and we can take the elaborate description as a formula that the author expected to happen in a siege, and is another example of Maccabean exaggeration to explain defeat.[17] Lysias was, in fact, quickly distracted from the situation in Judaea by bad news from Antioch.

Philippos, on his way back from the east, had now made his claim to the regency clear. By the time Lysias returned to the north Philippos had gained control of Antioch, so when the Jerusalem temple siege began he was probably quite close to the city. Lysias still had the king with him, and a larger section of the army than Philippos, but control of Antioch and its nearby cities was as important as the king's person, so Lysias had to return to the north.

He was also in difficulty over supplies. The sabbatical year in Judaea, and the earlier under-production of food because of the disturbed condition of Judaea, meant that local supplies of food that the Seleukid army must have hoped to collect did not exist. Together with the news of Philippos' approach, this predisposed Lysias to consider concessions. He could assume that the defeat and dispersal of the Maccabees' army was decisive. He had no wish to destroy the temple in Jerusalem, just to capture or kill a small group of rebels – it was, after all, Menelaos' temple.[18]

Negotiations took place, but who took part on the Jewish side is not clear, possibly whoever was in command in the temple. It does not seem that Judah was involved, though since the outcome was seen by the Maccabees as a defeat it may be that his participation has simply been written out of the record. The resulting agreement took the form of a letter ostensibly from Antiochos V to Lysias, and was presumably delivered to some authority in Jerusalem. It revoked the oppressive measures that angered the Jews, and returned the legal situation to that which had been obtained before the oppressive edicts of Antiochos IV's time. II Maccabees, logically, attributed Lysias' concessions to his supposed defeat.[19]

This return to previous conditions was interpreted by Lysias as applying to the temple as well as to the laws, and the fortifications were pulled down. I Maccabees claims that this was a breach of the agreement by 'the king', but since Menelaos continued as high priest and the Seleukid garrison continued to occupy the Akra, it did not make sense for the temple to go on being separately fortified. The accusation of bad faith is wilful Maccabean misinterpretation and disappointment rather than royal (that is, Lysiad) oath-breaking.[20]

The revocation of the oppressive measures was not communicated directly to anyone on the Jewish side. The measures had originally been instigated by the high priest and the *gerousia* of the city. These were now ignored, presumably because they were unhappy at the revocation. Nor could Judah and his followers be told directly, for they were still in rebellion; hence the device of a letter from the child king to his first minister – which neatly emphasized that Judaea was still a Seleukid province – though no doubt copies were made available to them.

The result was that nobody was really satisfied, though the Seleukid government was the obvious winner. The defeat of the Maccabees, at Beth Zur, at Beth Zakaria, and at the temple, was clear; yet the hellenizers were hardly victorious, since they had been confined to the single fort of the Akra, and had had to be rescued by a major Seleukid expedition. It is unlikely that anywhere in Judaea was particularly safe for the hellenizers after all this, but the Maccabees had suffered a severe blow to their prestige. Lysias could claim success in that he had won battles, camped in the enemy's headquarters, captured the city, and dictated peace terms there. He could march away reasonably satisfied. When he reached Antioch he was able to take the city from Philippos with little difficulty.[21]

It was during these events that the Jews, or some of them, first encountered Romans in the east. A letter quoted in II Maccabees[22] seems to encourage the Jewish envoys to get to Antioch quickly. Problems abound with the letter, its date, the names of the Romans (who are otherwise untraceable), who the Jewish and envoys were, and what the contact meant. It may be a complete fabrication.[23] It has, of course, provoked enormous quantities of discussion, in the end to little purpose. Its effect on events in the east was nil. Rome was uninterested in events in Judaea, and had little or no influence. The letter is best seen as no more than a diplomatic courtesy,[24] if it is not a fabrication.

Lysias took the high priest Menelaos away with him when he returned north. It was clear that he could not continue in office with any safety, and to leave him in Jerusalem and in power would only attract local enmity. He was sent, so Josephus says, to live at Beroia, in North Syria, but was then executed.[25] Menelaos no doubt disagreed with Lysias' assessment of his prospects, and his (presumed) continued agitation of his restoration to power may have persuaded Lysias to eliminate him.

Lysias had so many problems at the time that one may sympathize with his wish to get rid of a turbulent priest (unless his execution was another Maccabean action). He returned to Antioch in July 162 or thereabouts, and had to drive out Philippos from the city and re-establish himself there. He was then faced by an unpleasant Roman envoy, C. Octavius, and soon after he was overthrown by the arrival of a successful claimant to the kingship, Demetrios I, who had both Lysias and the boy Antiochos V killed.

It is possible that Lysias appointed a new high priest, or it may be that Demetrios did so soon after his accession. On the whole it seems more likely to have been Lysias, who at least had some familiarity with the situation in Judaea and had been responsible for the execution of the previous high priest. It cannot be supposed that Demetrios knew much about the Judaean problem until he was on the throne. Whoever made the appointment, the man chosen was Alkimos, who was not of the hereditary line from which all earlier high priests (except Menelaos) had come, though he was of a priestly family.[26] There was a candidate from that family, another Onias, son of Onias III (referred to as 'Onias IV' at times), but he was probably still too young. (He went to Egypt, presumably seeking political support, but Ptolemy VI was a friend of Demetrios and, for the present, was not minded to interfere in Syria.[27])

Alkimos was chosen partly because he was neither Onias nor Menelaos, both of whom were identified with earlier political positions, and partly because he was a hellenizer of the moderate sort, perhaps of the same persuasion as Jesus/Jason. He was, it turned out, acceptable to the hellenizers of the city, and at first to the Hasidim, who had been aligned with the Maccabees until then.[28] He was not acceptable to the Maccabees, but at the beginning this did not appear to matter. No appointee by the royal government is likely to have been acceptable to them, for their defeat had simultaneously marginalized them and made them still more intransigent.

Demetrios, if he did not appoint Alkimos, certainly accepted his appointment. He then became fully preoccupied with royal affairs elsewhere. The Roman Senate reacted with displeasure to his quick success, so when Timarchos, the governor of the eastern province, came out in rebellion, he gained Rome's backing, at least in words if not in any effective way. Timarchos had the assistance of his brother Herakleides, who had been removed from his office by Demetrios. This royal crisis continued into 160, when Demetrios finally defeated and killed Timarchos. Herakleides went off to plot revenge.[29]

The situation in Judaea, meanwhile, deteriorated. The Maccabees reverted to their old methods: assassinations, overthrowing altars, and general terrorism.[30] This time the process was easier, since their previous successes had either gained them support or had given them a reputation for violence that cowed opposition. In the country areas any support for the hellenizers evaporated, and Alkimos found he was, like Menelaos, confined to Jerusalem. He complained to Demetrios, by way of a delegation of men who were classed as 'godless renegades' by I Maccabees, reflecting the propaganda put out by Judah.[31]

Demetrios responded as a new king must: with decisive, even overwhelming, power. He called in Bakchides, the governor of Mesopotamia, gave him a large army, and sent him to sort out Judaea. Bakchides attempted to negotiate with Judah, who refused to reply, relying on his inaccessibility in the Gophna Hills.[32] Some of the Hasidim did respond but, after a meeting during which they apparently made it clear that they did not accept Alkimos' authority as high priest, they were then killed.[33] This was a mistake, since the Hasidim really did represent a strand of moderate opinion, less extreme than the Maccabees, just as Alkimos was on the less extreme side of the hellenizers. If these two could not agree then the extremists must fight it out. The Hasidim had support among the country people, and their followers now swung round to support the Maccabees. The Maccabees in turn were handed a useful propaganda point by these deaths.[34]

Bakchides now concentrated his forces on attempting to root out the Maccabees in their Gophna Hills base. Before he had finished – he had killed a fair number of men, but none of the Maccabee brothers – he was recalled to Antioch. Perhaps, indeed, he felt he had finished the task of suppression, since, in the face of his power, the best thing Judah and his people could do was to lie low until the storm passed.[35] The rebellion of Timarchos had grown more serious and Bakchides' army – and perhaps his military skills – were required.

This new respite allowed the Maccabean cause to revive once more. This time any possibility of a reconciliation was out of the question after the killing of the Hasidim, so when the Maccabees emerged from their hills they found much support. 'Alkimos fought hard for his high priesthood', I Maccabees acknowledged, but he was soon confined to the city again. He appealed once more to the king.[36]

Demetrios responded by sending another envoy-cum-governor-cum-commander to Judaea. This was Nikanor, who had formerly been the commander of the elephant corps.[37] Nikanor may have been one of several men of that name recorded as being in the Seleukid government at this time: the son of Patroklos who was defeated at the battle of Ammaus, a friend of Demetrios who helped him escape from Italy, or a man who had acted as agent in Samaria in the time of Antiochos IV. II Maccabees thought he was the man defeated at Ammaus; Josephus thought he was identical with the Italian Nikanor.[38] Neither had any proof, and neither was anywhere near these events in time, so they were merely guessing. But the odds must be on one of these identifications. The fact that he was sent to Judaea with plenipotentiary powers, and appears to have acted as governor there for some time, does suggest that he was close to the king, which would incline one to identify him with the man who was active in Italy. His command of the elephant corps has suggested to some that he was out of a job because the elephants had been killed at Octavius' orders. If so, he had been appointed to that post by Lysias, and so was not a natural Demetrios supporter. But we do not know that all the elephants had been killed. Some certainly had died, but the Seleukid government was under no obligation to ensure that Octavius' demand had been fully met. It is very likely that some elephants had been spared, in which case it would not be beyond the bounds of possibility that a trusted friend of the new king was given a high status post in charge of the elephants and then sent to Judaea to solve a different political problem.

II Maccabees makes Nikanor's remit rather more aggressive at first than does I Maccabees, but both indicate that he aimed at a negotiated settlement with Judah[39] – that is, he was pursuing the same policy as Bakchides. He had to fight a Maccabean force under the command of Simon and then the main army under Judah at Kefar Salama, and won[40] (though I Maccabees claims it as a victory).[41] This is not a place whose location is known, but it may have been at the climb up to the Judaean plateau from the lowlands to the north, possibly in the same general region as the battle against Apollonios. Negotiations with Judah followed this fight, which suggests that the Maccabean defeat had been serious, and negotiations were a means of putting off another attack. On Nikanor's side the negotiations were conducted by Poseidonios, Theodotos and Mattathias,[42] a trio of names, which implies that he appointed supporters of Alkimos as his envoys. The names suggest the participation of both hellenizers and non-hellenizers: there seems to have been a fair spread of Jewish opinion behind Nikanor.

There are differing reports of the result of the negotiations. II Maccabees says they were successful and that Judah recommended them to his followers. A subsequent ceremonial meeting between the two leaders sealed the agreement. But the two men are then portrayed as becoming friends, with Nikanor recommending Judah to marry. Judah did marry and settled down, apparently living in Jerusalem. Part of the agreement was that Judah was to become a King's Friend, that is, one who could be an adviser to King Demetrios. A fairly substantial period of time is suggested by all this, several months at least.[43]

This is the problem – apart from the sheer unlikeliness of it all – for Nikanor was in office no more than three or four months, a period that began with his journey south, and included the battle of Kefar Salama, the negotiations, the breakdown in relations, and finally two battles and Nikanor's own death. There is not time between the negotiations and the breakdown for the peaceful interlude described in

II Maccabees. Yet an interval there was, and it seems likely either that the negotiations took a long time, or that an agreement was reached but then quickly broke down. I Maccabees omits the negotiations, Judah's agreement, and the peaceful interval, and condenses the whole period from the arrival of Nikanor to the breakdown into a single sentence, blaming the break on a plot by Nikanor to kidnap Judah.[44] But this will not do either, for some time certainly elapsed, and has to be accounted for. Further, King Demetrios was also involved. II Maccabees' explanation is that he was annoyed at Nikanor's proposal of Judah as a King's Friend, an idea that is as unlikely as the marriage idea, and may be discarded. But the king's annoyance was a fact.

The only indication of what happened is in II Maccabees. If we can discard the peaceful episode of Judah's relaxation and marriage, and the proposal of Judah as a King's Friend, then the account of the breakdown of relations as given in II Maccabees can make some sense: the talks took place between Judah and the three negotiators, and then the agreement was sealed by the meeting between Judah and Nikanor. But when Alkimos got a copy of the agreement he was annoyed and complained to the king in person at Antioch. Demetrios reacted angrily and wrote to Nikanor, revoking the agreement. This in turn led to the break between Judah and Nikanor. Judah fled back into hiding and collected up his people once more.[45] Nikanor blamed the temple priests for the breakdown, reasonably enough. It all suggests just how difficult it was to reach any settlement. At one point Nikanor threatened to sack the temple,[46] a threat perhaps designed to deter Judah from attacking the city. It is a sign that most of the Judean population, even those in the city, and even at least some of the priests at the temple, now supported the Maccabean cause. The best hope of moderates everywhere had been the negotiations, and these had now failed, compelling a choice of sides by those in the middle. Judah as a result had become confident enough, and his forces large enough, to confront Nikanor's troops in battle, and win, even if not decisively.

The Seleukid authorities could agree with one or other of the parties in Judaea, but the Judaean parties were unable to agree among themselves. An agreement between Judah and Nikanor would certainly affect Alkimos and the hellenizers adversely, and Alkimos' action in undermining Nikanor by a direct appeal to Demetrios is credible. If that is accepted, there must have been an interval of peace between the meeting of Judah and Nikanor and the resumption of fighting. It may only have been a month or so, but it does lend some credibility to the account in II Maccabees.

When the breakdown came Nikanor marched out of Jerusalem to attack Judah's people. Whatever agreement had been reached, the Maccabean forces had not disbanded, but had remained in control of their Gophna Hills base, and probably of much of the countryside. II Maccabees refers to Judah's forces being 'in the region of Samaria',[47] which is actually a fair description of the Gophna Hills area. But Judah came out to meet the Seleukid attack.

The two armies met only ten kilometres from Jerusalem, closer to the city than to the hills, at a place called Adasa, next to Gibeon.[48] The precise location is not clear, but it was in more or less open country. Judah was no longer using his ambush tactics. Instead, his army stood and fought a straightforward battle. Nikanor is credited by I Maccabees with 'a large army', but this may be seen as the usual exaggeration, to make the victory of Judah the more impressive. The fight was actually one between more or less equal forces, a few thousand on each side.[49]

This change in Judah's tactics may have been the result of the more equal sizes of the armies, which suggests that the Maccabean army had grown in number since Beth Zakaria. If it was able with confidence to face Nikanor's force, this in turn means that the men were equipped in much the same way as Nikanor's soldiers, with body armour, good swords, spears, and war horses, and had been drilled to fight in formation. It is a development that was clearly necessary if the Maccabean forces were ever going to win their war, but it also rendered them much more liable to destruction, if the Seleukid government could once again send a sufficiently large army into Judaea.

Nikanor had sent for reinforcements. This was the time during which Timarchos' eastern rebellion was at its most successful, so it is unlikely that many troops came from North Syria. However, the garrisons and militias of Palestinian cities could be combined into a relief force. These came up the Beth Horon pass, and Nikanor's first move in coming out from Jerusalem was to join up with them. He moved to Beth Horon, presumably the upper village, and then, with the two forces united, moved back towards Jerusalem. Judah was out in full force. He may have permitted the junction to take place, or Nikanor may have moved too fast for him.

Numbers on both sides are, as usual, uncertain. The only number quoted that may have any credibility is in Josephus, who gives Nikanor an army of 9,000 soldiers. Judah's willingness to fight in the open, and not in ambush, suggests that this time he had an equal or even a larger force. I Maccabees claims Judah had 3,000 men, as usual understating Judaean forces to demonstrate that god had supplied the balance of power on the Maccabean side. The fact that Nikanor had needed reinforcements suggests he faced a larger Maccabean force than before.

The fight was once more an open pitched battle. Nikanor was killed early on in the fight, no doubt the first target of Judah's force. He would be easily identified in the forefront of the cavalry, and his death disrupted the Seleukid force, which disintegrated as the news of Nikanor's death spread. The troops fled westwards, for Judah's force was between them and Jerusalem, the nearest refuge. Gezer was their aim, which meant going back down through the Beth Horon pass. The local people, alerted to the Maccabean victory by trumpet signals, came out and harassed the fugitives, many of whom had discarded their weapons the more easily to run. I Maccabees claims that none survived, which is unlikely, but there is no doubt that the Seleukid army was destroyed. Nikanor's head and right hand were cut off and displayed, perhaps to convince the people of Jerusalem and the soldiers in the Akra of the extent of the Seleukid defeat. Celebrations followed, and became an annual affair ('Nikanor Day'; 13 Adar, March 161).[50]

Once more the Maccabees had gained control of all Judaea except the Akra, but after the celebrations, as after the cleansing of the temple, preparations had to be made to meet the next Seleukid attack. Two of these preparations can be identified, one diplomatic, one military. During 161 Judah sent envoys to Rome. He may have done so as a belated response to the request by the earlier Roman envoys that they be kept informed of events, or he may have been imitating that other rebel, Timarchos, who had already made contact and been given Roman encouragement. Either way he sent envoys to Rome, and received exactly the same response as Timarchos: encouragement in words, but no material assistance, not even any diplomatic assistance. Rome was not about to become involved in a war in the eastern end of the Mediterranean on behalf of rebels.[51]

By contrast with this diplomatic move, Judah's military preparations can only be assumed. He now commanded an army that approximated to the standard Hellenistic type, and that had won a couple of victories, though it was not very large. In the meantime, during the winter of 161/160 Demetrios had defeated Timarchos, and was therefore now able to send a new army, commanded once more by Bakchides, to deal with the Judaean rebels. The Maccabean army was no doubt recruited to a greater size, and the new men armed and trained in so far as that was possible. But a couple of victories and a short period of training were not enough. The coming fight would be very difficult.

Bakchides came south with a substantial army, said in I Maccabees to number 20,000 infantry and 2,000 cavalry, which may be only a little inflated. It included, presumably, part of the army which had just beaten Timarchos, and no doubt some of the soldiers had already fought in Judaea as part of Lysias' army, or even earlier. The author of I Maccabees systematically reduced Judah's force in the battle to an unbelievable 800 men, so there would be no need to inflate Bakchides' figures.[52] Bakchides had a well-trained, well-balanced force, and it was commanded by a skilful general.

Bakchides, already familiar with the region from his earlier commands there, approached with care and cunning. He climbed to the Judaean plateau by an unexpected route, coming along through the Jordan Valley and the Gilgal road, and before Judah could react he had planted his camp on the upland, in territory where he could deploy his army most expeditiously. He made no attempt to reach Jerusalem, for his aim was to compel the Maccabean army to come out and fight a set battle against heavy odds. To encourage this he sent out parties to ravage the surrounding land.[53] Thus the country people received the same treatment from Bakchides as Judah had meted out to them earlier.

Judah mobilized his forces and brought them to Elasa, a place not far from the earlier battlefields of Adasa and Kefar Salama. Bakchides moved forward to camp only a kilometre away, coming deliberately close so that neither army could now move without leaving itself open to attack. The battle came soon after. Both forces were arranged in the standard Hellenistic way, with cavalry protecting the flanks of the infantry phalanx. The Seleukid phalanx advanced to push-of-pike with the Jewish infantry. Judah led his cavalry (on the Jewish left) in a charge against the Seleukid right wing cavalry, aiming, as usual, to kill the enemy commander. Bakchides had laid out his plan in advance to cope with what had now become the standard, even obvious, Maccabean tactics. He retreated, drawing the Jewish cavalry after him. Having thus lured Judah away from the infantry battle, part of the Seleukid left-wing cavalry came across to join in, so that Judah's cavalry force was surrounded. They, with their commander, were all killed. Meanwhile the Seleukid infantry were driving back the Jewish foot. The news of the defeat of the cavalry and the death of Judah – though I Maccabees does not mention this – no doubt caused the usual demoralization. The Jewish infantry formations broke up, and the survivors fled.[54]

Bakchides, now in control of his province, set about rooting out the main Maccabee supporters. He was assisted by the revival of the hellenizers' cause: those who had been terrorized into subjection and silence by Judah's terrorist methods made certain that the Seleukid authorities found as many of their prominent enemies as possible. In addition there was famine in the land, hardly surprising after the recent troubles.[55]

The Maccabees chose Judah's brother Jonathan as their new leader. He took refuge first in the wilderness of Tekoa, south-east of Jerusalem, and was then pushed across the Jordan.[56] Bakchides, meanwhile, set about fastening the Seleukid grip firmly on the whole of Judaea, fortifying a series of places chosen so as to control the communication routes: Beth Zur, controlling the approach from the south; Beth Horon, at the upper end of the pass; Bethel, at the junction of several routes north of Jerusalem; Ammaus at the entrance to the hills; Tekoa, where Jonathan had first taken refuge; and Jericho and Gezer in the lowlands to east and west – all these imposed a strict control over the whole region, and each was not more than ten kilometres from its neighbouring fort. In addition, the Akra was strengthened; it housed hostages collected from the main Jewish families.[57]

The high priest Alkimos was overshadowed by Bakchides, whose task it was technically to support him, yet it was clear to the Seleukid authorities that Alkimos was in part the source of the trouble. So when he died in 159, he was not replaced.[58] Jonathan and his band made the mistake of seizing a fort, perhaps with the intention of sending out a call for a popular rising, but Bakchides blockaded them there, at a place called Bathbasi, and no rising took place. The network of forts, and the deaths of Judah and Alkimos, doused a good part of the Maccabean fire. Jonathan and Bakchides were able to reach an agreement, which was all too clearly based on Bakchides' overwhelming victory. The non-replacement of the high priest was a useful development, and Jonathan settled down and stopped fighting. Maccabean prisoners were released.[59] 'So the war came to an end in Israel,' I Maccabees says.[60] But this was so only for a short time.

This sequence of events, from the murders by Mattathias at Modiin to the capitulation of Jonathan, is described in many modern accounts as a 'war of Independence' or a 'war of liberation'. Neither of these, nor any other term that suggests success or freedom, is remotely accurate. What occurred was partly a terrorist campaign within the community of the Jews in Judaea with the aim of establishing a dictatorship, partly a rebellion against the Seleukid kings, and partly a war of imperial conquest during the brief moments of Maccabean success. In only the first of these conflicts were the Maccabees partly successful, presumably because many of those opposed to them had been killed, while the rest were terrorized into submission. But as soon as the Maccabean army was decisively beaten, and terror was no longer available, the terrorized rose against their oppressors. The Maccabean cause was fully supported by relatively few amongst the Jewish population, which was why their only method was brute force and terror. And brute force can only succeed if it is never met by greater force. Once the Seleukid army arrived in real strength and without distraction the Maccabees' forces were rapidly defeated. Bakchides' network of forts was the real liberation for the Jewish population – from the terror inflicted on them by the first of the Maccabees, Mattathias and Judah.

Chapter 6

Achieving Independence

The defeat of the Maccabean rebellion left Judaea once more under Seleukid rule, and this time, thanks to Bakchides' forts, it was rather more firmly planted than before. Yet the Maccabean cause was not dead. Judah's brothers, Jonathan and Simon, lived on, and Jonathan established himself at Michmash, a place no doubt carefully chosen for its historical resonance – Saul and Jonathan beat the invading Philistines there – and for its position close to the main route from the plateau towards Jericho; it was a high point of the plateau, relatively remote yet still only a dozen or so kilometres from Jerusalem.[1]

I Maccabees, and Josephus following him, claims that Jonathan 'ruled the nation'. This is, of course, a contradiction of the actual political situation. The Seleukid governor, in the name of the king, ruled Judaea, backed up by the garrisons in the forts. For some time, it would be impossible for Jonathan to assert himself, since he was surely watched very carefully. The governor knew where he was and no doubt ensured that he knew what he was doing. And yet the term used – 'ruling the nation' – is not altogether inaccurate. Jonathan, having become his brother's acknowledged successor, had an authority denied to any other man in Judaea. And he exercised that authority in the same way as his brother had.

The actual method and process is revealed by a supplement to that claim of 'ruling': Jonathan 'rooted the godless out of Israel', which Josephus expanded to say that he 'punished the wicked and godless and so purged the nation of them'.[2] These chilling words show that Jonathan carried on his brother's work and continued to use his methods. Under cover of the peace agreed with Bakchides and enforced by the Seleukid occupation forces in their forts, he was busy among the population of Judaea at the old programme of murder and terrorism. No doubt matters remained relatively quiet for a time, with only the occasional murder and beating, but from 154 onwards the Seleukid government of Demetrios I became fully preoccupied with a much more important threat, and from then on Jonathan was able to set about the purging of Judaea more openly.

The problem that faced Demetrios I was one of the results of his own seizure of the throne, but also of his subsequent political mistakes. By his usurpation he had alienated the Attalids who ruled much of Asia Minor, and had sponsored Antiochos IV's earlier adventure; he was always out of favour with Rome; and in 154 he used intrigue to gain possession of Cyprus, which alienated his former friend Ptolemy VI of Egypt. These enemies came together in support of a man, Alexander, who claimed to be a son of Antiochos IV. This may or may not be true, but it suited Demetrios' enemies to believe it.[3] Alexander and his sister Laodike were promoted by Herakleides, the brother of the deceased rebel king Timarchos, defeated and killed by Demetrios. From 159, the year after Timarchos' death, Alexander was active in a stronghold in the Taurus Mountains, publicizing his claim and gradually gathering friends.[4]

Demetrios, with enemies in Asia Minor, Cyprus, and Egypt, was therefore pinned down in Syria. There were troubles elsewhere, particularly in the east, where the Parthians were becoming hostile once more, but the enmity of his western neighbours prevented him from going east to attend to them. By 153/152 Alexander had gained enough troops, money, and ships to launch a wider attack. He descended on Palestine and seized control of Ptolemais-Ake. No doubt this was all arranged beforehand. The garrison at Ptolemais joined the invader, who proclaimed himself King Alexander.[5]

Demetrios came south with his army to contest Alexander's position, and the situation of everyone in Palestine at once became dangerous. There were numerous cities, on the coast, in the Vale of Jezreel, across the Jordan, there were the garrisons in the forts established by Bakchides, and there were the non-Greek communities, the Ituraeans, the Nabataeans, the Jews of Judaea, and all of these had to tread very carefully in the midst of this royal dispute, for a wrong step might well bring disaster. I Maccabees and Josephus say that Demetrios communicated with Jonathan,[6] but he must have communicated with everyone else in the region as well. I Maccabees' usual narrow view of events ignores the majority of the people of Palestine, just as earlier it had tended to ignore the larger picture in Lysias' time.

Above all, after the defection of the governor at Ptolemais Demetrios needed to ensure the loyalty of the other Seleukid garrisons, those in the cities and those in Bakchides' forts. The size of the forts is not known, but there were at least ten of them. A garrison of only a hundred men in each meant a thousand soldiers, and one would have thought they would be larger than that. But in garrison they were of little use to Demetrios in his fight with Alexander, and to get them out of the forts meant that he had first to reach a new settlement with the Jews, that is, Jonathan. His continuing campaign of purging and terrorism had made him, like Mattathias and Judah before him, the master of the countryside. The alternative would be for Demetrios to launch a hunt for Jonathan and so secure his suppression, but this, as Bakchides' campaign had shown, would take time. The place where Jonathan was living, Michmash, was one from which he could get away fairly easily into the Jordan Valley or back into the desert, or he could be hidden almost anywhere in the Judaean countryside. And this was hardly the moment for Demetrios to begin yet another new campaign.

Whatever Demetrios said to the other inhabitants and communities in Palestine, he gave concessions to Jonathan. The process is summarized in I Maccabees in a single letter from the king,[7] but the subsequent events imply that a negotiated bargain had been reached. Jonathan became an 'ally' of the king, but such a designation cannot imply Jonathan's independence. He was permitted to raise an army, though its size is not stated, and he was allowed to move to Jerusalem. These are all gains for Jonathan. In return he must have agreed to fight on Demetrios' side when his army had been constituted, and so Demetrios was now able to withdraw some of the garrisons – characteristically said by I Maccabees to be 'making their escape'[8] – though subsequent notices indicate that some were not withdrawn. Beth Zur and Gezer were certainly still garrisoned ten years and more later.

So far both sides had benefited, but there were further clauses to the agreement. The Jerusalem Akra was not evacuated, so that, even though Jonathan controlled Jerusalem (for this is implied by his presence in the city and his possession of an army), his authority was still visibly limited by the continued presence of a Seleukid garrison in Akra. The Seleukid king was, in effect, making Jonathan the local governor in Judaea. The hostages held in the Akra were released. It is claimed that Jonathan returned them to their families, which was presumably part of the agreement. These families were not necessarily Jonathan's supporters, and now that the hostages were free, their families were able to make their own decisions. Beth Zur was similarly retained by the king, and became a refuge for those subjected to the renewed purge by Jonathan, as were other places garrisoned by Seleukid troops. 'Godless and renegade Jews'[9] – that is, the political opponents of the Maccabees – took refuge there and in the Akra. So Jonathan's authority was by no means complete, and the internal disturbance of Judaea continued, and may even have intensified. No doubt this aspect had not escaped Demetrios' calculations. One modern historian has referred to 'Jonathan's potential in helping to stabilize control of Judaea', which is one way of putting it, though the victims, dead, mutilated and expelled, might have had different words for it.[10]

When he was established in Jerusalem, and by implication after the garrisons in the outside forts had gone, the old fortifications around the temple, demolished by Lysias, were rebuilt.[11] Their purpose, when built by Judah, had been to separate the Akra from the rest of the city, and no doubt this was the main purpose of the new walls. Whether this was part of the agreement with Demetrios is not known. It may have been done independently, some time after the agreement with Demetrios had broken down.

This all took some time. No doubt the negotiations occurred when Demetrios had come south, and perhaps the rebuilding of the temple walls went on for some time after the talks ended – they were still unfinished two years later – but we must assume that some weeks at least elapsed between Demetrios' arrival in Palestine and the arrival of Jonathan in Jerusalem. After all, the king had probably negotiated with many other local authorities as well. There was time enough for Alexander in Ptolemais to hear what was going on, though it was surely obvious what Demetrios' policy would be. Alexander, or his backers, made contact with Jonathan (and presumably with other communities in the Palestine region), and made a better offer than Demetrios. This time all that Demetrios gave was increased by the offer of the post of high priest for Jonathan personally.[12]

This appointment was the prerogative of the king, and by accepting it Jonathan was recognizing Alexander as the rightful king. It provoked a reply from Demetrios, who offered a cancellation of taxes, and control of three areas north of Judaea, which was actually part of the Samarian sub-province. He also confirmed the award of the high priesthood, agreed to permit an enlargement of Jonathan's army, and offered the revenues of Ptolemais and its lands to support the temple in Jerusalem.[13] At least this is what I Maccabees claims, followed by Josephus. This all might seem a worthwhile offer, but both of the rival kings were, in fact, offering what they did not control. It seems evident that Alexander had gained general control of Palestine. The offer of the high priesthood cost Alexander nothing, and Demetrios' lavish offers of territory were at Alexander's expense, but implied that Jonathan would certainly campaign on Demetrios' behalf; Alexander's offer did not require any fighting. The Jews are said to have ignored the later offer from Demetrios as being uncollectable,[14] which, if Alexander controlled all Palestine, was an accurate assessment.

Nevertheless, despite its rejection by Jonathan, Demetrios' offer had subtle undertones. The city of Ptolemais was already hostile to the Jews, so the news of the offer might undercut Alexander's authority, or at best compel him to make expensive assurances to the citizens. The three territories Demetrios offered to add to Judaea – Lod, Apharaema and Arimatheia – might well become a threat to the nearby Greek cities. But being on the lowland they would also make part of Judaea vulnerable to attack. The increased Jewish army would, if Jonathan accepted these terms, be at Demetrios' disposal, but it would also mean increased power for Judaea, and the surrounding lands had already been raided by Judah's guerrilla forces. Most of all Demetrios had addressed these new terms not to Jonathan, but to the Jews as a whole, which would include the hellenizers – the 'renegades' and the 'godless'. By rejecting them Jonathan laid himself open to criticism that he was putting party advantage above that of the nation. The offer therefore might just provoke a counter-revolution in Judaea that would distract Jonathan sufficiently to render useless any support he might give to Alexander.

One result was that a definite break occurred between Jonathan and the 'Teacher of Righteousness', who was the originator of the Jewish sect that was eventually settled at Qumran. The 'Teacher' had to leave Jerusalem when Jonathan became high priest, in part because the two men recognized a different calendar, which meant they carried out the required sacrifices on different days. Jonathan – whom the documents refer to as the 'Wicked Priest' – made an attempt to murder the 'Teacher' when he was celebrating the Day of Atonement by his own calendar. Of course, resorting to the murder of a political opponent was a typical Maccabean action. The 'Teacher' escaped, but he and his followers went into exile, probably to Damascus.[15]

There is also the issue of just how genuine all these offers were. The documents supposedly quoted in I Maccabees are hardly the normal products of the Seleukid royal chancery. We are dealing with Jewish compositions, or at least adaptations, in other words, in which Demetrios' second offer is in fact a bundle of points that may well have been made by Demetrios I, but which seem also to be attributable to his son Demetrios II several years later. The offer of the three districts north of Judaea looks especially doubtful, for it is exactly these areas that were actually handed over by the second Demetrios. Yet an offer of some sort was certainly made by Demetrios I with the aim of undermining Alexander, just as offers will have been made to other peoples and cities in Palestine, even if we do not know what they were, and even if the offer to the Jews is distorted, probably exaggerated, and recomposed to enhance Jewish self-regard.

Demetrios' second offer was rejected, putting Jonathan firmly in Alexander's camp. In 150, after over a year in which it seems that no fighting took place (though we depend on I Maccabees and Josephus), Alexander had gathered sufficient armed strength to march north. It seems probable that he had military help from his Ptolemaic and Attalid allies, and he certainly had enough money, presumably from them, with which to hire a large force of mercenaries to reinforce his army. He did not have to worry about his Egyptian border, while Demetrios had to be concerned over the east, and about his Asia Minor frontier, as well as Alexander's advance. A battle took place not far from Antioch in which Demetrios was killed.[16]

Jonathan and his new army were not involved, so far as we can tell, in the fighting. Alexander married the daughter of Ptolemy VI, Kleopatra Thea, at Ptolemais, and, at least according to I Maccabees, Jonathan was there given extraordinary honours.[17] Since he had done nothing to deserve them, the account seems unlikely, and at least exaggerated. However, he was soon to be put to the test.

Demetrios I sent two of his sons, Demetrios II and Antiochos, out of the kingdom before the final battle to preserve their lives, no doubt remembering how he himself had treated the son of Antiochos IV.[8] (He kept one son with him, Antigonos, who was killed by Alexander's minister Ammonios.[19]) The eldest of the boys, Demetrios II, energetically set about gathering forces to return to Syria, and by 148 had recruited a substantial mercenary army, largely from Crete, and was able to do unto Alexander as Alexander had done unto his father, by establishing himself in Kilikia.[20] Alexander hurried north from Ptolemais, whereupon Demetrios successfully suborned Alexander's governor in Koele Syria, thereby cutting Alexander's communications with his father-in-law, Ptolemy VI.

This governor, Apollonios Taos, had been one of Demetrios I's officers, appointed governor of Koele Syria by Alexander, presumably in a commendable attempt to reconcile former enemies with his rule. But as soon as Demetrios II arrived in Syria Apollonios joined him, and Alexander's rule crumbled elsewhere. The Antiochenes disliked Alexander, ostensibly for his manners, and in Iran the Parthians had begun a serious campaign of conquest. He appealed to Ptolemy VI for assistance, and demanded that Jonathan bring his new army into the fight.[21]

Not surprisingly, given his and his family's record so far, Jonathan intervened in his own interest rather than that of his suzerain. He brought his army down into the lowlands and laid siege to Joppa: access to the sea was in Judaea's interest. This action presupposes that a number of new political conditions now obtained. First, Jonathan's army was considerably larger and more professional than the army Judah led to defeat at the end of his life. Jonathan had had several years – since 152 – in which to recruit, train, and arm the soldiers. He could use as a basis those men who had survived from the failed rebellion, and he and they could remember their defeats when they faced the well-armed and well-led Seleukid armies of Lysias and Bakchides. I Maccabees gives Jonathan a force of 10,000 men, and in this case it is quite possible that the number might be roughly accurate,[22] but the main point is not their numbers, but their training and discipline.

For the second point to be made about the siege of Joppa is that Jonathan clearly had no fear of being attacked during the siege by Apollonios Taos' own army; he was thus confident that he had the stronger and probably the larger force. The only number given for Apollonios' force is 3,000 cavalry. (He is credited with 8,000 infantry as well,[23] but this is clearly a number derived from the supposed casualties later, which are probably exaggerated.) This Jewish numerical superiority is confirmed by the campaign that followed.

Joppa did not resist for long, despite having a garrison of Apollonios' soldiers to reinforce the citizens. Apollonios would not have been able to spare many men for such duty. No doubt after some negotiations the citizens capitulated.[24] Apollonios, who had gathered his army at Ashdod, might have hoped Joppa would hold out longer. Alexander had presumably taken most of the soldiers north to confront Demetrios – thus leaving the way open for Apollonios to be able to come out against Alexander, but by taking the local forces north, Alexander had also deprived Apollonios of any real strength. So Apollonios' army consisted only of those men remaining in the cities of Palestine, and these would surely be reluctant to provide many men in view of the fact that Jonathan had shown a new and surprising competence in aggressive warfare by the capture of Joppa.

Apollonios made a move towards Joppa during the siege, but then retreated southwards when Jonathan's army, released from the siege, approached. The two armies met near Ashdod. Apollonios posted a cavalry force in hiding, armed with javelins, according to Josephus, but according to I Maccabees with bows and arrows, perhaps a more likely weapon. The two infantry forces confronted each other, each flanked by cavalry on the wings in the normal Hellenistic mode, but Apollonios' mounted archers compelled the Jewish force to halt, and use their shields, interlocked, to protect themselves from the arrows. Apollonios, if he had even an equality in numbers, could have used this halt to attack the Jewish infantry but did not do so; nor was he strong enough in cavalry to drive off the Jewish mounted arm. The stalemate lasted until the archers had exhausted their arrows. The Jewish force could then advance. The Greek cavalry was driven off, and the Greek infantry retired rapidly to Ashdod.[25]

The Greek infantry is said by I Maccabees to have fought as a phalanx. This may be an assumption by the historian, but that is how the Greek armies usually fought. The Jewish cavalry is not mentioned in either of the surviving accounts, but there must have been some to deter a cavalry attack by Apollonios on the Jewish infantry square as it stood stationery under the archery attack. The battle therefore approximated to the normal Hellenistic battle, two solid formations of infantry each protected by their cavalry, and when the cavalry was beaten the infantry had to retire. Exactly how well drilled and competent the two infantry forces were is less clear, though the Jewish infantry's stoic stance argues good training and discipline.

The aftermath was decisive, rather more so than the battle itself. Apollonios' army took refuge in Ashdod, in part in the temple of Dagon. Jonathan's army, buoyed up by victory, got into the city, perhaps by the old and familiar method of arriving while the gates were still open to receive the fugitives. The city, its temple, and the surrounding villages were then subjected to a sack, and the temple was burnt. The casualties are put at 8,000. Jonathan was then free to march further south, where Ashkelon negotiated submission before it could be attacked.

This was not a campaign of conquest. Ashkelon was never under his control at all, despite the city's submission; Ashdod had been sacked, but there is no sign that Jonathan continued to hold it, and there was a sufficiently large and coherent population surviving in the city to complain vociferously about the sack a short time afterwards; Joppa had surrendered to him, but the terms are unknown, and there is no indication that he continued to control it – no Jewish garrison was imposed, for instance. On the other hand, King Alexander is said to have rewarded Jonathan with the town of Accaron, the former Ekron, and its territory.[26] This was a town bordering on Judaea and on the lands of Iamnia and Ashdod. It had little real importance in itself, but it was the first country the Maccabeans came to control in the lowland, which might be an advantage in an attack, but might also be a hostage to fortune in adversity.

Alexander needed friends, for his campaign against the young Demetrios in the north did not go well. His father-in-law, Ptolemy VI, now came into Palestine to render assistance, though he was as intent on gaining advantage for himself as was Jonathan. He marched along the coast, seizing control of all the cities, including Joppa. At Ashdod, Ptolemy listened to complaints about Jonathan's conduct, but did nothing about it yet. The two men were still both allies of Alexander, and Jonathan took part of his army and joined Ptolemy's march as far as the Eleutheros River.[27]

This was a significant place, for it had formed the boundary between Ptolemaic and Seleukid territory until Phoenicia and Palestine were conquered by Antiochos III. The fact that Jonathan turned back when the two armies reached that point rather suggests that he knew that Ptolemy intended the recovery of the old Ptolemaic lands, and that they had reached some sort of understanding. Almost as soon as Ptolemy passed that river and established himself in the city of Seleukeia-in-Pieria, he abandoned Alexander's cause and allied himself with Demetrios, by transferring his daughter Kleopatra Thea from Alexander to Demetrios.[28] But then he was persuaded by the Antiochenes to abandon Demetrios, according to Josephus, for they detested the memory of Demetrios' father. Ptolemy allowed himself to be proclaimed king of the Seleukid lands to add to the kingship of Egypt.[29] A month or so later all three kings met in a battle near Antioch in which Ptolemy was mortally wounded, Alexander was defeated, pursued and killed, and Demetrios emerged, perhaps to his own surprise, triumphant.[30]

This manoeuvring took place in and around Antioch, with no reference to, and no input from, Jonathan. The result was, however, very dangerous for him. His alliance with Alexander continued, so Ptolemy's break with him left Jonathan stranded. Had Ptolemy survived and maintained his grip on the coastal cities, a new negotiation, at the very least, would have been needed. The deaths of Alexander and Ptolemy relieved one set of anxieties, but he was surely apprehensive at the prospect of dealing with the Demetrios II, whose father he had betrayed. He was therefore no doubt further relieved when the Ptolemaic position in Phoenicia and Palestine instantly collapsed.

In some places the citizens drove out the garrisons, in others the soldiers simply left and returned to Egypt.[31] Demetrios II, the new king, came south to tidy up. Jonathan took advantage of the confused situation to attack the Akra in Jerusalem, but his internal opponents swiftly reported this to Demetrios, in the knowledge that control of the Akra had always been a crucial element in Seleukid policy. Demetrios and Jonathan negotiated, each having worthwhile cards to play, and both having demands to make. The result was that Jonathan accepted Demetrios' authority as king and, by implication, abandoned the siege of the Akra, though neither I Maccabees nor Josephus, in line with their policy of not reporting minor setbacks, mention this. Demetrios confirmed Jonathan as high priest, thereby making it clear that it was an office in the king's gift, and transferred three small territories to Jonathan's rule – Apharaema, Ramathaim, Lydda – giving Judaea an extension northwards. These were the territories I Maccabees claimed had been offered by Demetrios I. Ekron, similarly ceded by Alexander, apparently remained to Jonathan. Some tax concessions were given as well.[32] It is a measure of Demetrios' political weakness that Jonathan gained so much.

Demetrios' authority in North Syria was no greater than Alexander's had been, and he soon faced a rebellion, having disbanded his Seleukid forces. He had hoped to rely on the mercenaries he had recruited abroad, but this did not work, and he called on Jonathan to supply soldiers to join the mercenaries in suppressing the rebels in Antioch, which was the centre of opposition to him. Jonathan's price was the Akra and the forts of Judaea, some of which were apparently still garrisoned, or perhaps had been re-garrisoned. Demetrios gave a vague promise, and the Jewish soldiers went to Antioch and helped to suppress the rebellion, using considerable brutality. Jonathan demanded the payment he thought had been agreed, only to be refused.[33]

Demetrios now faced another, more formidable, rebellion, which was raised by Diodotos of Kasiana, formerly an officer of Demetrios I and Alexander. He was also one of those who had prclaimed Ptolemy VI as king of the Seleukid lands just before his death. He brought the baby son of Alexander out of hiding and proclaimed him king ('Antiochos VI'), and succeeded in having him accepted in some parts of the kingdom.[34] Here was another chance for Jonathan.

This new Seleukid civil war was at first fought in the north, so that both sides were concerned that no help should come to their rival from the south. Jonathan was already annoyed that Demetrios had not provided the rewards he had expected, though even in the Jewish sources Demetrios' promise was extremely vague. Hence Diodotos, in the name of the child Antiochos VI, was able to offer confirmation as high priest, gifts of gold trinkets and purple robes, and confirmation of the cession of the four districts given by Alexander and Demetrios. Alexander had already made Jonathan governor (*strategos*) of Judaea, and now Diodotos made Simon governor of the land (*strategos*) 'from the Ladder of Tyre to the borders of Egypt'.[35]

Exactly what this meant is not really clear. Superficially it seems to define Koele Syria, but it was not so stated. Therefore all 'Koele Syria' was not Simon's province, but probably just the coastal districts. Even so, it is highly unlikely that he was given authority in, say, Ptolemais, where he and Jonathan were already unpopular, and Simon would hardly be welcome in any of the other Greek cities. In fact, Demetrios had established his power there after Ptolemy's death, so Simon's appointment was only a political gesture. Jonathan had also been bought off once more by a mere form of words – the 'concessions' to Jonathan himself were actually no more than he already held. Simon is never seen exercising authority in his province except as a conqueror, not as a governor.

Jonathan used the Seleukid civil war to expand his territorial power, though this was achieved above all at the expense of his internal enemies. Josephus and I Maccabees are vague on what Jonathan's first move was, but it seems that he attempted to persuade cities nearby to join him in supporting Antiochos VI against Demetrios. Josephus says none of them did; I Maccabees says 'all the forces of Syria gathered to his support'.[36] In this case Josephus is to be preferred, for at this point he was using a different, less committed source, probably Nikolaus of Damascus.

Despite the fact that it was Simon who was appointed governor, it was Jonathan who moved down into the coastlands to attempt to establish his power there. He faced resistance. Ashkelon submitted again (unless Josephus is simply repeating the original submission), but Gaza was obdurate and refused. The city is said to have deserted Demetrios, but still refused to join Jonathan and Antiochos. The city was perhaps, like Jonathan, attempting to use the Seleukid crisis to gain its independence; if so, it was isolated and so was a tempting target. Jonathan blockaded it, harrying the surrounding countryside. Jonathan's conduct clearly pushed the city into Demetrios' camp, but he was unable to help, so the Gazans finally gave in, accepted an alliance, and gave hostages.[37] Jonathan had not conquered the city, and it is clear that neither side trusted the other; otherwise the hostages would not have been necessary.

One reason for Jonathan to conclude this agreement with Gaza was that Demetrios' army was at last approaching, presumably with the aim of reasserting his authority in Palestine by 'rescuing' such cities as Gaza from Judaean menaces. Josephus has a comment that Jonathan went through Syria as far as Damascus,[38] but this is more likely to be a garbled reference to the fact that Demetrios' army was approaching by way of that city. Jonathan took his army north to contest its passage.[39] Demetrios' army, coming by way of Damascus, will have marched the same route used by Antiochos III in 200 before his victory at Paneion. (Demetrios' army may also have come by way of Phoenicia, based on the fact that his camp, at Kadesh, was in Tyrian territory, but there is no reason to connect this with the army's route of march.) Demetrios' army turned south at Paneion or thereabouts, aiming to reach the cities in and about the Vale of Jezreel – Skythopolis, Samaria, and others – who apparently supported him. Jonathan's march to the north was thus an attempt to prevent an invasion of Judaea, for the general support of the Greek cities of Palestine for Demetrios left him isolated. Once the army reached the Vale of Jezreel it could approach the northern border of Judaea without difficulty. By facing the invasion well to the north Jonathan was displaying good strategic sense.

Demetrios' army, said to be 'large', whatever that meant, was commanded by a set of generals rather than the king himself. From Kedesh in Galilee, above the marshy Jordan Valley, north of Lake Huleh, it had the choice of marching south either east or west of the Jordan Valley. On the east it was restricted to a limited number of crossings over the river, which could be blocked fairly easily; west of the river there was more scope for marching southwards or for crossing the hills through Galilee towards the coast.

Jonathan's strategic dilemma was awkward. He had neutralized the enmity of Gaza and Ashkelon, and presumably Ashdod was in no condition yet to fight, while the defeat of Apollonios Taos had, temporarily at least, removed the threat of attack from him. There was still a considerable enemy force at Beth Zur, which had become a rallying point for Jonathan's Jewish hellenizer enemies. Simon was sent to blockade the place with part of the Jewish army. He had to fight to establish the blockade, which suggests that the people at Beth Zur were fairly numerous, and that they were taking advantage of Jonathan's preoccupation in the north to attempt a move towards Jerusalem. This whole process at Beth Zur clearly took some time, for a blockade is a slow business.[40]

Jonathan camped by the Sea of Galilee, probably by its northern edge, say at about the site of the later Capernaum, and then marched northwards. The two armies met in the plain below Tell Hazor, an open but scarcely level area of land. Demetrios' generals' concealed part of their army in the hills to the west, engaged the Judaean army, and then sprang the ambush. The Judaean forces collapsed and mostly fled, though some men rallied long enough to prevent Demetrios' army from pursuing the fugitives – another indication of improved discipline in the Judaean army. I Maccabees and Josephus both claim a victory by the rallied force, but do not claim that Demetrios' army was seriously damaged – claims of 2,000 (Josephus) or 3,000 (I Maccabees) casualties among Demetrios' army are no more than imaginary figures. No admission of Jewish casualties is made, which rather suggests an embarrassingly large number.[41]

Jonathan retired from the battlefield, going as far as Jerusalem. The army of Demetrios is not said to have retreated at all, but 'wishing to make good their defeat', gathered reinforcements and returned to the attack. This is a Jewish interpretation. We may rather take it that Demetrios' generals rested their army after their limited victory, aimed to recover from the check suffered by Jonathan's rearguard, and wanted to investigate conditions ahead of them before advancing again. Jonathan's return to Jerusalem was perhaps to gather more troops, but it is also likely that he aimed to ensure that his authority was not damaged by the military setback. He may also have wanted to see if Simon needed help. Jonathan is then said to have advanced his army to meet Demetrios' army again, and did so in the area of 'Hamath'.[42]

This sequence is disrupted in our sources by a discussion of communications between Jonathan and Rome, so implying a lengthy interval between the fight at Hazor and the confrontation at Hamath. But there cannot have been much time between the two fights. Jonathan returned to Jerusalem, and then came out to meet the renewed attack by Demetrios' generals, journeys that might take only a few days, perhaps a week at most. Demetrios' army stopped for only a short time. It is said to have been reinforced, and then advanced again. In other words, it stayed at the camp close to the Hazor battlefield, and, after a fairly short time, moved to the attack once more. The confrontation did not result in a battle, but it cannot have taken place at 'Hamath'.

Hamath is the modern Syrian city of Hama, which in the second century BC was called Epiphaneia. It was a town fairly recently upgraded to *polis*-status, whose new name commemorated Antiochos IV. It lies 270 kilometres from the Hazor battlefield, as the crow flies, along a road through mountains and deserts and past several cities, none of which feature anywhere in the accounts as we have them. Even if we take the name as it is actually given in Josephus – Amathitis – and assume that this is the Hama region, which stretches some way south from the city, rather than the city itself, the distance involved for Jonathan's army's journey is simply not believable. (It does, of course, suit pro-Jewish historians to believe that Jonathan's army could march that far without opposition, but a more objective view is that it is nonsense.)

On the other hand, there is a place called Hammath on the south-western shore of the Sea of Galilee, a short distance south of the site of the later Tiberias – it is now called Hammat Tiberias, where, as the name suggests, there are hot springs.[43] This is at a narrow passage between the lake and the western hills, which here are even steeper than to the north. Assuming, as seems to be the case, that the first battle of Hazor was a limited victory for them, Demetrios' generals did not need to retreat, so this Hammath would be a good place to confront their new advance, a place that Jonathan's army could block.

The meeting, as noted, did not produce a battle. Instead, after an unknown period of time, Demetrios' army turned back. By leaving their watch fires burning, the army got away without being noticed, despite Jonathan supposedly having spies in the enemy camp. I Maccabees, followed by Josephus, attributed their retreat to Jonathan's superior generalship, his army's valour, the support of their god, and the cowardice of the army; in actual fact it was more likely due to some military development in the north. Jonathan did not relax his guard until he heard that the enemy army had crossed the Eleutheros River. This implies a march along the Lebanese coast. (Note also that a retreat northwards from Syrian Hamath would not require a crossing of the Eleutheros.)[44]

Once relieved of the immediate threat from Demetrios' army Jonathan took his own army on a raid into Arabia, perhaps at the expense of the Nabataeans, though this is Josephus' correction of I Maccabees' term 'Zabataeans'. This is all very odd, for the Nabataeans at this time were centred well to the south of the Sea of Galilee, and Jonathan is then said to have sold his rustled cattle – not a Nabataean animal – in Damascus. There is clearly something seriously amiss about all this, and all we can do is accept that Jonathan carried out a raid somewhere.[45] Its strategic purpose is unknown, and it may have been merely an expression of frustration at the lack of success against Demetrios' army. Meanwhile, the blockade of Beth Zur by Simon and his detachment of the Judaean army had succeeded in forcing the surrender of the town, whose inhabitants, Jewish enemies of Jonathan and Simon, were driven out as part of the peace terms. A Maccabean garrison was installed.[46]

Simon followed this up with a march into the southern coastlands, first towards Ashkelon and then north. Presumably he bypassed Iamnia and Ashdod, but at Joppa, which was intending to defect to Demetrios, he put a Maccabean garrison into the city, presumably in the name of Antiochos VI, though this was, in effect, the annexation of the city to the Judaean state. He then reinforced the Maccabean position in the area by fortifying the town of Adida,[47] halfway between Modiin, on the edge of the Judaean Hills, and Lydda in the lowland, which was one of the areas acquired recently. Adida was an advanced post in front of the Beth Horon pass. In control of Joppa, Lydda, and Adida, the Maccabean state now had a firm grip on the route to the sea.

It is the frustrated intentions of the people of Joppa that is perhaps the key to all this. Had Jonathan really won the 'brilliant victory' over Demetrios' generals at the plain of Asor, it is unlikely that the Joppans would have picked the aftermath of the fight as the moment to desert the victor, no matter how unpopular Jewish influence was. So we may assume that the news was that Jonathan's army had in fact been worsted. Hence the two simultaneous marches of Jonathan's and Simon's forces, to 'Arabia' and along the coastlands respectively, which can best be interpreted as showing-the-flag exercises, to demonstrate to potential local enemies that the army was intact. The claim to victory was also no doubt made, the evidence being that Demetrios' army had retired – 'retreated' or 'fled' would be the characterization. Simon's army really had, of course, won a victory, though the expulsion of the inhabitants from Beth Zur might be one of the reasons why the Joppans wanted to escape from Jewish clutches.

This military crisis therefore resulted in the annexation of Beth Zur and Joppa, and so a strengthening of Judaean defences. It did not result in the extension of Judaean control across the Jordan or north to the Sea of Galilee. Neither the raid across the Jordan nor the fighting near Hazor and Tiberias resulted in any annexations. The acquisition of Beth Zur on the other hand was very valuable in that it drove away the hellenizing Jews who had gathered there and, the place having been newly fortified in the past decade, it now stood a strong guard on the southern approaches to Jerusalem. Similarly Joppa's importance to the inland state was clear. The whole sequence of events since the arrival of Alexander shows that we can now speak clearly about the Judaean state, even if it still owed some allegiance to a Seleukid king.

The message Jonathan sent to the Romans at this time was of no great significance, but it may well be part of the same political purpose, to intimidate others, to assert statehood, and to wave the existence of the relationship with Rome in the faces of any enemies. There is no sign that any of them paid much attention.

Whereas the Jews claimed to be allies of Rome, Rome merely accepted Jewish friendship.[48] The Jewish envoys are said to have been given letters to send to their neighbours notifying them of Roman friendship, which would be the more valuable since Roman annexation of Macedon and Greece and Carthage in 148–146, but the claimed friendship with the Senate could scarcely be turned to effective political advantage. Rome was still uninterested in any action in the eastern Mediterranean. (Still less useful was the connection with Sparta, a land that was of no political consequence at the time.[49])

Jonathan, more usefully, set about establishing his regime on firmer political foundations, perhaps another indication that his military campaign had been less than successful. So far his government had been, in effect, a military dictatorship. Having conducted what could be seen as a successful military defence of the land he ruled, and gained some victories, he now turned to consult the Jerusalemites. Presumably, the successive purges had removed the surviving hellenizers and other opponents, and their eviction from Beth Zur had pushed them even further into exile. It would also seem that, judging by the Greek names of the envoys he sent to Rome (Numenios son of Antiochos, and Antipater son of Jason), a process of reconciliation between the Maccabees and some of the hellenizers had taken place. His repeated confirmation as high priest by recent kings had no doubt helped, as did his defence of Judaea against Apollonios Taos' and Demetrios' armies. Simon's conquests in the south and on the coast were even more convincing. The presence of the hostile garrison in the Akra could be turned to political advantage, and an assembly of 'the people' (Josephus) or 'the Senate' (I Maccabees) was persuaded to initiate further defence works. The Akra was to be walled off from the rest of the city, and forts were to be constructed in various parts of Judaea. These last were no doubt mainly the forts established by Bakchides fifteen years before, most of which had been evacuated. Having been built to control Judaea, they were now to be reconstructed as its defence. But, of course, they would also be Judaea's controllers once more.[50]

The child King Antiochos VI died in 142 – murdered by Diodotos, his enemies said – whereupon Diodotos proclaimed himself king, taking the throne name Tryphon ('Magnificent'). This reduced the pressure on Demetrios, though Tryphon remained powerful enough to withstand Demetrios' renewed attacks. Demetrios, rather than fighting on in a futile civil war in Syria, went off to the east to attempt to recover the lands lost in the last few years to the Parthians.[51] All this changed everyone's perspective, and new loyalties had to be sorted out.

Tryphon came south, presumably intent on clearing out Demetrios' supporters, but also on establishing his own clear authority as king over the former supporters of Antiochos VI. Jonathan, clearly apprehensive, met Tryphon at the head of an army, said by I Maccabees to be 40,000 strong. The size of Tryphon's army is not known. The two men, neither of whom could afford a defeat or to lose many soldiers, agreed to negotiate, and Josephus was persuaded to go to Ptolemais with a bodyguard of a thousand men, leaving another 2,000 nearby in the Galilee Hills. He is said to have had supporters in that area, presumably Jews, but that is not a sign that he ruled the area.[52]

At Ptolemais the citizens attacked Jonathan's bodyguard, and seized him. Josephus claims this was done at Tryphon's order, and both Jewish sources have preliminary comments designed to show that Tryphon had been plotting this all along. But I Maccabees implies that the capture was at the initiative of the citizens of Ptolemais themselves.[53] Ptolemais' political allegiance before this is not clear, and it may be that Tryphon's authority there was very recent and not at all firm. But the city was well known for its hostility to the Jews, and Jonathan's bodyguard of 1,000 men should have been enough to protect him – just as it was a clear sign that he did not trust anyone.

Whether he instigated the capture or not, Tryphon certainly made use of his prisoner. The news encouraged other cities to make their hostility to Judaea and its rulers clear. Tryphon could ride this wave by putting himself at the head of the movement. He began by sending out a force to drive away the 2,000 Jewish soldiers Jonathan had left in Galilee. The flight of these men to Judaea brought the news to Jerusalem, both of Jonathan's capture and of Tryphon's hostility.[54]

In Jerusalem Simon executed a neat *coup d'état*. He summoned an assembly, probably of the general population rather than the *gerousia*, pointed out that he was the last of a line of brothers who had all died for the cause, and was answered by an approving shout. He took this as his election as war leader, which could be temporary, if Jonathan returned, and a platform for the succession to the high priesthood if he did not, and instigated immediate military measures. The walls in Jerusalem, presumably in particular the wall begun a couple of years before between the Akra and the city, were hurried on.[55] He put a stronger garrison into Joppa, and then 'expelled its inhabitants',[56] by which we should understand the inhabitants who were his opponents, both gentiles and Jewish hellenizers – no doubt the news of Jonathan's capture had produced anti-Maccabean unrest. But this was the second place where Simon had driven out a population – Beth Zur was the first – and it was an ominous sign of his policy intentions. As a measure it can only have solidified hostility to him and Judaism in the surrounding non-Judaean region.

Tryphon came south from Ptolemais with his army. Simon and the Judaean army took station at Adida, in front of the Beth Horon pass. Tryphon offered to release his captive in exchange for a hundred talents of silver and two of Jonathan's sons as hostages. Simon agreed, and handed over the ransom, but Jonathan was not released.[57] This, of course, was to be expected, and it suited both Tryphon and Simon. Tryphon now held the head of the Judaean state in his hands and could assume that it was now less than stable; he might still release Jonathan at a moment of his own choosing, when he felt it would be most useful to him. Simon's advantage lay in the fact that he was now free of contenders for his power (the sons) while the anger produced by Tryphon's breaking his word obviously reinforced Simon's own authority inside Judaea.

It is clear from Tryphon's movements that he did not have an army large or strong enough to tackle Simon's army; at the same time Simon was not strong enough to risk a direct attack, quite apart from the fact that his brother would probably be the first casualty of any battle. The campaign that followed is not recorded in detail, though it would be fascinating if it was. Tryphon moved south along the coastal lowlands, marching along the old great road, the Way of the Sea. He passed between

Adida and Joppa but did not attack either. Simon took his army back into the hills and marched parallel with Tryphon's movements. The first march, up along the Beth Horon pass to the plateau and then south to block any possible move by Tryphon uphill by another route, must have been an exhausting effort for the Jewish army, but the way was blocked successfully. Tryphon moved on south, presumably probing along each pass and being blocked at every one. He moved into Idumaea, no doubt using the route by which Lysias had approached two decades earlier, but this time Beth Zur was strongly held and was covered by Simon's much more substantial army. Tryphon camped eight kilometres or so south at Adora.[58]

There Tryphon received news from the Akra, indicating that the Maccabean blockade meant that the garrison was now short of food. A cavalry raid to put in supplies was arranged, but it was prevented by a surprise snowstorm (this was the winter of 142/141). The cavalry raid had been intended to go 'by way of the desert', which would seem to mean that from Adora the raid would evade Beth Zur and Simon's army by riding along a route between Beth Zur and the Dead Sea,[59] while Tryphon's main force pinned Simon's army down. This has led to the assumption that the whole army marched by that route. This is highly unlikely. Such a route, in dry country (even in winter), and crossing many ravines, was, for a large army, far too dangerous. Apart from that, and any shortage of supplies, the danger of ambush in the hills was far too great. Further, some of Tryphon's soldiers were from the coastal cities and their absence left their homes vulnerable. If Tryphon's army made its slow way along the edge of the Dead Sea, Simon could well launch raids into the coastal lands and perhaps seize one or more of the less well-defended cities there.

Tryphon's retirement took place therefore by the way he had arrived, from Adora westwards towards the coastal cities and then north. He is said to have gone onto Galaaditis/Gilead, which would mean he marched east between Judaea and Galilee, ensuring the safety of such cities as Samaria and Skythopolis, and incidentally reinforcing his own authority there. When he got beyond Jordan, he killed Jonathan, at a place called Bacsama, perhaps north of the Sea of Galilee.[60] Jonathan's life had been forfeit, of course, ever since Tryphon had refused to release him on payment of the ransom. We do not know what became of his sons. His enemy, the follower of the 'Teacher of Righteousness' decided that 'god gave into the hand of his enemies to humble him with disease for annihilation in bitterness of soul, because he had acted wickedly against his chosen one'.[61]

Tryphon moved off to the north. Simon communicated with King Demetrios, who was either in North Syria or in Babylonia. In Judaea the death of Jonathan left the office of the high priest vacant. Josephus says that Simon was chosen by the people as the next high priest. The letter from King Demetrios confirmed a set of tax concessions and is addressed to 'Simon the high priest, and the Senate and nation of the Jews'. This is a precise formulation of the political arrangement in Judaea that had existed at the end under Jonathan. Demetrios, with nothing to lose as he set off to the east, and wishing to leave a major difficulty for Tryphon, now had no compunction in recognizing Judaean independence.[62] The election of Simon as high priest by the people, instead of being appointed by the king, marks the moment of independence for Judaea. Having gained it, it had now to be maintained and defended.

Chapter 7

The Defence of Independence

Jonathan Maccabaeus had done his work well, and must be accounted the true founder of the Maccabean state. Judah had led rebellions but had failed at the end, his only real achievements being a certain reputation, which his family could exploit, and the recovery of the temple, for a time. Jonathan, on the other hand, had secured the removal of most of the fort garrisons, founded a professional army, won at least one clear military victory, and had fought on equal terms against armies led by Demetrios' generals successfully enough to prevent a new invasion of Judaea. He had acquired the office of high priest as well as that of *strategos*, and the combination of these gave him dictatorial powers inside Judaea. He had developed what seems to be a partnership between the *gerousia* of Jerusalem, the people of Judaea, and himself as leader, which in effect constituted a state system. He had continued the purging of elements of the population of Judaea that were deemed to be inimical, but had, so it seems, also successfully effected a reconciliation of his Maccabean followers with at least part of the hellenizing tendency. All this had been done by extracting concessions from successive Seleukid kings. Yet this policy suggested deviousness and unreliability, and it was surely this part of his reputation, as well as his success, which induced Tryphon to keep him in captivity and eventually to kill him.

Simon's inheritance, therefore, consisted of a state that was more or less properly founded, though perhaps it was still somewhat unsteady. He had a reasonably capable army that could respond to danger and conduct a sustained campaign of marches without losing its discipline, and which could claim a rather tendentious tradition of victory. It is all summarized in the set of titles which I Maccabees gives Simon at his accession: high priest, *strategos*, and leader (*hegemon*) of the Jews.[1]

There was one blot on the landscape: the continued occupation of the Akra by a Seleukid garrison, which served also as a refuge for diehard hellenizers, and so was a standing reproach to the Maccabean regime and its ideology. The blockade of the fort, which had already been in place for a year or so, was continued. Since it had already recently provoked cries for help to Tryphon – which he had been unable to answer – it was clearly only a matter of time before its final capitulation, but the process could not be hurried.

Simon also attacked Gezer. This was a town on a ridge that extended out westwards from the highlands and provided extensive views over the coastal plain 'from Ashkelon to north of' Joppa, and up into the hills to the east. It was well fortified, having been one of the forts developed by Bakchides. It stood between two towns already in Judaean control, Lydda and Ekron, and commanded the main north-south coast road (the 'Way of the Sea'), and that from Joppa towards Jerusalem.[2] For a strategist in Palestine, Gezer was an essential acquisition.

The successful establishment of Simon in power in Judaea called for a military campaign and a victory to confirm his suitability to rule, and Gezer was a prime target. Like the Akra the place was now isolated, with Judaean territory on three sides. There was now no royal army available to come to its assistance, and none of its neighbours would be able to do so either. Simon attacked it, using a 'siege engine', which battered a hole in a tower. (This sounds like a ram, but may have been no more than a particularly sturdy ladder.) At this point the city surrendered to avoid a storm, but Simon expelled the inhabitants as he had at Beth Zur and Joppa.[3]

Again, this process of expulsion needs to be understood. Later the city was Jewish and subject to Jewish law, as a circle of boundary stones attests.[4] The expulsion, however, need not have affected the whole population, despite I Maccabees' words. For example, a *graffito* survives in which a man with a Greek name, Pamphras, cursed the building of a palace for Simon. Whether he was Greek or Jew (or a citizen or a captive), he was clearly a political opponent of Simon's,[5] so we may assume that the expulsion was selective, applying presumably to those who could be identified as Simon's political opponents, and so to Jewish hellenizers and prominent gentiles; anyone who could be fingered as anti-Maccabee would suffer. Another purge, in other words, though the Greeks and the poor need not be affected.

The acquisition of Gezer gave Simon a solid and well-fortified position in the lowlands, and a well-protected route now connected Jerusalem and the Judaean plateau with the sea at Joppa. The capitulation of the Jerusalem Akra, which followed later in 141, finally cleared the last enemy position within the Judaean boundaries.[6] The taking of the Akra was, of course, followed by another expulsion, hardly surprisingly given that it had been an anti-Maccabean refuge for twenty years. The expellees went, presumably, to nearby places, at least at first. They may not have been particularly welcome in their new homes, as is often the case with refugees, nor especially well liked, but they were a clear warning to other cities that the newly independent and clearly very militaristic state of Judaea had arrived. It was clear what fate would be meted out to them should they also be conquered. The definition of political enemies clearly included hellenizing Jews, but it could easily be extended to anyone who fought against the Judaean state, even in defence of their homes.

Simon had achieved power after Jonathan's captivity partly by a species of popular election, an acclamation in an emergency, but also by emphasizing his relationship with his deceased brothers – that is, he claimed to be the Jewish leader (*hegemon*) by hereditary right, and this now in large part became the basis for his rule. He began the construction of a palace at Gezer, which was referred to by the disgruntled worker Pamphras in his *graffito* as 'Simon's palace'. The captured Akra was refortified. The dead members of his family, including Judah and Jonathan, whose bodies had been recovered, were commemorated by a grandiose mausoleum at Modiin, which was visible from as far away as the coast.[7] His office as high priest might have been technically awarded by 'the people', and confirmed by King Demetrios, but it had also been inherited from his brother. Simon was evidently intent from the beginning on creating a hereditary monarchy. After a royal succession it was one of the necessary elements for the new ruler to conduct a successful military campaign; Gezer and the Akra filled that bill very nicely.

It was inevitable that the state should adopt the usual trappings of a Hellenistic polity – monarchy, bureaucracy, palaces, fortifications, monumental family mausolea, and so on – since this was the only model available. The men Simon sent out as envoys, such as Numenios and Antipater (who had been used previously by Jonathan) had to speak and think in Greek, for Aramaic was not the language of diplomacy, and no one outside Syria spoke it. Simon sent an embassy to Rome once he was in firm control of the country, which elicited a round-robin letter to a variety of states in the eastern Mediterranean, purporting to extend Roman protection to the Jews in those places. Whether it is accurately transcribed or not – and its date is uncertain – it had no more effect than earlier Roman documents.[8]

Simon's achievements and the bases of his political authority, were inscribed on a stele, in the best Hellenistic style.[9] From its origin in a peasant rebellion, Judaea rapidly became a fairly typical Hellenistic state. This inscription is quoted at length, and probably almost in its entirety, in I Maccabees. It is dated to September 140, and was the memorial of an assembly of the people and the elders at which Simon's precise position was regulated. A preliminary recital of his achievements makes it clear that his authority was based above all on his military successes and his heredity. His titles are stated to be high priest and *hegemon*, and these positions were his 'in perpetuity'. It was forbidden to abrogate the decrees that granted him these powers, and only he could convene assemblies, which were the only authority that could compete with him. His position was thus legally very strong, but it relied above all on continued success. Despite the provision against abrogation, however, it was clearly stated that these powers were delegated to Simon by 'the people'. The implication was that any successor would need to be similarly accepted by a popular assembly. No doubt it was this limitation that was part of the impetus behind Simon's drive for hereditary power.

He was fortunate that, during his initial period of rule, King Demetrios was away in the east, and King Tryphon was fully occupied in North Syria, but the Seleukid civil war stalemate would not last for ever. When Demetrios was defeated in Iran in 139, his brother Antiochos VII arrived to take up the gauntlet. He was a more accomplished soldier than his brother, and probably a more attractive man, and a much cleverer politician. The first thing he did was to marry his brother's wife, Kleopatra Thea (her third husband), which gave him control of Seleukeia-in-Pieria, where she had been besieged by Tryphon. Tryphon's support collapsed. Antiochos drove him south. He took refuge in Dor, just north of Joppa, and there Antiochos besieged him.[10]

The limits of the independence that Simon had gained were quickly shown when such a determined and accomplished Seleukid became king. Judaea's sphere of operations depended on Seleukid disunity, and Antiochos, having all but destroyed

Tryphon's power, was able to compel Simon's obedience. A letter supposedly written before his landing at Seleukeia is quoted in I Maccabees, but it shows so many anachronisms that it was evidently composed later.[11] Antiochos apparently confirmed whatever concessions Demetrios had awarded, yet he set limits to these concessions; he repudiated whatever Tryphon had offered – which included the appointment as governor of the Palestinian coastlands, and he insisted on reverting to the conditions as they had existed at the time Demetrios went to the east. Joppa and Gezer and the Jerusalem Akra were to be returned to Seleukid control; Judaea could purchase them, but Antiochos set so high a price that neither Simon nor his treasury could pay it.

While Antiochos was besieging Dor, Simon offered assistance, in the form of cash and a force of soldiers. Antiochos refused the help,[12] for it was offered without acknowledgment of his suzerainty. Antiochos regarded Judaea as a subject province, for his monetary demands, made when he rejected Simon's offer of help, were 500 talents for the cities and another 500 as compensation for destruction and loss of tribute.[13] To pay would be to admit Antiochos' political authority, and would also bankrupt the state. Simon offered the same hundred talents he had offered before, and when Antiochos' envoy Athenobios came to negotiate he was told that Simon regarded the cities as his by right of inheritance from the past.[14] In effect, Simon was offering to buy Joppa and Gezer for a hundred talents.

During these talks Tryphon got away from Dor by ship. Antiochos went after him, leaving a new governor, Kendebaios, in command in the coastlands.[15] He operated from the southern zone, south of the Judaean-occupied area between the hills and Joppa, but this clearly restricted his powers. He made his first base at Iamnia and built a forward base at Kedron from which he could block any Judaean moves south from Gezer and Ekron, and raided into the hills by way of the Kidron valley.[16] This route led directly to Jerusalem. Kendebaios was clearly a dangerous man.

Simon used this threat to further his plans. He had already placed his son John Hyrkanos as governor in Gezer to guard the western approaches. Hyrkanos reported the situation to Simon, who was in Jerusalem. A Judaean army, said to be '20,000' strong, was mustered at Modiin,[17] which was both the place the original revolt had begun and a strategic location overlooking the western approaches. Command was given to two of Simon's sons, Hyrkanos and Judah, while it seems that Simon commanded another force.[18]

The accounts of Simon's measures are not clear, but the main fighting took place between Ekron/Gezer and Kedron, and between the armies of Kendebaios and Hyrkanos and Judah. Simon, according to a thin account in Josephus (who no longer based his work on I Maccabees at this point), posted soldiers to guard the routes into the hills. This combination makes military sense. On the assumption that the Judaean army was superior in numbers, half the men formed the main force and the rest were on guard to prevent raids into the homeland.

The guards blocking the valleys were successful in preventing Kendebaios' forces penetrating very far. Josephus says that 'Simon did not lose a single engagement', which means that there were several raiding attempts.[19] Presumably, fairly small mobile cavalry forces were used by Kendebaios, and Simon's guards were able to block their raids in the narrows of the valleys. The fortified posts Simon had organized – some of them Bakchides' old forts – no doubt also constrained the Seleukid forces. The advance of Hyrkanos' and Judah's army into the lowland compelled Kendebaios to concentrate his army to face this attack.

The strength of Kendebaios' force is not known. The only figures given are 20,000 for the Judaean army and 2,000 for Kendebaios' casualties, which are not much help.[20] The Seleukid cavalry was superior to the Judaeans', which is likely enough since Kendebaios' horsemen had been raiding up to the plateau. His infantry was presumably partly Seleukid professionals and partly local levies. The fact that he was superior in cavalry does not mean that Kendebaios was also superior in infantry, and it seems obvious that his infantry was in fact much inferior in numbers to the Judaeans. Given that the main royal army was still in the east or with Antiochos, this is not surprising.

I Maccabees gives a peculiar account of the battle.[21] It took place at a gully, no doubt a fairly steep-sided wadi, probably the Kidron, though this is not stated. The Judaean army is said to have been drawn up with cavalry in the centre of the infantry, but I Maccabees also says that part of the Judaean army crossed the gully separately from the rest. Which part of the army did so is not stated, but it could be more of the cavalry. The brothers presumably divided the command, one, probably Hyrkanos, with the cavalry and the other with the infantry. This is all rather a matter of guesswork, but it would help to make sense of the battle. Phalanx infantry could defend itself against cavalry if their flanks were protected and if the soldiers kept their formation, but if Hyrkanos' cavalry crossed the gully first, he may have been able to drive Kendebaios' horse away from one wing. At a guess the force that crossed in advance, whatever it was, took the Seleukid army in flank. The distracted Seleukid phalanx was then charged by the Judaean cavalry, which had been stationed, most unusually, 'in the centre of the infantry'.

A victory for the Judaean army is claimed, with the Seleukid forces retiring to 'the fortress', probably Kedron, or perhaps Iamnia. The casualties of the defeated force are put at 2,000, which can have been no more than a guess, and is not really very many for a defeated force of perhaps five times that to have suffered. Some of the Seleukid army retired as far as Ashdod, taking refuge in towers in the countryside. Hyrkanos is said to have set fire to Ashdod itself, but if the towers and the Kedron fortress had not been captured first this is unlikely, and the story of burning may be no more than a repetition of Jonathan's burning several years before. Hyrkanos (Judah had been wounded) then led the army home to Judaea.

The battle was hardly a decisive victory. Most of Kendebaios' force survived, even if defeated and had suffered 2,000 casualties, and the Judaean army did not continue the campaign. The battle with Kendebaios took place at roughly the same time that Antiochos finally cornered and killed Tryphon, at Apamea in Syria. The strategic result was the establishment of military and political superiority throughout Syria and Palestine by the Seleukid king. The indecisive victory over Kendebaios was therefore probably followed by a negotiated peace.

Seleukid diplomatic practice was that peace agreements were concluded between rulers and lasted until the death of one of them. It would seem therefore that an agreement was made between Antiochos and Simon, as independent rulers, in or shortly after 138, the year of the defeat of Kendebaios and Tryphon. The terms are not known, though territory did not apparently change hands – Joppa, Gezer, and the Akra remained under Simon's control, but he gained no territory. Perhaps Simon paid tribute. We do not know, but it seems clear that a peace of some sort was agreed, with Simon acknowledging that his state was part of the Seleukid kingdom. This is the minimum Antiochos would accept if he was not to recover any lost territory into his own direct rule. Such an acknowledgment, of course, meant that Judaea was vulnerable to further Seleukid pressure.

Given the fact that I Maccabees is intent on praising Simon above all his brothers, it is likely that a veil of silence was drawn over what was a political defeat. Antiochos left Simon in peace for the rest of his reign, so the king had been appeased in some way. The peaceful period lasted until Simon was killed four years later, and this fact is the clue to the peace agreement.

Simon fell victim to his own success in establishing his control over the state and his promotion of the hereditary succession. A son-in-law of Simon, Ptolemaios son of Abubos, entertained him, his wife, and two of his sons at Ptolemaios' castle at Dok, east of Michmash and overlooking the Jericho plain, of which Ptolemaios was governor. Getting Simon drunk he had him killed and then kept the children and their mother prisoner.[22] He aimed to seize power in Jerusalem, and he set about it systematically, in a series of steps that show that he had planned his *coup* carefully.

He made four moves, no doubt simultaneously. His obvious competitor was Simon's eldest son Hyrkanos, who had a similar post to Ptolemaios', at Gezer, on watch over the lowlands to the west, and was already a successful commander. Assassins were sent to dispose of him. The approval of Judaea's overlord was required, so a message was sent to King Antiochos, 'asking him to send troops, and to give him authority over the country and its towns'. Messages went to army officers inside Judaea, offering presents in return for their support. Soldiers under Ptolemaios' command went to gain control of Jerusalem.[23]

This is a very revealing set of actions. The rulership of Judaea was clearly seen as a settled monarchy, so that the killing of Simon and his sons left it possible for a daughter's husband to accede. Ptolemaios saw clearly that he also needed the acquiescence of the army and that he could do this through the officers by promising rewards. The Judaean polity, despite the recent partnership of *gerousia* and people with the Maccabean leader, was still a military state; in this, of course, it was a fairly typical Hellenistic kingdom.

The message to Antiochos is the most revealing action of all. Ptolemaios understood that Antiochos, as Seleukid king, had the authority to confirm the Judaean head of state, a continuation of that required by the high priests, which was Simon's main office. This has to have been one of the provisions of the peace agreement between Antiochos and Simon. Ptolemaios was clearly aware that Antiochos' acquiescence, even assistance, was needed if his *coup* was to be successful, and by sending his message before news of the doings at Dok could reach the king, it was probable that he would gain both. After all, Antiochos was unlikely to be keen on appointing Hyrkanos, who had fought and defeated one of his armies. Ptolemaios, by killing Simon (and perhaps Hyrkanos) might even claim to be eliminating the king's enemies.

Ptolemaios did not ask for the high priesthood. He did ask to be made ruler of 'the country and its towns' – *strategos*, in other words. He was therefore identifying clearly where the real power lay. Appointment as high priest might then follow. It is his immediate reference to the king for ratification of his *coup* that makes it clear that Simon had earlier accepted the king's overlordship as part of the presumed treaty of 138.

Ptolemaios was well prepared and had executed the *coup* well. He was foiled by the single fact that he was unable to keep what he had done secret from Hyrkanos. Ptolemaios needed to control the city and the army before Hyrkanos could move, because Hyrkanos had been identified by Simon as his chosen successor, and the army officers and the citizens in Jerusalem would first of all look to him when they heard of Simon's death. Hence the assassin sent to remove Hyrkanos. But Hyrkanos was told what was happening by a man who got away from Dok and reached him before Ptolemaios' assassins could kill him.

Hyrkanos reacted with commendable speed, intercepting and killing the assassins sent by Ptolemaios and reaching Jerusalem before Ptolemaios, so that when Ptolemaios tried to enter the city his way was barred by the citizens, roused by Hyrkanos. Ptolemaios had been too slow. He had to do more than Hyrkanos to gain control. Hyrkanos had only to turn up at Jerusalem, but Ptolemaios had to get his elaborate plan working. He moved too deliberately, and so lost the contest. It is evident that Hyrkanos did not bother about communicating with Antiochos, not at least not until he was installed.[24] His priority was Jerusalem and installation as high priest. Appointment as *strategos* he saw as only secondary.

The two rivals now fortified their respective political positions. Hyrkanos had himself made high priest, presumably by some sort of popular election, but he was the only candidate, and had a clear hereditary claim: Josephus says he 'assumed' the office.[25] He mustered an army and went after Ptolemaios, who was at Dok. Hyrkanos laid siege to the fort (remains of siege works have been found by archaeologists), but was prevented from mounting a serious assault by threats to his mother and brothers.[26] It was very similar to the situation Simon had faced when Tryphon held Jonathan.

Simon was killed in February 134. The siege went on for some time, but is said to have been suspended at the beginning of the sabbatical year, which is supposed to have begun in October 135.[27] Yet other calculations put the death of Simon more definitely in 134, in which case the sabbatical year did not intervene. The chronological indications are confused in other ways as well, but it might be that Josephus or his source was simply using the sabbatical year argument as an excuse for devaluing the intensity of the political crisis.[28] Ptolemaios eventually killed his prisoners and got away across the Jordan to take refuge with Zenon Kotylas, the ruler of Philadelphia.[29] This city had drifted into independence in the wake of the Seleukid civil wars and the Judaean revolt, both of which would increase the need for local vigilance – Judah's enemy Timotheos had been acting as an independent ruler a generation earlier. It may be that Ptolemaios was permitted to escape from the siege and that the sabbatical year was later suggested as a reason for ending the siege.

All this had wider implications. A civil war inevitably attracted enemies, and Antiochos VII now intervened. Any peace he had made with Simon ended with the latter's death. The dispute between Hyrkanos and Ptolemaios for the succession gave the king a clear opening to move into Judaea with a colourable excuse that he was intervening to bring peace to a vassal state; this would allow him to assert his suzerainty over the winner.

Hyrkanos was able to eliminate Ptolemaios before Antiochos arrived. The siege of Dok lasted for several months, so it seems likely that Hyrkanos was simultaneously negotiating with Antiochos, which is to say he was playing for time. If Antiochos arrived during the siege he would be in a position to make an ally of either of the contenders, not to mention catching the Judaean army in the open. He had clearly taken his time, no doubt content to see the troublesome Judaean state dissolving into internal dissension. Hyrkanos, however, had to gain power exclusively before Antiochos arrived. When Ptolemaios escaped Hyrkanos was established as his father's successor – Ptolemaios' escape was, of course, an admission that his *coup* had failed. Antiochos' delay was surely deliberate, to allow Hyrkanos to win; he would not necessarily wish to support a man who had murdered one of his tributary rulers.

As Antiochos approached, Hyrkanos prepared Jerusalem for a siege, and the city had enough supplies to hold out for several months. (The chronology is unclear yet again.) The sabbatical year of the time now ceases to matter in our sources, but if it really existed Hyrkanos' supplies were probably less adequate than it seems. Antiochos reached the plateau and the city without being obstructed in any way. Hyrkanos evidently hoped that a siege in a land whose supplies had been brought into the city would present Antiochos with an impossible logistical situation. Antiochos' siege of the city gives Josephus a chance to include various stock siege stories in his account: double ditch circumvallation, 'useless mouths' expelled and left to starve between the lines, a hundred towers built, frequent sallies by heroic Jewish soldiers.[30] All these are so often described in the literature that they cannot be accepted as descriptions of this particular siege.

Various indications in Josephus imply that the siege lasted nearly a year, which seems hardly likely. The Seleukid army was not unpractised at sieges and it would not take so long to capture a minor city, nor would Antiochos wish to be pinned down for a year in such a siege. Its end is related as a curious story whereby Hyrkanos requested and was granted a truce to celebrate the Feast of Tabernacles, and Antiochos sent in sacrificial animals, spices, and gold and silver vessels, which in turn led to Hyrkanos asking for terms.[31]

This is, of course, highly unlikely, and cannot be accepted. It is much more probable that the siege was fairly short, since both sides knew full well what terms Antiochos would insist on, and Hyrkanos was in a weak position. He was the survivor of a civil war, in which his opponent had some local support – amongst the army officers he had offered to enrich, for a start. Ptolemaios was still at large, and if Hyrkanos proved to be obdurate Antiochos might well bring him back. The alternative account of the siege in Diodoros says nothing about events during the siege, but that it lasted 'for a time', which is exceptionally vague, but does imply considerably less than a year.[32] In other words Antiochos was in a strong position, both militarily and politically, and Hyrkanos had few advantages.

Terms were therefore agreed without much difficulty, once Hyrkanos indicated that he would negotiate, and once Antiochos indicated his acceptance of Hyrkanos as high priest, which is implied by the Feast of Tabernacles story. Antiochos was relatively lenient. He did not insist on recovering Simon's conquests, but he did require that tribute be paid for them, which was an acknowledgment that they were part of his kingdom. Arms were to be surrendered, and though such a provision was virtually unenforceable, it did mean the effective demobilization and disarmament of the Judaean army. A garrison was to be placed once more in the Akra. This last provision produced such strong objections that in its place Antiochos agreed to accept a tribute of 500 talents (presumably a sum separate from that owed for the cities in the lowlands), hostages were to be surrendered, and he required that the walls of the city be taken down. This last was overseen by Antiochos himself, and he insisted on collecting 300 of the 500 talents on the spot.[33] (So much for the pleas of poverty uttered by Simon in the negotiations of 138.)

These terms collectively reinforced Judaea's status as a vassal state of the Seleukid kingdom, paying tribute and giving hostages. With its main city now without fortifications it was clearly vulnerable to any attack. It was an object lesson in what could happen when the internal conditions broke down. This subordination was made even clearer when Hyrkanos was compelled to join Antiochos in the war with Parthia the king started in 131.[34] Hyrkanos is said to have used his treasury to hire mercenaries[35] – his army having been disbanded – and it was presumably these men he took to the east, though he surely had some of his own Jewish soldiers with him as well, if only as bodyguards. Hiring mercenaries may have spread the burden away from the Judaeans in the fighting in the east, but it also may imply a lack of support for Hyrkanos among his Jewish subjects, as a result of the civil war. No doubt Judaea, after a civil war, an invasion, and a sabbatical year (if there was one) was exhausted. Yet Hyrkanos had been able to pay Antiochos' fee, and was able to pay for his mercenaries; taxation in Judaea must have been ferocious.

No details of Hyrkanos' war in the east are known beyond a supposed request to Antiochos to halt operations so that a Jewish feast could be celebrated,[36] and the fact that Hyrkanos escaped when the Parthians killed Antiochos and captured much of his army. Hyrkanos returned to Jerusalem during 129.[37]

The death of Antiochos released Hyrkanos and Judaea from the obligations of the peace concluded in 134. Hyrkanos no longer had to supply forces to the king, pay tribute, either for Joppa or the other cities, or in place of a garrison in the Akra. One would expect that the re-fortification of the city was one of his priorities on his return, and he is credited with this by I Maccabees.[38] The death of Antiochos VII, in other words, made the Judaean state independent once again.

Chapter 8

Early Conquests

The Maccabean state as it reached true independence in 129/128 was geographically small. It consisted of the upland plateau centred on Jerusalem, together with some neighbouring lowlands. The upland stretched from the Gophna Hills to Beth Zur, no more than fifty kilometres; from the edge of the plateau looking west towards the Mediterranean to the steep edge of the Rift Valley looking east over the Dead Sea was about forty kilometres. In addition, Hyrkanos' predecessors had acquired the small territories of Lydda, Arimatheia and Apharaema along the edge of the plateau to the north-west and north, the fortified town of Gezer on a projecting hill to the west, its smaller neighbour Ekron to the south, and Joppa on the coast. These acquisitions increased the area of Judaea by about half. They were valuable partly because they were wealthier than the lands of the plateau (Joppa in particular generated wealth as a busy port), but they were also forward defensive positions. The Jordan valley from the plateau edge to the river had been acquired as well – it was Ptolemaios' province in 134. Even with these lands added it was only forty kilometres from Jerusalem to Joppa, thirty to the crossing of the Jordan, thirty to Arimatheia, and even less to Beth Zur. (There is no sign that any of Hyrkanos' predecessors ruled beyond the river, despite raids by Judah and Jonathan.) It was possible to walk to any of the borders of the state from Jerusalem in a day or a little more. Judaea was the size of a large Greek city state.

The possession of Joppa remained disputed. One of the aims of Antiochos VII had been to recover that seaport. It seems he succeeded, though he handed it back to Hyrkanos in return for tribute. The death of Antiochos VII in 129 cancelled that arrangement, unless his successor was able to reinstate it, which would require at least a threat to attack Judaea. There is a sign that Demetrios II, on his return from captivity in 128, at first intended such a move but, as Josephus says,[1] he did not have the time or the opportunity, for he was fully occupied during his brief second reign with other and bigger problems. So Hyrkanos' independence, acquired by default when Antiochos VII died, continued through the contested reigns of Demetrios II and Alexander II and into the early years of Antiochos VIII, that is, from 129 to 121.

This is the period during which we may locate the early wars of Hyrkanos, described without much detail by Josephus.[2] He gives an initial misleading statement that Hyrkanos 'marched out against the cities of Syria'. In fact, Hyrkanos carefully avoided fighting any of the 'cities of Syria' until the last years of his reign. These were the cities that lined the Mediterranean coast from Gaza northwards, occupied the Vale of Jezreel, and populated a large area east of the Jordan, from Philadelphia-Amman north to Damascus. None of these places and cities figures in any military activities by Hyrkanos until the last half-decade of his reign after 110.

The dating of Hyrkanos' first wars of expansion is not clear.[3] Josephus implies that all the wars took place over a fairly short time, beginning as soon as he heard of the death of Antiochos. However, Hyrkanos must have 'heard of' the king's death while he was still in the east, and it will have taken him some months to get home. Antiochos died early in 129, during the winter, so Hyrkanos could have got home during that year. The impression that his conquests took place quickly is just as misleading. One of the wars involved a siege said to have lasted for six months, and other sieges may be implied as well. The date of the earliest attack cannot be earlier than 128, since Hyrkanos cannot have reached Judaea until middle or late 129; the end of his campaigns was probably 122, because from the next year the Seleukid King Antiochos VIII was no longer distracted by challengers, and then it would be far too dangerous for a minor ruler like Hyrkanos to attempt anything aggressive. Josephus makes the wars occur in a clear sequence. Again, this may or may not be accurate, for they clearly do make a coherent group. We must always bear in mind that the sequence could be either wrong or, at the least, much less clear than it seems.

The first war was centred on the siege of the town of Medaba, the modern Madaba, across the Jordan, twenty-five kilometres from the river crossing near Jericho. The purpose of this attack is difficult to discern. The town itself was of little importance, nor did it command a wide territory. It was on the Belka Plateau, above the Ghor, the Rift Valley containing the Jordan and the Dead Sea. It was also close to Mount Nebo, a site holy for its association with Moses, but that does not seem a particularly good reason for capturing the nearby town. It lay south-west of Philadelphia-Amman, but there is not even a hint that Philadelphia was involved. (Zenon Kotylas had ruled in 134, when Ptolemaios took refuge with him, and he may have still ruled in the 120s; his son Theodoros appears to have succeeded him, so presumably one of these two was the ruler at the time.) The town, or village, of Samoga, thought to be Samak, twelve or thirteen kilometres north-east of Medaba, was also attacked and captured. This was a place of minimal size and importance, no more than a village, and possibly only a hill. Samoga, however, if it was Samak – the identification is uncertain and disputed – was on a direct line from Medaba towards Philadelphia, and lay halfway between the two places. It was a high point, the highest between Medaba and the upland just south of Philadelphia, so it would be a useful observation post.

The conquest of these two places raises another question: what was the status of Heshbon, north of Medaba and west of Samak, and so between Hyrkanos' original territory and his conquests? Heshbon was sited in a useful and productive plain on the plateau, on a route up from the crossing of the Jordan, and beside the upper stretches of a perennial stream, the Nahr Hesban. It had been re-occupied from about 200 BC when a rectangular fort had been built on the hill, and a settlement had grown round it. It was, however, still small – and the fort must have been a deterrent.[4] But without Heshbon, the two other places could be only precariously held by a state whose main centre was west of the Jordan.

It is not clear what the situation was in the region vaguely called the Peraia. This was a variable area across the Jordan from Palestine, the valley between the river and the steep rise to the plateau. This was the area Judah is said to have raided early in the rebellion, and it was the area where the Tobiad Hyrkanos built his palace-temple at Iraq el-Amir. It clearly had a population that was at least partly Jewish, and may well have received more Jews as refugees from the troubles in Palestine since 166. But who controlled the land by the 120s is not obvious. The Seleukid government appears to have evaporated from Philadelphia by the 130s, given that Zenon and Theodoros are described as 'tyrants', that is, independent rulers. Perhaps several of the cities to the north had also slipped into independence. But the Peraia was outside all of these places. Perhaps the best guess is that the region might have been loosely attached to Judaea, though there is no direct evidence for this, until Hyrkanos attacked Medaba. He had no difficulty reaching the town, so his forces were able to march unobstructed through the southern Peraia; this episode therefore marks its definitive annexation. Later, in the reign of his son, the area was certainly part of the Judaean state; possibly it already was, even before Hyrkanos' reign.

It looks as though Hyrkanos was probing into the area, attacking places such as Medaba, which were politically isolated, or others like Samoga, which had no value in themselves, except as outposts of his conquest. The stronger cities, of which Philadelphia was the most important in this region, were left alone, even though that was where Hyrkanos' enemy and rival Ptolemaios had fled. Heshbon was similarly ignored, despite its more useful situation. Josephus remarks that Samoga was captured 'with its environs', which cannot have been very extensive, but which would include, presumably, the hilltop on which the village stood.

The political status of Heshbon is not known, but since it is no more than twenty-five or so kilometres from Philadelphia it may have been part of that city's territory. Hyrkanos was operating outside Philadelphia's lands, and clear of any of the cities that occupied much of the territory east of the Jordan. He kept clear of any dispute with the Nabataeans who dominated much of the land east of Philadelphia and southwards as far as Petra and the Gulf of Aqaba.

Gaining Medaba gave Hyrkanos an interest in what was happening in the Belka and other parts beyond the Jordan. Philadelphia was his new neighbour, independent of the Seleukid kingdom under the rule of its 'tyrant'; Medaba was close to the old route called the King's Highway, which ran along the plateau from north to south. Holding Medaba gave Hyrkanos the possibility of later seizing control of part of the road, and so milking it of customs' revenue. But the road, being valuable, was at this time under the firm control of the Nabataeans and the cities.

This war was thus against the politically isolated town of Medaba. No one came to its assistance, it was of small size, and of little importance. Yet it took Hyrkanos' army six months to capture the place. (We are not told anything of Samoga except that it was captured.) To take six months over the siege of a small town suggests very strongly that Hyrkanos' army was both small and without much in the way of specialist expertise. He is said to have been the first of his family to employ mercenaries, and this unenterprising episode indicates why he needed them. If he already used them in the Parthian campaign they cannot have been very numerous, for they were expensive and Judaea was poor. The Judaean army in the 120s was apparently a good deal less professional in its training and attainments than its predecessor had become under Judah and Jonathan thirty years before.

There had, of course, been cases in the past when it was reported that machines had been used in sieges by the Judaean forces – in Jerusalem in Judah's time, at Gezer by Simon – but these were isolated cases. Indeed the battering in Jerusalem was unsuccessful; that at Gezer had produced a fairly quick surrender, but was only one machine. The general principle of siege artillery was apparently well enough understood, but was only employed when other methods would not work, and it required expensive expertise to construct and work the machines. There was clearly no artillery establishment in the Judaean army. In a siege, blockade and improvisation was the preferred method.

The second of Hyrkanos' early wars was a raid northwards. He attacked Shechem and the nearby site of Mount Gerizim, on which, Josephus says, was a temple of the Samaritans. He calls these people Cuthaeans, the name of a community removed to the region from Babylonia by the Assyrians centuries earlier, so implying their alienness. The temple was supposed to be a version of that of Jerusalem, which made it a competitor. Archaeological investigations have shown that the temple, and Shechem itself, had been developing since about 200 BC.[5] Both Shechem and the temple were captured, and the latter was destroyed. The region was, however, not annexed to Judaea. To do so would push a salient of Judaean territory well to the north, and Shechem town lay in a valley, and to hold it would require a strong garrison capable of dominating the hostile population. This was merely a raid. The real power in the area lay in the cities of Samaria and Skythopolis, in the Vale of Jezreel to the north. But by destroying the temple, Hyrkanos was making a clear statement of both political and religious intent.

The difference between the campaigns against Medaba and Shechem is noteworthy. Medaba, despite its long resistance, was eventually captured and annexed; Shechem, quickly captured, was then destroyed. The reason for the difference is that Shechem's temple was a challenge to Maccabean ideology. Samaritans were a separate branch of Judaism, and so they were competitors for the loyalty of the Judaean population, and possibly more sympathetic to hellenization than the Maccabees.[6] Medaba, inhabited by non-Jewish Semites and by Greeks, constituted no such threat. Competitors for Jewish loyalty were the prime target, hence the repeated campaigns to drive hellenizing Jews out of Judaea, the earlier destruction of the Tobiad temple at Iraq el-Amir, and now the destruction of the Shechem temple.

The third region of Hyrkanos' aggression was to the south. Here Judaea already held the fort at Beth Zur, but this had been captured twice by armies coming from the coastlands. In what must therefore be seen as a defensive move, Hyrkanos attacked and captured two places through which these Seleukid attacks had come.

Due south was Adora (now Dura) and west was Marisa,[7] through both of which Lysias' army in the 160s, and Tryphon's in 142, had approached. The capture of these two places was clearly aimed at setting up a wider defensive perimeter to protect the main part of Judaea from further attacks.

This, in fact, would seem to have been Hyrkanos' main agenda. The three regions he attacked were all bases from which Judaea could be menaced – and both the Shechem area and Idumaea had seen invading forces passing through to attack Judaea. Yet Hyrkanos had to avoid stirring up any powerful enemy. He was assisted, of course, by the continual strife within the Seleukid kingdom, but it seems clear that even a single Macedonian city such as Philadelphia was an enemy to be avoided, judging by the campaign east of the Jordan, as were the Nabataeans.

The other areas Hyrkanos attacked were the homes of communities that were perceived by the Judaeans as sworn and inveterate enemies. The Idumaean lands had been the route through which Judaea had been invaded several times. The inhabitants may not have been able to prevent the passage of the Seleukid armies, but it seems probable that they had assisted with some enthusiasm. Judah had turned on them, but only in a destructive way, and the southern border of Judaea had remained at the newly fortified Beth Zur since its conquest by Simon in Jonathan's time. Adora and Marisa were the main Idumaean political centres, and therefore their conquest by Hyrkanos brought all of northern Idumaea into the Judaean state.

There is, however, a problem. In the wars in Judah's time this area had been a sub-province of the Seleukid state, governed by Gorgias. He had controlled a wider area than Idumaea, but Marisa was certainly one of his bases, and possibly his governing centre. If Hyrkanos was concerned to avoid attacking places that were part of a major polity, we must assume that the Seleukid state's power in Idumaea had faded away since Gorgias' time. It is certain that there was no Seleukid reaction to Hyrkanos' conquest.

In the north the area of Shechem and Mount Gerizim was the centre of the Samaritans, viewed by the main Jewish community as heretical. Their temple was a version, perhaps a copy, of that at Jerusalem, so Josephus reports.[8] Excavations show that considerable development took place from about 200, so the Samaritan community was flourishing. When Samaria became a Macedonian city in the time of Alexander the Great the new temple for the Samaritans developed just below their holy mountain. This was Hyrkanos' target, not necessarily because it was a major political threat, but because it was an apparent alternative to Judaism. By destroying that temple and their main city he presumably intended to destroy the Samaritans as a community. In this he failed.[9]

Hyrkanos, in these attacks to north and south, certainly succeeded in identifying the crucial local enemies of his state and his regime, and at the same time he avoided antagonizing any serious enemies who could retaliate. His victims were carefully chosen as being weak and isolated, notably the well-rooted Idumaean and Samaritan communities on Judaea's borders. To remove the threat they posed to Judaea, which amounted to permitting invasions to come through their territories, he destroyed their urban centres and attacked their communal existence. The temple of the

Samaritans on Mount Gerizim, which had become a substantial building, and was perhaps larger and better built than the temple at Jerusalem, for it was a more recent foundation, was destroyed. It was certainly the emotional and religious heart of the Samaritan community, but, of course, as the Jews should have known from their own history, its destruction would very likely only solidify that community's existence.

The Idumaeans perhaps did not have the same identification with a religious centre, and Hyrkanos took a leaf from his father's work and compelled the people to Judaize. That is, he destroyed them as a separate community, incorporating those who submitted and driving out or killing those who resisted. This proved to be a successful political move, and those who stayed became loyal to Judaea, but how many died and how many fled to avoid that fate is, however, not known. There seems to be no record of Idumaean refugees later, but there must have been some, perhaps many, who left to hold to their old gods and avoid becoming circumcised. One of those who may well have been affected was Herod's great-grandfather who was supposed to have lived at Marisa; his son became governor in the area, so the family very quickly assimilated to the new religion and regime.

In terms of military achievement, nothing Hyrkanos had done so far was particularly notable. The communities he had attacked were all weak or defenceless or both; only Medaba had made a serious resistance. Certainly he had conquered territory, though only small areas. The area he had taken over east of the Jordan was only the land about Medaba and down to the shores of the Dead Sea and the lowest crossing of the river, though by controlling Medaba he consolidated his hold over a larger part of the Peraia.

In Idumaea he had pushed Judaea's borders south and west, but how far is not clear. Adora is only six kilometres south of Beth Zur, and Marisa only twenty to the west; these were certainly annexed. Adding some land to the south of Adora and west of Marisa to these conquests would push the boundary further out, but not all that far – and that was dry, near-desert land. In the north no territory at all was annexed. It is likely that the Greeks of the city of Samaria would have reacted with some hostility to a Judaean annexation, and Samaria was still part of the Seleukid kingdom. They could perhaps tolerate a Judaean raid against the Samaritans, but not a conquest of any land. Possibly the Samaritans were as disliked by the Macedonian citizens of Samaria as they were by the Jews.

The Maccabees had succeeded in destroying two competing Jewish temples, at Iraq el-Amir and at Shechem. Their reasons were essentially political, since these places were competitors with Jerusalem for the loyalty of all Jews. By now, however, another temple had been established, at Leontopolis in Egypt, by the son of Onias III, known as Onias IV. This, protected by the Ptolemaic state, was out of Hyrkanos' reach, but its importance could be reduced by building up the devotion among Jews to *the* temple in Jerusalem. Onias' temple lasted longer than that at Jerusalem, being closed by the Romans in AD 74, four years after the Jerusalem version was destroyed.[10]

The conclusion to be reached from these minor wars is that the Judaean army was still small, and unable to accomplish much. The long siege at Medaba suggests that the event was less an active siege and more a blockade. The army itself is said to have suffered severe hardships in the siege, which also suggests that its logistical support was poor – no doubt the resources of the land around were quickly consumed or destroyed by the besiegers, and it is doubtful that Judaea could supply much. The raid on the Samaritans was mere destruction and did not necessarily take very long, especially if it was a surprise attack. The conquest of the Idumaean area was a solid achievement, but was not very difficult, and it may be that the places captured were not even fortified – there is no fortification at Beit Givrin (Marisa). We must conclude that the Judaean army remained small. The land itself was not wealthy, so the number of mercenaries Hyrkanos could hire would be few. The army therefore consisted of a small professional mercenary force accompanied by a larger, perhaps almost untrained, mob. This was not a military force very much to be feared by its neighbours.

These wars are, as noted earlier, undated. Josephus' implication of speed cannot be accepted. The raid on Shechem was probably quickly accomplished and soon over, but the campaigns of Medaba and Adora/Marisa clearly took some time. The siege of Medaba, having lasted six months, was followed by the capture of Samoga, and presumably by a subsequent military occupation that must have lasted for some time in order to prevent a rebellion. Similarly, the Idumaean campaign involved the capture of two towns, the second of which must have been prepared for attack, even if the first was taken by surprise, and all this was followed by another necessary military occupation, the unpleasant business of forced conversion, and presumably the expulsion of the recalcitrants.

Neither the Medaba nor the Idumaean campaigns can have taken less than a full campaigning season, and it would be easier to see each of them as lasting for two. The Mount Gerizim campaign could have been over in perhaps a month, but a second campaign in that year seems unlikely – the possibility of a revenge attack had to be guarded against. It is thus possible to account for five years by these campaigns without much difficulty. This in turn fills up much of the time available between 128 and 122. From 121 onwards the Seleukid king was not distracted, and any further Judaean aggression would probably impinge on his territory. It had become too dangerous to indulge in more wars.

Chapter 9

The Samarian War

The Seleukid king Antiochos VIII Grypos had surmounted his most immediate problems by 121, when his domineering and threatening mother was compelled to kill herself. He did, however, have a younger half-brother, Antiochos IX Kyzikenos, who constituted a new threat. Seleukid brothers had not fought each other for a century – though Alexander I claimed to be a son of Antiochos IV, and so a cousin of Demetrios I and II. Recently, however, the family's record had been violent and murderous – Demetrios I and Antiochos VII were killed in battle, Alexander I and Demetrios II were murdered, Seleukos V was murdered (by his mother), Alexander II (not a family member) was either murdered or a suicide, and Kleopatra Thea was forced to suicide.

Kleopatra was killed, in effect, by her son Antiochos VIII, who insisted that she drink the poison she had prepared for him.[1] The other son, Antiochos IX Kyzikenos, could claim the right to revenge, and had presumably been intended by her as Grypos' successor. There is a hint that Kyzikenos emerged as a threat right away, but this is a comment by Josephus that looks like a brief summary of a much more detailed source, and cannot be dated.[2] Certainly one explanation of the apparent passivity of Grypos between 121 and 114/113 must be that he was under a constant threat that his half-brother would take advantage of any preoccupation to attack him.

The significance of this period of Seleukid peace will be evident when Maccabean history over the previous half-century is considered; when the Seleukids were preoccupied with major problems – civil war, foreign war – the Maccabees were active. Thus Hyrkanos made war on his neighbours between 128 and 122 when the Seleukid civil war distracted the kings; from 121 onwards he remained quiet; when Seleukid troubles came again, in 113, Hyrkanos became active once more.

The period of Seleukid quiescence may be because Grypos was unwilling to go to war. He made no attempt to recover territories lost to the various Seleukid enemies, even when this would have been comparatively easy, and he later had a reputation as a pursuer of pleasure rather than a devotee of duty.[3] Josephus points out that the period of peace under Hyrkanos, which coincided with Grypos' early rule (121–c.109), enabled Hyrkanos to 'exploit Judaea undisturbed)'.[4] The same could be said for Grypos on a larger scale. The Seleukid kingdom had suffered grievous manpower losses and the loss of its richest province, Babylonia, in the Parthian war, and there had then followed several years of civil war. A period of peace and rest was indicated, and it might be this that was behind the accusation that Antiochos VIII was lazy and a dilettante – though the report in Diodoros is only an excerpt, and is quite likely the result of hostile propaganda. He is said to have had no military ability, but he did in the end defeat his rival and recover much of his kingdom.

The peaceful time did not last, of course, and in 114/113 Kyzikenos launched his attempt to seize the kingdom. He almost succeeded, but Grypos recovered during 113/112, and then the two men settled down to a prolonged civil war. Antioch changed hands four times between Kyzikenos' first attack and the final recovery of the city by Grypos in 109/108, and the same could probably be said of other cities.[5]

The early years of the fighting saw each king gaining sudden but often fleeting successes; only from 109 or so onwards was it clear that they were locked into a paralysis, in which neither could win. Josephus memorably likened it to two wrestlers who had exhausted each other but neither would yield.[6] The result was a further decisive weakening of the kingdom; local civic autonomy increased – a process that had begun in the 120s – and neighbouring powers were increasingly willing to intervene in Seleukid affairs. These neighbours included the Hasmonaeans, the Ptolemies, and the Parthians.

This period of apparent peace in Syria – it may be only apparent because of the lack of sources covering these years – was also, it seems, a time of peace in Judaea. But in this case this was the time during which the conquests of the previous decade – Medaba and Idumaea – were digested and became fully part of the Judaean state. This process was useful, in that both areas never showed any signs of wishing to secede. Hyrkanos must also have been on his guard against all his neighbours, whose reaction to his successes and methods could well be very hostile.

After Hyrkanos' attack on the temple at Shechem in the 120s the Samaritans' centre shifted back to the city of Samaria. This therefore became a more cosmopolitan city whose population included the descendents of the original Macedonian military settlers, Samaritans, and Jews (and probably Greeks and other Syrians as well). It appears from Josephus that the Samaritans took out their resentment at their defeat and the destruction of their temple on the Jews in the city. Hyrkanos came forward as the Jews' protector and champion.

This is an interpretation of a mangled notice in Josephus, when the dispute is said to have taken place in 'Marisa'.[7] This, of course, had been one of Hyrkanos' Idumaean conquests. It is highly unlikely that Samaritans would live there or that they could ill-treat the Jews of that city. Samaria may therefore be regarded as the correct name.[8]

We do not know the sequence of events that led up to the war that followed, but presumably Hyrkanos would first protest at the Jews' sufferings, which would force the citizens of Samaria – the Macedonians, that is – to take sides in the dispute in their city. They appear to have taken the part of the Samaritans. (A distinction must be kept between 'Samaritans' who were the religious group, dissidents from Judaism – 'heretics' or 'apostates' to the Jews – and 'Samarians', who were the citizen inhabitants of the city.) The choice of the Samarians about who to support was dictated by their own interests. To accept that Hyrkanos could intervene in the city's internal affairs would be to admit his overall authority. This would conflict with the city's allegiance to the Seleukid king, whose authority was more acceptable than that of Hyrkanos. The latter had, after all, compelled the Idumaeans to forcible conversion. The Samarians therefore made the situation clear to their Seleukid suzerain. According to Josephus in the *Jewish War*, this was 'Antiochos Aspendios', who was Antiochos VIII Grypos (who had briefly taken refuge in Aspendos in Pamphylia before returning in 111 to recover control of North Syria). But much of the south – that is, the Palestine area – was still controlled by Kyzikenos.[9] It is not known to which king the Samarians reported.

The city, having (presumably) adopted the cause of the Samaritans, Hyrkanos sent his army to attack it. The date is not altogether clear, but references to the participation of other parties narrow it down to between 111 and 107. Since the siege lasted a year, so we are told, and ended soon after the intervention of Ptolemy Lathyros, who was co-regent with his mother until about 107, it seems best to put the start of the war in 109 or 108.[10] Hyrkanos began the war and set up the siege, but then left the conduct of the war to two of his sons, Antigonos and Aristoboulos.[11] Hyrkanos was now old, probably in his sixties, so one explanation would be that he was feeling his age. Another, for which only conjecture exists, might be that the sons were keen on the war and the father less so. Certainly Hyrkanos is not mentioned again in the account of the war, and, in fact, Antigonos also drops out. However, since Aristoboulus was Hyrkanos' chosen successor and was a warrior and conqueror during his brief reign, this preference may merely be the result of assumptions by Josephus (or his source).

The Samarians' defiance of Hyrkanos must have included the assumption that he would attack them in retaliation. The Jewish-Samaritan hatred had long existed, and Hyrkanos' destruction of the Gerizim temple had no doubt driven that hatred to even greater heat in the city, especially since the Samaritan refugees had been deprived of their homes as well as their temple. When the Judaean army attacked it was wholly unable to make any effect on the city. Evidently Samaria was fully prepared.

Excavations at Samaria have shown that the acropolis area was newly fortified in the mid-second century BC with a substantial wall. There was also an outer city wall, which was probably that which established the limits of the city at its foundation at the time of Alexander the Great. Only a fragment of this has been located, but it was substantial enough so show that the city was well defended. If the acropolis received extra protection in the period following the aftermath of the Maccabean revolt, which took place only a short distance to the south, no doubt the outer wall was also well maintained.[12] The timing of the improved fortification fits with the activity of Apollonios, Judaea's first enemy, who was governor in Samaria. It is also an indication of the apprehension generated in the surrounding areas at the Judaean rebellion.

The Judaean army failed to capture the city at its first attack, then settled to a siege. The city was hardly large or strong enough to hold up a professional army – it is only a kilometre across at its widest part – so it seems that the Judaean forces were no larger or better trained and equipped than at the siege of Medaba twenty years before. The only siege technique attempted was a trench of circumvallation, said to have been eighty stades long (about sixteen kilometres), reinforced with a double wall.[13]

This would put the wall-and-trench a good kilometre outside the city wall, and perhaps more, which seems a long way. (This is assuming the figure of '80' is accurate, and accurately reported; it may well be a considerable exaggeration.) If this is correct, the siege was clearly not being actively fought; the city was subjected to a blockade intended to starve the inhabitants out, as was the case at Medaba. The population of the city is not known, but it was not more than twenty-two hectares in area, and so we must assume a fighting population of only a few thousand at most.[14] The Judaean army was probably larger in numbers, and was no doubt composed in part of a professional core of mercenaries and a larger force of partly trained Jewish levies, recruited mainly from the Judaean countryside. The mercenaries, no doubt recruited up to a larger number than before in view of the crisis, and as a result of the wealth Hyrkanos had gathered in the years of peace, would need to be numerous enough to stand off attacks by the citizen militia. The Judaean levies, however, cannot have remained on duty for a year, for they were farmers in most cases and would need to attend to their work; hence, no doubt, the wall-and-trench surrounding the city, which could be constructed by unskilled labour. It would enable the professionals and that part of the levy on duty to block any breakout by the city troops, and could institute the blockade which would make it difficult to put supplies or reinforcements into the city.

Relief attempts from outside had also to be faced. Josephus in his *Jewish War* ascribes one attempt to Antiochos VIII 'Aspendios',[15] who is fairly certainly the king who was in control of the area at the time. In the *Antiquities* he describes two attempts, both by Antiochos IX Kyzikenos,[16] in the second he had the assistance of a force borrowed from Ptolemy Lathyros.

The relief attempt by Grypos/Aspendios described by Josephus in the *Jewish War*, is also given in very similar terms in the *Antiquities*, but with command given to Kyzikenos. The king, whoever it was, came to the assistance of the city 'readily'. He was thus available, had a considerable army, and was not too far away. He was, however, defeated by Aristoboulos and retreated eastwards by way of Skythopolis; this was therefore presumably the direction from which he had come.

The second attempt at relief is different. By this time the siege had continued for some time. Antiochos was appealed to once more, for, according to Josephus in the *Jewish War*, the citizens had been reduced almost to starvation. He came with a force of his own, together with 6,000 men contributed by Ptolemy. This force adopted a different strategy, trying to break the siege by invading Judaea and harrying the land, clearly aiming to draw the Judaean army away from Samaria. However, the attackers dispersed to undertake the task of destruction and theft, lost men in ambushes, and failed to disturb the siege. They were then withdrawn, and Antiochos himself went off to Tripolis, a destination implying a march along the Phoenician coast.

It is usually assumed that Josephus made a mistake in ascribing the first relief attempt to Antiochos VIII Aspendios in the *Jewish War*; it is equally likely that he made one in *Antiquities*, by conflating two attempts and putting them under the same king. The second attempt was clearly a very different affair than the first, in its size, its composition, its methods, and in its line of retreat. So there really were two separate attempts at bringing relief to the city. They came from different directions, in different forms, and perhaps by a different king, and I shall here assume that this is so.

Josephus was, of course, writing from the point of view of the Jews, Judaea, and Hyrkanos, but neither of the two Seleukid kings had that priority. They were mainly concerned with gaining advantage over their rival; for neither was Samaria itself his main concern. Either king would be pleased to relieve Samaria of its siege since the city would then become his, and he would gain prestige by the success, but both had to avoid a serious defeat, in which they lost many soldiers. This viewpoint helps to explain two elements. First, there is the question of why Aspendios brought in the reinforcements from Ptolemy, whom he no doubt used in the front line to preserve his own forces. (It is said that Ptolemy's mother, Queen Kleopatra III, was furious when she heard what he had done;[17] the waste of Ptolemaic military manpower may well be one of her main grievances.)

The second result of the adoption of a Seleukid point of view helps to explain the ease with which the relief attempts were defeated. Neither king was prepared to fight a full-scale battle. Their 'defeats' were not the result of battles, but of ambushes and a withdrawal. Josephus says that in the first relief attempt 'Aspendios' (Grypos) was defeated, but he and his army largely survived, so no large battle had happened. (Had Aristoboulos defeated a Seleukid king in a serious battle we can be sure that Josephus would have said so, probably at length.) Once Grypos had failed to bring relief, Kyzikenos' attempt was less to assist the Samarians and more to gain control of the city. Neither king was concerned for the Samarians themselves.

Kyzikenos left two generals and part of his army to continue the war.[18] The generals, Kallimandros and Epikrates, seem to have divided the work. Kallimandros was in charge of trying to break the siege; Epikrates garrisoned Skythopolis. This means that Skythopolis, last heard of as the refuge of Grypos' army in its retreat several months earlier, was now in Kyzikenos' hands, no doubt acquired when he arrived to assist Samaria. He may have regarded this southern expedition, therefore, as a success.

Kallimandros' attempt to break through to Samaria failed. He died in the attempt, and his force was, according to Josephus, routed.[19] This left Epikrates in a difficult situation, for his duty was to take up where Kallimandros had left off. According to Josephus he did so by accepting money to leave the city of Skythopolis, which was later captured by the Judaean army.[20] A second version of this event seems more acceptable, for the first asks us to believe that the Judaean army, which was unable to capture Samaria, was nonetheless capable of capturing the bigger city of Skythopolis. Epikrates, on the other hand, is said to have been short of money, which he would need to pay his soldiers, and by accepting money, probably from Hyrkanos, he could abandon Skythopolis but still continue attempting to break the siege of Samaria.

90 *The Wars of the Maccabees*

This was a fairly desperate strategy, and it failed. Epikrates was as unable to break the siege as the other commanders. The Samarians had assumed that if they held out long enough they would be rescued. They also assumed, reasonably, that since the war had begun with a dispute over the ill-treatment of Jews in the city, then their defeat would be the occasion for, at the least, the sack of the city, and quite possibly the massacre of the Greek and Samaritan inhabitants; hence their long resistance. But the failure of Epikrates, who certainly made some attempt to relieve the city after coming out from Skythopolis, no doubt disheartened the Samarians and at the same time encouraged the besiegers.

In the end the fate of the Samarians was even worse than a mere sack. Combining the information in both of Josephus' accounts, it seems that the inhabitants were first reduced to starvation, then the city was captured. How exactly it fell is not stated, but an assault is surely probable, once it was made relatively easy by the weakened state of the starving inhabitants. (Though it is not stated, this presumes that Epikrates and his army had left the region.) The city was sacked, the surviving inhabitants were sold into slavery, the site of the city was razed, and a stream diverted to run over it.[21] There are signs in the archaeological record that the walls of the acropolis had been damaged, though how is not known.[22]

The references to Skythopolis in these accounts seem to suggest that Hyrkanos' forces gained control of that city. A closer examination shows that this is a conclusion that is not supported by Josephus' words. It appears three times in his two narratives. The first occasion is when Grypos' relieving force was driven away from Samaria; he was pursued 'as far as Skythopolis' by Antigonos and Aristoboulos, but got away.[23] Whether he controlled the city itself, or entered it, is not stated, though it seems likely that he did. His eventual object was presumably to cross the Jordan at one of the crossings south of the Sea of Galilee.

The second appearance of the city is in the episode of Epikrates. He is said to have been short of money, and to have 'betrayed Skythopolis and other places near it to the Jews'. Yet Hyrkanos' army is not said to have taken the city, and was kept fully occupied for some time yet by Epikrates' attempt to relieve Samaria by using his (now presumably well-paid) army.[24] Skythopolis was a major city, and would need a considerable garrison to hold it. The Judaean army surely could not afford to transfer a force into Skythopolis large enough to hold the city and at the same time maintain the siege. Whatever is really meant by Josephus' words, they cannot be taken to mean that Skythopolis was captured by the Judaean army.

The third reference tends to confirm this conclusion. After the capture, at last, of Samaria, the Judaean army went toward Skythopolis where it 'overran the district, and raided the whole country as far as Mount Carmel'.[25] It explicitly does not claim that Skythopolis was captured or under Judaean control. Indeed if it had been, then the ravaging was done to Judaean subjects. So Skythopolis, though it was unfriendly towards Judaea, remained independent or subject to one of the kings.

Skythopolis is forty kilometres north-east of Samaria. The army could clearly reach it, and, in the absence of a defending force, could ravage the Vale of Jezreel (from Skythopolis to Carmel) 'in the flowing tide of success', after at last taking

Samaria, but that was not a conquest, merely a raid. The territory around the obliterated Samaria was probably annexed to Judaea, but other areas to east and west were not.

This fall of Samaria will have convinced the non-Jews all around Judaea that the new state was dangerous, if they had not yet already reached that conclusion. Hyrkanos had attacked his neighbours on three sides, east, south and north, captured and destroyed a Macedonian city, and ravaged the land as far as Carmel and Skythopolis. He and his father had twice forced a conquered people to undergo conversion to Judaism. And when a dispute between Hyrkanos' Samaritan victims and some Jews living outside Judaea occurred, Hyrkanos used it as an excuse to attack the city in which that dispute had taken place, and to destroy it, which could only be seen as a disproportionate reaction. Any community in which Jews lived, therefore, had to regard themselves as being under Hyrkanos' protection. This hardly made for comfortable or even peaceful communal relations.

This political behaviour was, of course, an inheritance from the methods used by the Maccabee brothers in the rebellion in the 160s. This had bred into the ideology of the state a contempt for non-Jews, and a determination to remove perceived threats both to the state and to the religion. It made Judaea a most uncomfortable neighbour.

Chapter 10

Internal Upheavals and the Ptolemaic War

It is not possible to detect a settled or formal mode of succession in the Hasmonaean house. The death of every ruler produced a crisis in which more than one member of the extended family laid claim to power, and these contests struck at the very foundation of the new state. The death of Judah brought the early extinction of the rudimentary state he had built. The capture and later death of Jonathan led to the seizure of power by Simon, to the exclusion of Jonathan's sons, a process that was accomplished peacefully, in part thanks to the threat from Tryphon, so that Simon filled in while negotiations went on for Jonathan's release. Simon's murder produced a war for the succession between his son and his son-in-law, which opened the way for the re-establishment of Seleukid authority, and the reduction of Judaea once more to the status of a Seleukid province. The long reign of Hyrkanos I seems to have been sufficient to restrict the succession to his own immediate family, but he had five sons. This was a guarantee of disputes, and his dispositions for the succession were a recipe for more trouble.

Hyrkanos' long reign (134–104) also allowed disputes to develop within Judaean society. The foundation of the state had been based on a particular interpretation of the Jewish religion, which the original rebellion had aimed to protect from contamination by Greek influences. Hyrkanos was the representative of that interpretation, above all as high priest. This was a post that had now been hereditary in his family for three generations, as it had been, for even longer, in that of the Oniads.

This religious foundation naturally produced disputes between men who interpreted the writings on which the religion was based in different ways. The debate over interpretation thus shifted away from hellenization, but became more intense, for there was now the added element that if the ruling family could be persuaded to a particular point of view, then power and its privileges would flow to the adherents of that group. Jonathan's dispute with the 'Teacher of Righteousness' had begun when he rejected the Teacher's persuasions.

At least three distinct groups can be discerned at this time. Pharisees and Sadducees were the most vociferous; Essenes were less obvious.[1] There was also the rival temple in Egypt, established by one of the Oniads; the Tobiad temple at Iraq el-Amir had been another. The Samaritans can perhaps be seen as another group. The sources of the differences between them were their varying interpretations of biblical writings, but from the point of view of this study it is the political dimension that is important. In Hyrkanos' reign this difference reached the royal family.

The Maccabees, originally centred on rebellion in favour of the restoration of the old religion and the removal of hellenized contamination – a process of 'restoring' past practice – were generally sympathetic in their first decades towards the Pharisees, whose *metier* was a strict interpretation of the law. This was similarly the stance of Hyrkanos, though his allegiance to Pharisee notions was helpfully modified by his reputation as having the gift of prophecy, which could be used to subdue disputes and override the less devout Sadducees – for prophecy implies direct connection with one's god. By such means, by his success as a military commander, and by the foreign threat implied by the peaceful and united Seleukid kingdom, Hyrkanos kept the lid on the internal disputation until the last years of his reign, though Josephus alluded to one dispute that produced a brief rebellion, though he does not date it.[2] But then a dispute arose in which Hyrkanos felt that he and his family had been insulted by a Pharisee. So he turned for support to the Sadducees.

The precise point of the dispute was, in fact, not the insult but the interpretation of the law relating to the erring Pharisee's punishment. (The Pharisees, being the accused, recommended a lighter sentence than Hyrkanos wished).[3] Of course, this was not the cause but the culmination of disputes over a much longer period during which Hyrkanos had gradually become alienated from the Pharisees and more sympathetic to the Sadducees – the rebellion was part of it. These were more secular in their outlook, a condition that Hyrkanos as ruler found more congenial. The Essenes, who were more to the religious side even than the Pharisees, and were fewer in number and less assertive, were never in contention for the ear of the rulers.

It is also worth noting that the Pharisees in this dispute were attempting to establish their own political authority over the high priest. For if they became the established interpreters of the laws, they would have removed that function from the high priest, and since that function was the essence of the state, the state would therefore be run by the Pharisees. No doubt Hyrkanos fully appreciated this threat, hence his abandonment of the Pharisees in favour of the Sadducees. The problem then changed, for the Pharisees, posing as the righteous group, turned to cultivate popular support as against the richer, aristocratic Sadducees.

Perhaps to sort out this potentially dangerous situation Hyrkanos divided his powers in his testament, though the reason may also have been familial. Of his five sons, Aristoboulos and Antigonos had already been entrusted with command of the army during the war of Samaria; Absalom was so wholly uninterested in political power that he was able to live on quietly for years. Alexander was apparently disliked by his father and was sent to Galilee to grow up in a sort of exile. The fifth son is never named, but was certainly politically ambitious.

Each of these men had two names, one Jewish, one Greek – Aristoboulos was also Judah, Alexander was Iannai – a sign of the continuing attraction of Greek culture. Indeed, the Sadducees were generally somewhat sympathetic to the defeated hellenizers. They were the priestly aristocracy, members of families who had survived the troubles, no doubt deftly shifting their political stance to accommodate the current victors. But they were also essential to the state: they often had a Greek education and were able to communicate with the Greek-speaking states all around, from the Parthians to Rome. It is men such as these who were employed from the start in foreign embassies. Almost all those so recorded, from the time of Judah onwards, had Greek names.

Hyrkanos apparently understood that the concentration of power in his hands was unhealthy, and seems to have tried to subdivide it, separating the high priesthood from the government of the state, which would also sideline any Pharisee domination. Presumably, he also understood his sons well enough to see their limits and impetuosity. He therefore assigned to his widow a general supervision over their children and the government: 'mistress of the realm' is the translation of Josephus' term.[4] At times modern historians extend this implying that she had 'secular authority', even rulership. It was also an attempt to perpetuate Hyrkanos' own authority over the family after his death, and to provide a referee for the inevitable disputes between the sons.

Whatever purposes Hyrkanos had in mind, it did not work. Aristoboulos, the eldest son, was made high priest. This was automatic, given that he was the eldest, but it also gave him the real 'secular authority', which has been ascribed to his mother. Hyrkanos' rulership derived from that high priestly office, and so did that of Aristoboulos. Hyrkanos' personal authority had also developed over time and through his achievements, and Aristoboulos inherited all that in full, and was not prepared to accept the intended limitations. He carried through an internal *coup*, removing his mother and her three younger sons to prison, but keeping the second son, Antigonos, as his colleague.[5]

Or so we are told. Where the 'prison' was is never stated, and Josephus says that the brothers were held 'in chains'. In fact, this may merely be a hostile version of Aristoboulos' action in removing them from power, and then keeping them in the palace under guard. If he was seriously threatened by them he could have had them killed, but by imprisoning them he kept his brothers alive. (The whole story, in fact, has so many similarities with the *coup* of Ptolemy against Simon and John Hyrkanos one wonders if it has been manipulated to fit it. Note also that the number of a Hyrkanos' sons, five, is an echo of one version of the number of Mattathias' sons.[6])

The two elder brothers had worked together already in the War of Samaria, and Aristoboulos implemented his own division of authority, sending Antigonos into Galilee on campaign while Aristoboulos himself remained in Jerusalem. This made good sense, for the *coup* he had conducted after succeeding to the high priesthood implies that the situation in Judaea was still somewhat unsettled. Aristoboulos then carried through a second *coup* by proclaiming himself king.[7] This was only a formalization of the position he already held,[8] but it looks very much as though Aristoboulos was carrying out a programme he had worked out before his accession.

Antigonos' success in war in Galilee was perceived as a threat by Aristoboulos, so he had him killed. The deed is blamed on his wife and a group of interfering courtiers,[9] a scenario reminiscent of greater royal courts than that at Jerusalem. Meanwhile, their mother died in her prison, a fact that was elaborated by his enemies claiming that he starved her to death.[10] (She must have been elderly; her husband had been in his sixties when he died.[11]) Aristoboulos became ill, which was god's retribution for his misdeeds, said his enemies. He died after reigning for about a year.[12]

The wars that had been conducted by the brothers are referred to only incidentally in Josephus, the only source for these events, for he was much more interested in the gory conflict within the Hasmonaean family. Antigonos campaigned in Galilee where he received military decorations;[13] Aristoboulos campaigned against the Ituraeans, and brought some of them into the new Judaean kingdom, by means of the usual forced conversion.[14] These are two separate notices, but they are usually conflated and used to indicate Judaean conquests in the north. That is, however, not what they say, and considerable doubt must surround both.

Let us take the Ituraean conquests said to be by Aristoboulos first.[15] This was a people who first emerge into the records about this time. They lived in the mountains of southern Lebanon, and began to colonize the lands around, including to the south of their homeland. The war made upon them by Aristoboulos is referred to by Josephus only in his obituary of the king; he quotes Strabo quoting Timagenes, a historian living within perhaps half a century of the events, so it is reasonable to accept his account as based on the facts as Timagenes knew them. But Josephus expands this notice, and claims that Aristoboulos 'acquired a good part of their territory', which is not actually supported by the quotation from Timagenes.[16]

The curious thing about this notice is that it is at third-hand (Josephus from Strabo from Timagenes). If the campaign was as great a success as Josephus suggests it is surprising that it is not expounded in more detail in his account of Aristoboulos' reign. The conclusion must be either that the whole thing was of only minor importance, or that Josephus was downplaying Aristoboulos' achievements, though he had wallowed in the unpleasant details of his reign. It is also possible that Aristoboulos had no direct part in the campaign; the clash with Ituraeans could have occurred as a by-product of Antigonos' campaign, with Aristoboulos being credited with it because he was king, in the same way that Roman emperors accepted salutations as *imperator* after a victory by a subordinate general.

Indeed, it is difficult to see how Aristoboulos himself could have conducted any campaign at all. He ruled for only a year, during which his hold on the throne was clearly uncertain. He organized two *coups* in order to establish his authority, and he then had to ensure careful control of Jerusalem and Judaea, whence he faced opposition. It was clearly necessary for him to be on the spot in Jerusalem to prevent threats from developing: he was at odds with all his family, the obvious source of any trouble. It does not seem likely that he was able to get away from the city for long enough to conduct a campaign as far away as the northern parts of Galilee, which is where the Ituraeans lived.

Antigonos' exploit in Galilee is just as obscure. All we have is a comment that Antigonos had acquired 'some very fine armour and military decorations in Galilee'.[17] The reference to 'military decorations' must imply some sort of victorious campaign with Antigonos in charge, but nothing is said of what he accomplished, and Galilee is a large area. There was a considerable Jewish population in the region, which grew and colonized until that whole land was Jewish, but this had not occurred yet, and the population was still mixed; it evidently included some Ituraeans and others. Two possible explanations are that Antigonos was establishing his family's authority in Galilee by conquest of at least part of it, or that he was driving back the enemies of the local Jews, opening up lands for more Jewish settlement. This in turn would require the local Jews' recognition of Hasmonaean authority. These suggestions are not necessarily irreconcilable, of course, but they must remain conjectural.

The campaign in the north, whatever it amounted to, did presumably result in the extension of Hasmonaean authority into parts of Galilee. Aristoboulos and Antigonos, after the capture of Samaria in 107, were able to ravage all the land north of Samaria, from Skythopolis to Mount Carmel; Galilee is the next land to the north. Access to Galilee from Judaea was clearly open. A couple of years after Antigonos at least two towns in the south-west of Galilee, Asochis and Sepphoris, were predominantly Jewish.[18]

Further, the War of Samaria had shown that part of the aspirations of the Hasmonaean state was to establish its rule over all Jews, and one of the methods Hyrkanos used for extending his authority was to claim the right to 'protect' Jews outside the boundaries of Judaea. Jews in Galilee who were under threat of attack, or who claimed to be under threat, had therefore a claim on Hasmonaean protection. Aristoboulos, as king, could therefore despatch his brother to provide that protection, and could then claim credit for doing so, by war on the Ituraeans.

(This was also, of course, the point about the stories of the curious campaigns of Judas Maccabaeus in the lands across the Jordan, and of the foray by Simon into the neighbourhood of Ptolemais-Ake.[19] The stories may well have originated at this period – I Maccabees seems to date from shortly after the end of Hyrkanos' reign[20] – as a supposed justification for Hyrkanos' and Aristoboulos' policy. The curious round-robin letter said to have been elicited from the Roman Senate early in Hyrkanos' reign, whereby a long series of Mediterranean states were enjoined to avoid persecuting Jews,[21] may be seen also as a reflection on this Hasmonaean imperialism; this point of view might suggest that the letter was in fact an invention.)

We must see this campaign in the north by either Antigonos or Aristoboulos, or both, as the definite extension of Hasmonaean hegemony into Galilee. No doubt there were areas where their authority was disputed or rejected, as by the Ituraeans, but Hasmonaean protection was shown to be effective, despite the problems in Jerusalem. This could well be an inducement to non-Jews to convert. This would explain the last part of the notice taken from Timagenes, that the Ituraeans apparently joined the Judaean state voluntarily, which is contradicted by the wording of Josephus' obituary of Aristoboulos, where the conversion is said to have been forced.[22] But a willing conversion, perhaps by a part of the Ituraean population after force had been used on others, would explain the fact that not long afterwards the population of Galilee was mainly Jewish.[23]

The death of Aristoboulos in 103 was followed at once by the release of his brothers from their prison. Aristoboulos' widow, Salome Alexandra (who had been credited, if that is the word, with organizing the plot to murder Antigonos) released them, and then put Alexander Iannai, the next eldest son of Hyrkanos, forward as the new king, and apparently married him.[24] (This was a recognized method of the transmission of royal power in both the Seleukid and Ptolemaic kingdoms, and so it would seem that the Hasmonaean family had adopted yet another contemporary Hellenistic royal practice; Hyrkanos' enemy Ptolemaios had based his claim on the same relationship a generation earlier, as the son-in-law of Simon; marriage of a widow to the next brother, however, was also a Jewish custom.) There were now three of the brothers left. Alexander Iannai's claim to power was successful because he was the choice of Salome; another brother, name unknown, disputed his succession, and was killed.[25] He had clearly felt that he was entitled to make such a claim. The fifth brother, Absalom, showed no royal ambitions, though he remained close to the family.

The upheavals in Jerusalem no doubt caught the interested attention of Judaea's neighbours, the cities along the Mediterranean coast from Ptolemais-Ake to Gaza, and east of the Jordan valley, from Philadelphia-Amman to Damascus, and further away the Seleukid kings in north Syria and the Ptolemaic rulers in Egypt. The intensity of these powers' interest depended on their closeness to Judaea. The Greek cities, having seen the fate of Marisa and above all of Samaria, were no doubt apprehensive of Judaean intentions. The kings were more interested in recovering control of Palestine, for Seleukids and Ptolemies could both lay claim to revive control of the area. The eventual victory of Hyrkanos in the War of Samaria had been at the expense of Seleukid armies. Their intervention had been a clear sign that the kings were interested in recovering control.

The new king, Alexander Iannai, had succeeded without any effort on his part. He was unknown – he had grown up, we are told, in Galilee[26] – and untried. It was therefore all the more necessary for him to achieve something notable in order to impress himself on his subjects as more than a man who had become king at the behest of his brother's widow. He was a member of a military dynasty: brothers, father, grandfather, had all been notable warriors. Clearly he needed to prove his military ability as well. A war was indicated.

He chose to do this by attacking the strongest city in Palestine, Ptolemais-Ake, and in doing so he set light to a fire which nearly burnt him up. Ptolemais was in no danger from an army that had taken a year to capture Samaria, but the attack was clearly awkward for the citizens. Alexander defeated the city's militia without difficulty but then he became stuck in a siege. The threat to this city alerted others who also felt menaced. The city of Gaza and Zoilos, a tyrant who ruled the towns of Strato's Tower and Dor, south of Ptolemais, joined Ptolemais in opposing Alexander, and the city government of Ptolemais appealed to Ptolemy Lathyros, who was now ruler of Cyprus.[27]

All of these allies had their own aims in this conflict. Gaza may not actually have been directly involved in the fighting, but when the Ptolemaians asked for Lathyros' help, Gaza was named as a likely participant. Zoilos was interested in gaining power in Ptolemais: he was thus a rival to Alexander in building up a little empire, but he was of little direct assistance.[28] Ptolemy Lathyros had been driven out of Egypt by his mother, Kleopatra III, in part because he had assisted Antiochos Kyzikenos in the Samaria War. She had replaced him with his younger brother as co-regent, Ptolemy IX Alexander.[29] When Ptolemais asked him to help, the citizens no doubt recalled that his earlier visit to Palestine had been to assist another city under Judaean attack; perhaps they thought he was sympathetic to their cause. In fact, his main aim was to recover power in Egypt, and Ptolemais' invitation opened the way for him to do so. The information that Strato's Tower, Dor, and Gaza were also involved would give him a clear route through Palestine as far as the boundary of Egypt. He might also be able to recruit reinforcements from those cities.[30]

Before he could arrive, the citizens of Ptolemais changed their minds, persuaded by a leading politician called Demainetos, and they refused Lathyros entry; perhaps he had made his real intentions all too clear. Nevertheless, he landed nearby, on the other side of Haifa Bay, at Sykaminos (Shikmona), halfway between Ptolemais and Zoilos' town of Dor, at the foot of Mount Carmel. The army he brought is described as 30,000 strong. This was probably the usual exaggeration, but the army was too much for Alexander Iannai; the Judaean forces swiftly retired from the siege.[31] Alexander attempted diplomacy, suggesting to Lathyros that if he deposed Zoilos, he would buy Strato's Tower and Dor from him for 400 talents. But he was also communicating with Kleopatra III. Lathyros found this out and turned hostile. He had already seized Zoilos, and presumably his towns as well, and from this base he attacked Ptolemais. He was able to leave a force to continue that siege and then take the rest of the army to attack Judaea.[32]

Lathyros marched up the valley of the Na'aman to Asochis, a town that was captured quickly because, Josephus says, it was attacked on the Sabbath (and so it is assumed to have been largely inhabited by Jews). Ptolemy then turned south and attacked the town of Sepphoris.[33] Both towns were mainly or wholly Jewish, so here we have evidence of the Jewish occupation of southern Galilee. It seems that he did not take Sepphoris, but marched off to the east in search of Alexander's forces.

Alexander, with a fully recruited army, including levies from Judaea and 8,000 mercenaries, had a total force of '50,000' or '80,000'.[34] He was positioned east of the Jordan, at a place called by Josephus Asophon or Asaphon, thought to be Tell es-Saidiyeh, south of the city of Pella. What he was doing there is not at all clear, though perhaps he was simply retreating from Ptolemy's more formidable army and had crossed the Jordan as a defensive move. But he permitted Ptolemy's force to cross the river without interference, and in the battle that followed the Judaean army was routed, though Josephus patriotically suggests a tougher fight. Ptolemy's force followed up the fleeing enemy and completed its destruction.[35] Meanwhile, his besiegers took Ptolemais.[36] Josephus includes some horror stories about the treatment of Jews by the victorious army, citing Strabo and Nicolas of Damascus as his sources, but they are fairly unlikely.[37]

At the same time the reaction in Judaea was that Ptolemy had intended to attack Jerusalem. This was equated in some scrolls from the Dead Sea with the invasion by Sennacherib of Assyria in 701. This does not mean that Ptolemy actually did mean to take the city, only that the Jews of Judaea could see no other purpose in the campaign into Judaea than to do so. His retreat and campaign against Egypt was, of course, regarded as a divine intervention to save the city, whereas it was actually due to the enmity of his mother Kleopatra III.[38]

Alexander's rescue by Kleopatra III, was due to her conviction that her estranged son had become too powerful. She came to Palestine to stop him, and in turn besieged Ptolemais, now garrisoned by Lathyros' forces (though Josephus says the 'inhabitants' refused her entry). Another part of her army was sent in pursuit of Lathyros. He in turn marched on Egypt, but got no further than Pelusion, from which he recoiled to Gaza. (He eventually escaped back to Cyprus.[39])

Kleopatra's army triumphed: Ptolemais fell to her forces[40] and Lathyros was confined to Gaza. She met Alexander, who arrived with gifts as a suppliant, and was accepted as an ally. The meeting took place at Skythopolis, and, since Kleopatra was the hostess, this makes it clear beyond any doubt that the city was not part of Alexander's kingdom, but was at this time an independent ally of Kleopatra's. Kleopatra is said to have been advised that it would be possible to conquer Judaea in its weakened condition, but was deterred by a veiled threat from her Jewish general Ananaias that by doing so she would make all Jews her enemies.[41] This threat seems unlikely (and not very potent) – Kleopatra was not the sort of ruler to welcome even veiled threats – but it may be a story put about to denigrate Alexander, who had clearly failed to protect the homeland. Ananaias is said to have been a descendent of the Onias who had founded the temple at Leontopolis in Egypt; another Jewish general, Chelkias, had been killed in the fighting against Lathyros.[42]

Kleopatra and Ptolemy Alexander returned to Egypt – where he murdered her later in 101. The alliance that Alexander Iannai had made with Kleopatra was presumably in her name and that of her son, who was the legal ruler, so even after she was dead he was constrained by that alliance. Rather more effective deterrents – for Alexander Iannai was not very good at keeping his promises – were the Ptolemaic garrisons that continued to hold the conquests Kleopatra had made, Ptolemais most notably, but also perhaps Skythopolis. Ptolemy Lathyros may also have left a force to hold Gaza. None of these forces was worth challenging after the disasters of the preceding year.

It cannot be said that Alexander had been in any way successful in his inaugural war. He had deliberately attacked, apparently without provocation, the main city of Palestine, and had been beaten by the mere arrival of a relieving force. His army had been destroyed in the battle at Asophon. His kingdom had suffered a ravaging by his enemy. He had been reduced, as Josephus puts it, to cunning, and to intriguing with both sides in the Ptolemaic conflict, for which he was punished by that defeat. He had in the end petitioned Kleopatra for a protective alliance, and was presumed to be so weak that a swift Ptolemaic conquest of Judaea was actively considered. He had not made a very promising start.

Chapter 11

Gadora and Gaza

The removal of Kleopatra III and her two sons from Palestine did not at once end their power in the area. The cities they had captured continued to be garrisoned by their forces for some time, and the cities themselves were therefore under their protection. So, while Ptolemy Alexander ruled in Egypt (after his murder of his mother) and Ptolemy Lathyros ruled in Cyprus, their power was still present in Palestine.

Alexander Iannai's power was bruised and his army largely destroyed as a consequence of his impetuous attack on Ptolemais-Ake, which was the ultimate cause of the intrusions once more of Ptolemaic power into Palestine. His throne was clearly under threat at home, and he must have been thankful that his last remaining brother had no political ambitions. Since the last year or so of the life of his father, the royal family had turned in on itself murderously, while the military pretensions of the kingdom had been shown to be based on very weak foundations. In order to recover, Alexander Iannai needed a victory.

It is this political requirement that is the uniting element in the two wars that are brought together in this chapter. They were, on the face of it, two distinct wars, one across the Jordan, one in south-west Palestine. But both were conflicts resulting from the previous war against the Ptolemaic kings. It was clearly necessary for Alexander Iannai personally to demonstrate that he could win a war, and this is the main justification for the trans-Jordanian attack. On a larger field, the Judaean kingdom needed better protection, which meant the acquisition of bulwarks at a greater distance from the homeland than before. Judaea was severely damaged by the defeat of its army, invaded, ravaged, and many of its men killed. It was well known that Kleopatra III had seriously contemplated a war of conquest, which at least would have inflicted more damage and killed more of its people, and might even have extinguished Judaean independence. These requirements – defence for the kingdom and a secure foundation for Alexander's rule – link the wars of Gadara and Gaza.

In this Alexander Iannai was operating in the tradition of his family. Idumaea, trans-Jordan, the southern lowlands, had all been invaded with the aim of driving enemies further off, and of acquiring defensible posts and borders. The conquest of Samaria had been aimed partly at removing a threatening ideological competitor, and partly at eliminating a Greek city which had been used in the past as a base for invading Judaea – similarly with Beth Zur and Marisa. Of course, the wider the

102   The Wars of the Maccabees

bounds of a kingdom the more there are apparent threats to those bounds. This was the logic of imperialism – but Alexander was operating within the parameters of his political inheritance as well.

Alexander first turned east. Beyond the Jordan was a series of cities that may well have seemed enticing. There was a group of small cities east and south of the Sea of Galilee, stretching as far south as Philadelphia-Amman. This last was now under the rule of Theodoros, the son of Zenon Kotylas. Part of the trans-Jordanian land, the Peraia, was already under Alexander's rule, as was Medaba, captured by John Hyrkanos.

Alexander's lands and those of Theodoros shared a common boundary in some places, always a likely source of dispute, though there were also some independent lands between them. Theodoros controlled a good deal of the country stretching north from Philadelphia, including the fort of Amathos, which was situated just north of the Jabbok River, close to where it joined the Jordan. This suggests that the Jabbok was the northern border of Philadelphia's territory, and that the city of Gerasa to the north was independent; close to the Ghor, the next city north was Pella, with several fairly small cities beyond it. The battle between Alexander and Lathyros had taken place at Asophon, which was in the Jordan valley between Amathos and Pella. Since Alexander had crossed the river to get to Asophon, this implies that this part of the Peraia was Judaean land. So the Philadelphia-controlled Jabbok valley separated two parts of the Judaean Peraia.

The cities of the north were probably under the distant control of the Seleukid kings. Damascus continued to be held by the Seleukids (it had been threatened briefly by Ptolemy Alexander during the late war) in some strength, and the cities east of the Sea of Galilee were well within the reach of the Seleukid forces there. They may also have controlled Pella, and possibly Gerasa as well, though these two were more distant from the certain Seleukid post at Damascus, and they may have slipped into independence. Across the river Skythopolis also may or may not have been under Seleukid control. It had been a base for the Seleukid King Antiochos Kyzikenos during the Samarian war, but Kleopatra III had been able to use it later; her power had largely evaporated from the inland areas; quite likely Skythopolis had been left without any royal master, abandoned, in effect, into independence. For the small cities east of the Sea of Galilee, such as Gadara, Dion, Hippos, and others, the political alternatives were Seleukid control or Judaean enmity. Independence would only make them a target for Judaean attack. If Alexander could assume that the great city of Ptolemais was vulnerable – as his attacks assumed – then these smaller cities certainly were. Philadelphia, however, was definitely independent, and Theodoros and Alexander Iannai regarded each other as enemies.

Alexander conducted a military campaign in this region, but the only reports of what happened are by Josephus, who provided a brief account in *Jewish War*,[1] and a slightly longer one in *Antiquities*;[2] even this longer account is no more than a paragraph. He states that Alexander attacked a place called Gadara, which he besieged for ten months; then he captured Amathos; then he was defeated by Theodoros.

The problem is that there were two Gadaras. One is a Greek city near the Sea of Galilee, sited just south of the valley of the Yarmuk, a place now called Umm Qais. (Much of the city has been excavated, but it is mainly Roman period remains that have been revealed.[3]) The other place, actually Gadora, is further south at the site of the modern Jordanian town of Es-Salt, little of which has been excavated. It is normally assumed that the northern Gadara was Alexander's victim. I would suggest, however, that it was the southern, Gadora.

Gadara is a comparatively long way from Judaea, though if Alexander Iannai ruled in Galilee (not a certainty), he could have had access across the bridge south of the Sea, the Jisr Bint Yaqub. But the city of Skythopolis and its territory lay in the way, and it is clear that Skythopolis was either independent or under Seleukid suzerainty at this point; it was also well fortified and so was neither a sensible place to attack nor one to leave in one's rear. Further, a number Greek cities were near to Gadara – Pella, Abila, Hippos, and others – and Damascus, the Seleukid stronghold, was relatively close. All these would feel threatened if one of them was deliberately targeted by Judaean forces for no apparent reason – for no explanation exists for Alexander's aggression; so far as we know, there was no previous relationship between Judaea and Gadara.

Gadara, in a geographical and political sense, was thus a very odd place for Alexander to attack. By taking his army there, and isolating himself amid a group of hostile Greek cities, in order to attack one of them, he would be rousing the automatic enmity of all the others. He also left his home base in Judaea at a time when his throne was unsteady, and put his forces (much reduced in size by the defeat by Lathyros) at great risk. Further, the siege was clearly difficult, since it lasted for ten months. He had been a failure as a military commander so far. A ten-month siege was not a great improvement on what he had done before, particularly since he was attacking a city of no importance to Judaea.

Gadora/Es-Salt, by contrast, was only twenty kilometres east of the Jordan, and only thirty from Jerusalem. It was close to Peraian territory that Alexander already ruled, with Medaba only thirty or so kilometres to the south. It was, it would seem, politically isolated, since it had to fight its own battle, though the people perhaps hoped for help from Theodoros at Philadelphia. Like Medaba the town lies on a spur of the plateau, not far from Iraq el-Amir, which may, like Medaba, already have been part of Alexander's kingdom. It was therefore an ideal target: isolated, small, close to Judaean territory, and weak.

In addition other places became involved in fighting, and these are significant in locating Alexander's target. Amathos is to the north of Gadora, and belonged, as it proved, to Theodoros. There was no connection between the northern Gadara and Amathos. To go from a long and difficult siege of Gadara to immediately challenge Theodoros, the major power east of the Jordan, makes no sense. But the conquest of Gadora was a clear threat to Theodoros, even if he did not intervene in the actual siege. Seizing Amathos, close to a crossing of the Jordan that linked the territory of Philadelphia with Skythopolis, makes much better sense. Gadora, the southern town, is clearly the more likely target.

The ten-month siege of Gadora is reminiscent of the long sieges at Medaba and Samaria, and no doubt for the same reason, that the Judaean army was competent only at blockade, not an active siege. It had lost many men in the defeat by Lathyros, so attacking a small place was probably the maximum effort it could make. Alexander perhaps hoped that the town would fall quickly, but he could not afford to lose the lives of more soldiers, so full-scale assaults were best avoided. Further, by holding the army with him at the siege he was both preventing any interference with its loyalty by his enemies in Jerusalem, and he had troops available should an insurrection or a *coup* be attempted in the city. Perhaps he did not mind that the siege took so long.

When the town finally gave in he tried another sudden attack. Amathos was to the north, thirty-five kilometres away and across the Jabbok, described by Josephus as the 'greatest stronghold' of the region beyond the Jordan. It was also a place where Theodoros of Philadelphia kept his treasury, or part of it. The Judaean army, having taken Gadora, now took Amathos, this time swiftly and without having to undertake a siege. But it was then immediately defeated by Theodoros' own army. This fight obviously took place as the Judaean army was heading back towards Judaea, perhaps before it had crossed the Jordan. All the loot collected from Amathos, together with Alexander's own baggage, was captured, and '10,000' of the Judaean army were killed. (The figure clearly means no more than 'a lot' of soldiers.)

Theodoros had clearly anticipated some sort of action by Alexander once he was free of the siege. Gadora is only fifteen kilometres from Philadelphia, and the progress of the siege had no doubt been watched carefully. Until Alexander's attack Gadora had been part of the neutral buffer between their lands, and Alexander's attack was destroying that buffer. (Heshbon may well have been another part of this buffer area, keeping the two states apart.) He surely knew, as soon as the Judean army marched away, which direction it was going, and since it had to march north to get to Amathos, whereas to go home it would have gone west or south-west, Theodoros could guess its destination almost at once. Even if Amathos was not the target, the Judaean army was clearly marching to cross the Jabbok, and that was a threat to Theodoros' territory. He may have instructed Amathos not to resist. Josephus says nothing of any fighting there. The 'greatest stronghold' east of the Jordan fell instantly to an army that had just spent ten months besieging a small town. It looks very much as though Alexander fell into a trap.

The conquered town, however – Gadora – remained in Alexander's possession, even if he had lost Amathos, his baggage, his loot, and part of his army. Yet except for the defeat at the end, for Alexander and Judaea the campaign had made sense, and the result had been a significant increase in the kingdom, a victory to brandish in the faces of his internal enemies and critics. And while he was busy in the east, the situation along the Mediterranean coast had changed in his favour.

The Ptolemaic garrison of Ptolemais was withdrawn some time in 101 or 100, and the garrison of Ptolemy Lathyros in Gaza was withdrawn about the same time – or so we may assume. This was the period during which Alexander was besieging Gadora. By the time he recrossed the Jordan, Ptolemaic power in Palestine had evaporated. It seems that the authority of one or other of the Seleukid kings had returned, for Ptolemais was under Seleukid control some years later, and neither Alexander nor his successors attacked it. But, south of Ptolemais, the Palestinian coast was now a power vacuum.

Alexander had tried to buy Dor and Strato's Tower from Ptolemy Lathyros in 103, but Lathyros discovered Alexander's double dealing before the transaction was completed. It is usually assumed that the towns were delivered, but Josephus' words can only be interpreted that way by adding that assumption; he doesn't actually say they were taken by Alexander.[4] The two towns probably fell into Kleopatra's hands as her army marched north along the coast. One of her aims in this campaign had been to block off Lathyros' ambitions to return to Egypt as king, and seizing any coastal ports he held – such as Ptolemais – was a priority. Lathyros had ships, which had carried his army from Cyprus, and from a Palestinian port he could easily reach Egypt; Ptolemy Alexander made that voyage each way during the campaign. There was, however, no point in keeping control of these small towns once Ptolemais was abandoned; they would then be abandoned in 101 or 100 along with Ptolemais. Their fate after that is not known, but they presumably reverted to independence. By the time of Alexander's death in 76 they had come into his hands, but we do not know when. Probably they could no longer resist an attack and might well have surrendered at the first pressure. Apollonia, the next town to the south, also fairly small, has no known history. Again, it was part of Alexander's kingdom by the time he died, but when and how he acquired it is not known. We are not entitled to assume he gained them at any particular time. (I will argue later that they did not fall to him until after the civil war.)

South of Joppa there was a string of towns and cities on or near the coast. Iamnia and Ashdod had suffered from Judaean attacks in the past, and were part of Alexander's kingdom by the time he died, though again, when they were taken is not known. Ashkelon, however, gained its full autonomy, according to its coins, in 104/103,[5] the very time that the several Ptolemaic rulers were campaigning in the area; this autonomy was, it seems, respected by Alexander.

When he returned from the trans-Jordan campaign, Alexander reserved his full attention to the next three places south of Ashkelon – Anthedon, Gaza, and Raphia. The importance of these lay in that they guarded the route to Egypt. Gaza was the real key, the other two being more or less fortified outposts of the main city. In the hands of the ruler of Egypt Gaza permitted an Egyptian invasion of Palestine; in the hands of the ruler of Palestine it was a powerful block against such an invasion, and at the same time it was the final staging post for an army on the way to Egypt. Its Egyptian equivalent was Pelusion. Held in determined Egyptian hands, an invasion force from Syria would be stuck in the Sinai desert. These places had performed this function repeatedly since the time of Alexander the Great (who had himself to besiege Gaza before he reached Egypt). Most recently, in 103, Kleopatra III had brought her army through Gaza to campaign in Palestine, and when Ptolemy Lathyros was at Gaza, an Egyptian army holding Pelusion prevented him from going any further. It had been an object lesson in strategy. It seems clear that Alexander Iannai took the point.

When he returned from his campaign in the east Alexander could see the possibilities for aggression against these several cities. The Seleukid king may have held Ptolemais and Damascus, but neither Grypos nor Kyzikenos was yet free of the other, and neither was likely to attack Judaea. In Egypt Ptolemy Alexander had shown ambition to revive the old Ptolemaic empire in Palestine, but he no longer had a foothold in the area, and was prevented from doing much by the standing threat from his brother Lathyros in Cyprus – again they neutralized. Therefore the way seemed clear to mop up any nearby cities that were outside the control of any of these kings. But Alexander could do little against such formidable cities as Gaza with an army that had taken ten months to capture a small town.

The dating of the events is not easy to sort out, but can give a clue as to Alexander's next move. The campaign in the east seems to have taken place in 101 or 100; it certainly lasted at least a year. The war he embarked on against Gaza took another year, and ended in 97 or 96, since his capture of the city is co-ordinated by Josephus with the death of Antiochos Grypos in 97/96.[6] There is therefore a space of perhaps two years unaccounted for. When he eventually tackled Gaza, Alexander had a much larger and better army. It would seem therefore that he spent that period recruiting a new force, which was, as will be seen, capable of defeating an enemy about 12,000 strong in open battle. It was thus probably getting on for double that in numbers, with a contingent of mercenaries perhaps a quarter of the total – though all these figures and proposals are probably wrong in detail, and mine are only guesses. What is quite clear is that Alexander's army was very much more capable in 96 than it had been five years before.

With his new army, Alexander initiated a campaign that proved to be well planned; this again suggests that serious thought had taken place. (One wonders if Alexander had recruited a skilled military staff: he had not displayed much military ability so far, and later he was often unsuccessful.) Gaza was a tough proposition, a major fortified city, as strong perhaps as Ptolemais-Ake, and far too formidable to be tackled directly. Alexander first isolated the city by capturing Raphia to cut the road to Egypt, and taking Anthedon, to separate Gaza from any possible assistance coming from the north or by sea. Probably neither exploit was difficult. Anthedon is said to have been taken by storm, which suggests fairly flimsy defences.[7]

Gaza itself was much more difficult. Alexander and his army settled down to another siege, which lasted a year. Josephus' account mentions only two incidents. At one point the Gazaeans made an night attack on the Judaean camp. This took place early in the siege, perhaps more or less as the Judaean army arrived, for the rumour spread among Alexander's force that they were fighting Ptolemy – Lathyros, that is. Only when dawn arrived was it realized that the enemy was only the Gazaeans.[8] The Gazaean army is stated to have been 2,000 mercenaries and 10,000 citizens, perhaps a fair approximation, and this is the basis of my calculation of the size of Alexander's army. The story implies that the Judaean army was larger, since, once it had got its nerve back, it won the battle relatively easily, killing 1,000 or 2,000 men.

The siege was, after the initial defeat of the Gazan army, a blockade. The city was governed by a council of 500, but the elected general, Apollodotos, dominated the city government. They hoped to be able to bring in help from the Nabataean King Aretas, for Gaza was a major outlet for Nabataean trade, which was no doubt badly disrupted by the fighting. This policy was not, however, successful, for Aretas would not intervene (another indirect indication of the new strength of the Judaean forces). This had, perhaps, been Apollodotos' policy and its failure undermined him. He was killed by his brother and rival, Lysimachos, who then let the Judaean forces into the city.[9]

This is the second event described by Josephus. Clearly most of the siege held no interest for him. In a blockade little happened other than the slow starvation of the citizens. Lysimachos and Alexander agreed between themselves to surrender the city, but when the Judaean army moved in Alexander gave his permission to sack the city. Maybe he could not stop his men from running wild, for they had finally won a victory after a series of defeats and long sieges. The inhabitants fought back, no doubt infuriated that the city had been surrendered by their commander without their agreement. The councilmen were caught in their meeting and massacred. The city was then destroyed.[10]

The treatment of conquered places had varied under Alexander. So far as can be seen, neither Gadora nor Amathos had been damaged, and Raphia and Anthedon had seemingly also been left intact, nor was conversion to Jewish practices forced on their inhabitants. Gaza was thus presumably destroyed because Alexander did not expect to be able to hold the city against the clear continuing enmity of its citizens. Maybe the absence of forced conversion was an attempt to persuade future Judaean victims to give in the more easily. But maybe it was also the result of the internal politics of the Judaean state, for forced conversion had been imposed while the Pharisees were the dominant group under Simon and John Hyrkanos I. Now that the Sadducees, who were less intolerant and more open to outside influence, were dominant this was a policy perhaps less to their taste. The actual internal Judaean conflict between them and others was, however, now leading into rebellion and civil war.

Chapter 12

War in the East

The victory at Gaza resulted from the improvement in the quality of the Judaean army, which had been accomplished since the lamentable performance at Gadora and Amathos, and before that at Asophon. The mercenary element, recruited from Pisidians and Kilikians (but not Syrians – that is, Greeks from Syrian cities), had probably been increased, and was decisive at Gaza. It now proved useful also for putting down a serious riot in Jerusalem. Supposedly 6,000 'insurgents' were killed in the riot's suppression.[1] Probably almost at once, Alexander took his army to fight across the Jordan again.

This move was no doubt partly to get the soldiers out of the city, where the mercenaries will have become even more unpopular than usual as the result of their riot suppression. As foreigners, as well-paid men, and as soldiers, they were disliked; their involvement in the killing of Jews in Jerusalem surely fired this dislike up to hatred. But the eastern expedition was also aimed at tackling serious problems that had developed there. Alexander campaigned to extend his boundaries and to straighten out those boundaries; he also attempted to see off a challenger. In the process the political geography of the trans-Jordan lands was decisively changed.

The situation across the Jordan had changed in the few years since Alexander captured Gadora. While he had been besieging Gaza, the Nabataean kingdom had emerged as a possible enemy of Judaea – and of all other states within reach, including the Seleukids and the Ptolemies.[2] The annexation of Gaza, the main Nabataean access to the sea, was one major element in their new hostility. At the same time the improved Judaean army now overshadowed Philadelphia, an equal only a few years before. The Nabataean king who had been unsuccessfully invoked by the Gazans, Aretas II, died about the time of Gaza's conquest – perhaps his age or illness had been the main factor in his failure to assist Gaza. His successor, Obodas I, however, was still more aggressive.

Alexander's new eastern campaign targeted groups of Arabs in Moab and Galaaditis.[3] (The date of this is not clear, but 94 or 93 is about right.) These regions were large, even diffuse. Medaba, inherited from his father, could be regarded as being in Moab. Galaaditis, however, was the name for a large area east and north-east of the Sea of Galilee and east of the Jordan, a name that seems to shift around. By specifying 'Arabs' as Alexander's enemies, Josephus implies that Alexander was attacking infiltrating Arab clans, who could well be regarded by Obodas as his subjects, in the same way that Jews in Galilee were regarded by the Hasmonaean kings as under their protection. Certainly this campaign led to a war with Obodas later.

Exactly where these preliminary campaigns were conducted is never stated. It would be fair to assume that in Moab the Arabs were moving into the lands under Alexander's rule, around Medaba and the area nearby. In the north the question is different. Galaaditis was not part of Alexander's territory. It was a land that was effectively divided up between several Greek cities from Philadelphia to the Sea of Galilee and beyond. Alexander held the land west of there, along the edge of the plateau and in the Ghor (the Jordan trench). His lands were thus not threatened by the infiltration of Arab groups into Galaaditis as they were in Moab. (Note also this was the region in which Judah Maccabee was supposed to have campaigned to 'rescue' persecuted Jews. This was the sort of activity that gave a state or people a claim to that territory – spurious though it was to others.)

The infiltrating Arabs, however, did threaten the Greek cities. If Alexander was campaigning there against the Arabs, he was doing so partly in support of those cities. From later accounts it seems that the area involved was where the small cities east of the Sea of Galilee (Hippos, Gadara, Dion, and others) were situated. This implies that the general policy of the Judaean state towards the Greek cities had changed since the War of Samaria. This had been already suggested by the lenient treatment of Gadora and Raphia and Anthedon, all of which were left essentially undisturbed socially after submitting to Alexander. (Gaza's obdurate resistance had earned it destruction, but this was normal in Hellenistic warfare.) The policy of forced conversion, which had been implemented under Hyrkanos and even under Aristoboulos, was clearly abandoned by Alexander.

The Jerusalem riot is relevant here. It had taken place while Alexander, in his office as high priest, was sacrificing at the altar in the temple on the festival of Tabernacles. The crowd barracked him, and then pelted him with citrons (a primitive sort of lemon), as a gesture of contempt. One of the insults they voiced was the very one that had led to the break between Hyrkanos and the Pharisees a few years earlier: that Hyrkanos' mother had been a 'captive' in the time of Antiochos IV. (The insult implies that she had been enslaved, and that therefore Hyrkanos' parentage was tainted, and he was thus not fit to the high priest. Sometimes the accusation was applied to Alexander's mother, but this is probably only the result of later confusion between the kings; but if the term applied to Hyrkanos, it did to Alexander as well.)

The insult shows that the crowd was mainly composed of Pharisee supporters. More popular than the Sadducees, and more rigorous in their interpretation of the law, they had been advisers of Simon and Hyrkanos when they carried out the ethnic cleansing at Joppa and Adora and Marisa and Samaria. Out of power, the Pharisees turned to the people for support. In power, the Sadducees were more concerned in foreign policy with expanding the kingdom than with converting gentiles. Alexander, and perhaps the Sadducees as well, could surely see that the expansion of the kingdom would be much easier if those communities he attacked were not in fear of

1. Petra - the High Place.
Petra was overlooked by a 'high place' where sacrifices took place. A long climb led to the mountaintop, with views in all directions. The high place itself is marked by these pillars, and the land has been carved and flattened.

2. Panias - the cave.
Panias' cave was an old holy place, which was further developed as a shrine to Pan in the Hellenistic period. The cave is now flanked by the remains of temples to, among others, Augustus. The place is a major source of the Jordan; its beauty and its water and its cave proclaim its holiness.

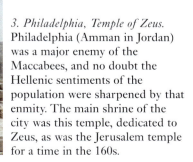

3. Philadelphia, Temple of Zeus.
Philadelphia (Amman in Jordan) was a major enemy of the Maccabees, and no doubt the Hellenic sentiments of the population were sharpened by that enmity. The main shrine of the city was this temple, dedicated to Zeus, as was the Jerusalem temple for a time in the 160s.

4. Caesarea – the Cardo. Caesarea, Herod's new city, on the site of Strato's Tower, was more a Roman than a Hellenistic city, and decidedly not Jewish. This is a view along the main street, the cardo, lined with opulent houses (under the modern roofing). At the far end was a Roman theatre, on the right a stadium was placed directly on the coast.

5. Caesarea – the Palace. Caesarea became the headquarters of the Roman governor, whose palace was on a small promontory, so that he could receive the sea breezes from three sides.

5.

6. Caesarea – the Bathing Pool. Even the bathing pool was excavated for his use. The sheer indulgence of having an artificial pool separated from the sea by a mere wall is a sign of the lavish resources deployed. The palace may in fact originally have been Herod's.

6.

7. Lachish and the way to Beth Zur.
Lachish was an Iron Age city devastated by the Assyrians. In effect it was succeeded by Marisa: this therefore is Idumaea. The valley floor is cultivable, the hills can be grazed. But it is not a valley easily defensible; Lysias' army marched along a valley such as this.

8. Marisa – the elephant.
An elephant in the Sidonian tomb wall at Tell Maresha. It is ironic that Lysias' army, passing this way, would have included elephants, though perhaps not so friendly-looking creatures as these. One of them, of course, killed Eleazar at Beth Zakaria, not many miles away.

9. Hazor.
A view north from the tell at Hazor. The remains here are Iron Age, and there seems to have been no inhabitation in the Maccabean period. The army of Demetrios II came from the north and was met somewhere near here by that of Jonathan. A draw resulted, though the Judaean army then retreated.

10. Hamath Tiberias.
The Ottoman fort marks the seaward side of Tiberias. The old road from the north ran along the shore, with the steep hills of Galilee to the right. The hot spring is about at the wooded shore on the left of the picture. Anywhere along this road would be a good blocking point to stop an invading army, as Jonathan did in 148.

11. Skythopolis.
Skythopolis (Beit Shean, Beisan) was one of the many cities revived by the Greek colonization after Alexander the Great. The ancient tell was abandoned and the new city laid out at its foot. This was fortified, and the tell formed an inner citadel. The city as visible now is essentially Roman, but the Hellenistic base is also quite clear. For an amateur army such as that of Hyrkanos I, capturing this place was impossible.

12. Sepphoris – the Nehovot Valley.
Sepphoris is on a low hill overlooking the valley of the Nehovot stream. Ptolemy IX marched his army up this valley in 103 to attack Alexander Iannai and his army in the Jordan Valley.

13. Iraq el-Amir.
The solid construction of the temple-cum-fort at Iraq-el-Amir suggests both the wealth of the Tobiads and their vulnerability.

14. The Yarmuk valley.
This is the valley viewed from the Umm Qais (Gadara). The view is to the north towards the Golan plateau. The formidable obstacle which this valley makes to an army is quite clear.

15.

Korazim.
Korazim was a small town north of the Sea of Galilee, built of the black basalt of the region. This is a territory well outside the original Maccabean base, but it was obviously colonized by the Jews, as the remains of this synagogue (of the first century AD) show (15, 16). The domestic buildings contained olive presses (17), an indication of the potential agricultural wealth of the region.

16.

17.

18. Gadora Mosaic.
A mosaic representing Gadora, from the church of St Stephen in Umm er Rasas (Kastrom Mefaa). The mosaic is dated to AD 785, and includes fifteen towns like this. The building is probably a church, and olive trees are shown on either side – the source of much of the wealth of the region.

19. Gamla.
Gamla was situated along the spine of a hill bounded on either side by steep valleys, and attached to the Golan heights (behind the camera) only tenuously. Presumably the inhabitants farmed the heights. The choice of such a hill for their town in a clear indication of their vulnerability.

massacre and/or judaization. After several conquests without forced conversion the message will have got home. For the Sadducees, more sympathetic to Greek culture than the Pharisees, the prospect of Greek cities, not subject to forced conversion, enclosed within the kingdom, was not as unnerving as it was to others. For the Pharisees it must have seemed that the Maccabean revolution was being undone.[4]

The campaign in Galaaditis, therefore, was directed against the Arabs, but it was also another element in Alexander's imperialism. His policy towards the Greek states was thus now to provide protection against enemies common to both, not conquest and forced conversion; however, if resistance to his will was encountered, the penalty would be destruction – the lesson, that is, of Gaza. The result was that some of the smaller cities in Galaaditis took shelter under Judaean power, which is to say that Alexander replaced the Seleukid kings as their suzerain. The cities involved in Galaaditis will be those which were listed in two sources, apparently independent of each other, which provide lists of the cities ruled by Alexander at the end of his life. One list is in Josephus, who in fact gives two complementary lists, and the other is in Syncellus, whose single list overlaps with that of Josephus. The cities in question are Gadara, Abila and Hippos. These three are all sited in the small region on either side of the Yarmuk valley east of the Sea of Galilee.[5]

Skythopolis finally succumbed about this time also. It had remained independent, or had acknowledged Seleukid suzerainty, since surviving Judaean pressure during the War of Samaria. With Galilee rapidly becoming judaized on a more or less voluntary basis, and Alexander including some of the cities across the Jordan in his kingdom, perhaps as allies, Skythopolis was becoming surrounded. The final straw might be when Alexander, after the campaigns against the Arabs in Moab and Galaaditis, seized Amathos from Theodoros of Philadelphia.[6]

Since Alexander's conquest of Gadora, Theodoros had taken control of Gerasa, the next city north of Philadelphia. This made a solid block of Greek territory along Alexander's eastern border, with Amathos as Theodoros' easternmost extension, reaching the east bank of the Jordan. This was also therefore his link with the lands of Skythopolis across the river. Skythopolis' territory stretched along the Jordan from about the mouth of the Yarmuk to about fifteen kilometres north of Amathos. On the east bank, north of Amathos, the land was divided between the cities of Gerasa and Pella, though it is likely that Alexander had taken over some of it earlier – as he now took more. When Alexander took the fort at Amathos, without fighting, and without apparent protest from Theodoros, it left Skythopolis more or less isolated, surrounded by Judaean territory, except for its neighbour across the river, Pella. An accommodation with Judaea by Skythopolis would therefore make sense. The city was not captured, nor even attacked, but accepted Judaean overlordship.

The fate of the city of Philoteria is relevant here. This was a Ptolemaic city, fairly small, sited on the southern shore of the Sea of Galilee, planted on an island between the sea and two outlets of the River Jordan. Syncellus indicates that it had been destroyed by Alexander[7] though Josephus does not mention it (another of his many omissions). One must presume that Philoteria had resisted Alexander's pressure, and that the Gaza policy was applied. If the conquest and destruction occurred about this time, during Alexander's campaigns in 94 and 93, then here is another reason for Skythopolis to seek an accommodation with the conqueror.

Theodoros did not resist the loss of Amathos. This was presumably because Alexander was militarily now too powerful. Perhaps also he appreciated what Alexander was doing in regard to Arab infiltration, for if the clans were moving in on Alexander's lands in Moab to the south, and into the lands of the Greek cities in Galaaditis in the north, no doubt the lands of Philadelphia and Gerasa were also being similarly threatened and harassed. He held much of the Jabbok valley still, for Alexander later attacked Ragaba (modern Rajib) only a few kilometres upstream, which was explicitly stated to have been in Gerasa's territory[8] – and so in Theodoros'. The taking of Amathos may thus have been only the occupation of a abandoned fort.

Theodoros' realm was now the main buffer between the kingdoms of Judaea and the Nabataeans, an ironic development in view of the earlier fate of Gadora, then a buffer between Judaea and Philadelphia. The two kingdoms had nearly clashed already over Gaza, and now Alexander's war on the Arabs provoked Obodas. The link is nowhere actually stated, but the timing of the Nabataean War, directly after the end of Alexander's campaigns against the Arabs, and the region where the fighting took place, east of the Sea of Galilee, where Alexander had earlier campaigned, makes the connection clear. Further, Josephus even refers to Obodas as 'King of the Arabs'.[9]

The fighting took place in Gaulanitis, the modern Golan upland. This land is partly the high plateau of the eastern Jordanian country, but also a series of steep valleys leading down to the Yarmuk valley in the south and to the Sea of Galilee on the west. (Philoteria had been a block on access to the Yarmuk south of the Sea; it had probably been destroyed by this time.) Alexander and his army were ambushed by the Nabataeans in one of these steep valleys, presumably while climbing up towards the plateau from the shores of the Sea. Obodas used a herd of camels to complete the ambush. The horses in Alexander's army recoiled at the sight and smell of the camels. The location is said to be near the village of Garada, which cannot be located. (The name has been emended to 'Gadara', but apart from the fact that there is no need to do so, Gadara was not in Gaulanitis.)

The disaster was total. Alexander himself escaped, as kings and commanders tend to do in these situations, but the army was destroyed, the men being prevented from escaping the ambush by the camels.[10] How much of the army of Judaea was involved in the disaster is not clear. Certainly it would seem that the force Alexander had with him was lost, but that is not to say it was all his army. Obodas was clearly not leading a large force, otherwise Alexander would hardly have been ambushed. Nor is there any information about how much of the mercenary force was involved. So Alexander escaped back to Judaea, where he took command of the rest of the army, and of those who escaped with him. His power would recover, for ambushes of parts of an army are rarely decisive, and often only make the victim the more determined. The defeat did not allow Obodas to conquer any of Alexander's territories, and he held onto his recent conquests in Moab and Galaaditis, at least for the present. But the loss of even a small force was just what Alexander's internal enemies had been waiting for.

Chapter 13

The First Civil War[1]

The return of Alexander Iannai to Jerusalem without his army, or rather without that part of it he had taken on campaign, persuaded his internal enemies to attempt to depose him.[2] It is assumed that the Pharisees or their sympathizers were the leaders of the rebellion, in part because Josephus, a sympathizer of the Pharisees – he had a Pharisean education[3] – implies it even if he does not name them, but also because Alexander himself is regarded at the end of his life as seeing that reconciliation with the Pharisees was necessary.[4] One of the scrolls from Qumran, a commentary on Nahum, also identified Alexander's enemies as the Pharisees, who were called the 'Seekers after Small Things', or perhaps 'Flattery-Seekers'. The scribe detested both sides, calling Alexander the 'Lion of Wrath', but the Pharisees' conduct earned them especial condemnation.[5] Josephus claims that 'the nation' rose against the king, which is evidently the usual political exaggeration of a partisan group, for Alexander was able to fight back fairly effectively.

Alexander had, of course, been putting a good deal of pressure on his people by his changes of policy. To committed Maccabee supporters the shift towards the Sadducees must have looked like a betrayal of the anti-hellenizing campaigns of the past seventy and more years. And now the army, which had also become hellenized, with a large contingent of Greek-speaking mercenaries, who had been used in Jerusalem to put down a Pharisee-inspired riot, had succumbed to an ambush – exactly the tactic that had given the Maccabees their first victories. Alexander had become dependent on his soldiers, and his soldiers had failed. An uprising is hardly surprising.

The course of the fighting in this civil war is barely known, other than a few incidents and the fact that it is said to have lasted for six years – this in itself indicates that both sides had plenty of support. The casualties are put at 50,000 Jews, but these are only those ascribed to the king's actions;[6] those inflicted by his enemies are not reported – and one is instinctively wary of any figures, especially such conveniently round numbers. No doubt most of the victims were the apolitical poor. Josephus implies that the fighting was between Alexander's mercenary army and the 'nation' in arms, who were the rebels; once again, clearly a distortion.

The questions concerning the rebellion begin with the leaders, include its causes, and ramify from there. None of the rebels, leaders or rank-and-file, is ever named. No mention is made of the attitude of the Greek cities that Alexander is said at the end of his life to have ruled. Only one of Alexander's foreign enemies took advantage of his predicament, though another also intervened, and neither of these happened until the later stages of the rebellion. One wonders just how serious the rebellion was. Josephus summarizes the events of the six years in no more than a paragraph, though he does take longer to explain the end. The whole affair certainly blocked Alexander's earlier attempts to conquer more territory. He surely longed to return to the fight with Obodas.

In keeping with the fact that this was a civil war it is probable that the fighting was very reluctantly engaged in on both sides, at least at first; it is also probably punctuated with attempts to end the conflict by negotiation, though neither side was prepared to give any ground. In the one example of a meeting between the two sides that Josephus mentions, Alexander is made to ask what the rebels wanted; the answer was they wanted him to die.[7] There was thus not much room for negotiation.

What else the rebels wanted is a problem for us as well as the king. Nowhere does Josephus specify the rebels' demands, but one may guess that, since they wanted Alexander to die, their most likely demand was for the abolition of the monarchy, and the implementation of a Pharisee-dominated government, presumably under a new high priest, a reversion, that is, to the theocracy that had ruled until 104, but without the Hasmonaeans.

The number of casualties reported seems large – '50,000' caused by one side alone – but for a war that lasted six years the casualty rate is not all that heavy. Combined with the lack of apparent interest by foreign powers, and the absence of concern over the Greek cities, this implies that the conflict was fairly low-key, and probably intermittent. At the start, for example, unless they had part of the army on their side, the rebels cannot have been very well armed, and the king, even if he lost men in the fight in Gaulanitis, still commanded an army. If after several years the king still had to ask what the rebel demands were this suggests that those demands changed during the conflict, or were perhaps incoherent from the beginning, or varied with the several groups of the king's enemies. Again this implied that removing the Hasmonaean dynasty was the main aim of a variety of rebel groups, perhaps the only measure they could all agree on. The fighting may well have been a long series of riots, ambushes, and brigandage rather than a full-scale civil war with armies marching about and fighting. Josephus mentions no battles until the end; probably none occurred.

After the conference that Josephus records the rebels felt that they were losing, so they turned to the Seleukid king ruling at Damascus for help. (It was this action, calling in a gentile army, which probably earned the condemnation of the scribe who wrote the Nahum commentary.) The king they invited was Demetrios III, called Eukairos (the 'seasonable', or 'well-timed') but Akairos (the 'ill-timed'), to his enemies. He was the son of Antiochos Grypos and had been ruling in Damascus for nearly ten years, ever since his father had died. He may also have controlled Ptolemais, though that is not certain. He was able to field an army of a reasonable size, but Alexander was also able to produce a force more or less equal to it in numbers, if not in quality.

Demetrios brought his army as far as Shechem, where he was joined by the rebel army.[8] Josephus gives two different totals for both armies. For the Seleukid army, in *Antiquities* he says it had 3,000 cavalry and 40,000 infantry; in *Jewish War* he says 3,000 cavalry and 14,000 infantry. The smaller figure is to be preferred, with the infantry figure in *Antiquities* a transcription mistake; if both are accurate, the difference is the number of troops the rebels brought to the meeting. Alexander met Demetrios with a force that is similarly given in two versions. In *Antiquities* Josephus gives the figures of 6,200 mercenaries and 20,000 Jews; in *Jewish War* he says Alexander had 9,000 mercenaries (1,000 horse and 8,000 foot) and 10,000 Jews.[9] One is inclined (always!) to favour the smaller figures again, given the tendency of all ancient historians to exaggerate, but the more interesting element is the make up of the army Alexander was able to field.

The proportion of mercenaries in Alexander's army was probably greater by this time than it had ever been, for he would need to recruit as many as he could find. In a civil war he would find it difficult to rely on a Jewish army, and after six years of fighting he could have built up a substantial force. At the same time it is clear from the number of Jews in his army, whichever number one might accept, that he had, even after five years of conflict, plenty of support in the kingdom. The classification of his mercenaries as Greeks, whereas he was earlier said to favour recruiting Pisidians and Kilikians, may indicate that he had recruited from the Greek cities in his kingdom – or it may simply be a shorthand for non-Jewish soldiers, and a reference to the language of command among mercenaries of all origins. No doubt the cities would support him against the more rigorous Jews of the rebellion, for their own well-being.

Demetrios, coming from Damascus to Shechem, had probably marched by the same route taken decades before by the generals of Demetrios II towards their battles with Jonathan, south along the western side of the Sea of Galilee. The alternative would be to march along the eastern side, past Golan, by which route he faced a bottleneck crossing of the Jordan south of the Sea, easy to block. Alexander, presumably based in Jerusalem and the main kingdom, camped close enough for the men on each side to communicate. Josephus has a vivid little description of the two forces each attempting to persuade the other's men to defect. The two kings issued rival proclamations encouraging deserters; Demetrios' Greeks attempting to persuade Alexander's mercenaries to change sides; the Jews on each side arguing with each other.[10] Neither side apparently had any success. In the battle that followed, Demetrios was victorious. It was, it seems, mainly a fight between Alexander's mercenaries and Demetrios' forces, and both of these groups suffered heavy casualties.[11] Demetrios won, no doubt because he had the greater number of trained men.

The result of the fight, as Josephus says, was unexpected on all sides.[12] Alexander survived, but had to take refuge in 'the mountains', otherwise unspecified, where a loyal group of 6,000 Jews joined him, probably gathering over a period of time.[13] It would be a good propaganda point if the 'mountains' were the Gophna Hills where his ancestors had maintained their resistance to Seleukid attack. Demetrios, even though he had won the battle, found that his rebel allies quickly faded away. He had lost a fair proportion of his army in the battle, and without local allies he was unable to make further progress. His own aims are not known. He was assumed by the Jews to be aiming to take Jerusalem, but they always assumed that of any gentile army. The promises made to him by the rebels that induced him to make the expedition are also unknown. The only thing, surely, which would bring him in would be the promise of the cession of land, perhaps some of the Greek cities Alexander had conquered, which would be no loss for the rebels. Demetrios' inability to persuade the Greeks in Alexander's army to change sides, however, and the fact that large numbers of them died in the battle at the hands of his army, may have convinced him that the Greek cities were loyal to Alexander and that to acquire any of them might well be more trouble than they were worth. It would seem that a generation of Seleukid absence had removed any residual loyalty to the Seleukids felt by the cities.

Demetrios, left with a damaged army in hostile territory and deserted by his allies, withdrew. His interventions had administered a salutary lesson to the two Jewish forces, royal and rebel. Alexander had been beaten, and much of his army was destroyed. This might make him more conciliatory. The Greeks he commanded now disappear. If they had been recruited from his Greek cities, no doubt the survivors made their ways home. The men collected in the mountains with him were clearly his diehard Jewish supporters and so they would form a formidable group. According to Josephus, he also found that many people – 'the whole nation', he claims – were returning to his support.[14] On the rebel side the use of a Seleukid army to fight the Jewish king and high priest in order to reimpose the full rigour of Jewish law had surely disgusted many of the rebels' sympathizers, for the outcome could well have been a new Seleukid occupation of Judaea. Hence their desertion of Demetrios in his moment of victory, and the fading of support for the rebels. Alexander's defeat was the moment of truth, and opinion swung his way.

It is at this point that another foreign enemy, Obodas of the Nabataeans, sought to take advantage of the rebellion. No doubt it was the reduction of Alexander to a fugitive in the mountains, together with the destruction of his main army, that was decisive in the timing of his intervention. It would also suggest that the rebels did not replace the king with much in the way of a government. Alexander was compelled to surrender territory to Obodas, who threatened to send his forces to assist the rebels. The lands involved are defined as the conquests Alexander had made in Moab and Galaaditis, which were the very areas he and Obodas had been fighting over before the rebellion.[15] Since it was the land Alexander himself had acquired that was given up it presumably did not include Medaba, a conquest made before Alexander's reign. The fate of the small Greek cities in the north is not clear. Alexander had not actually conquered any of them, so presumably they were not part of the agreement. Alexander's losses were thus not notably serious.

This can only have further reduced support for the rebels, when the full implications and events were understood. The rebels' rationale had been to return to the pure Jewish law. Alexander's reason for surrendering the territory had been so that Obodas would not help the rebels. Presumably the rebels had asked for Obodas' help, as they had asked for Demetrios' – or if not at least they would be assisted by his threatened invasion. This was therefore the second time a foreign intervention had affected this internal quarrel in the Jewish state.

The fighting within Judaea went on, but now it was between the most committed men on each side. As the victim of a notorious conspiracy to restore Seleukid power, and to give territory away to the Arab enemy, Alexander now could look to better support. He was able to win the various, presumably small, fights until he had the rebel leaders besieged in a place called Bethoma or Bemeselis, which may be the modern Misilye north of Samaria[16] – the precise location does not matter, but the result does.

The fort was captured, along with the rebel leaders. They were brought to Jerusalem and there executed, supposedly having seen their wives and children killed first. Alexander supervised the execution personally, feasting amid his concubines. These details have been doubted as being propaganda by his enemies; they could of course be true, thereby providing them with the propaganda. Indeed, the very fact that a Hasmonaean high priest could execute Jews has been doubted, an interpretation firmly refuted by the Nahum commentary. The problem then became the method of execution, hanging or crucifixion, as if it mattered.[17] Alexander's savage revenge is understandable. Josephus disapproved, but he had the honesty to admit that Alexander's policy was successful, for he had no further internal problems for the rest of his reign.[18] But Alexander's terrorizing of the population into submission may have produced peace – though 'peace' may not be good characterisation – but it is surely ironic that this was exactly the method used by the earlier Maccabees against the hellenizers: now the hellenizers' successors turned the method on the Maccabees' political successors.

The revenge taken by Alexander frightened off a large number of rebels who may or may not have been still in arms. Alexander executed 800 men (plus their families), and another 8,000 men at once fled into exile.[19] The symmetry of the numbers is suspicious, but the general fact is not. The revenge Alexander took on those who opposed him, and who, in his view, had subjected his kingdom to six years of civil war, might well have been a warning not only to the rebels but to those, such as Demetrios and Antiochos his heir at Damascus, and Obodas, who sought to intervene.

Chapter 14

The Second Eastern War

When Judaea emerged from its civil war in about 87 BC, the land and its people were exhausted. Casualties and exiles, taxation and destruction, had weakened them. Further, it was obviously necessary for Alexander Iannai to maintain a considerable army, both to prevent further uprisings and to deter external enemies, and for both of these reasons that army had to be at least partly recruited from foreign mercenaries. This would in turn require heavy taxation. The 8,000 men who fled abroad at the end of the civil war would obviously wish to return, and they had already shown a willingness both to fight and to call in foreign help. Their place of exile is not known, though Damascus has been suggested.[1]

Damascus would, in fact, be a particularly suitable place for the exiles to take refuge. There were alternatives, of course – Egypt, the Nabataean Kingdom, the Phoenician and North Syrian cities, but it is likely that, at least at first, most of them would want to remain close to their homeland with the intention of seeking any opportunity of returning – and indeed some or all of them did go back after Alexander died. Damascus was a good place to wait. It had been Demetrios III's headquarters, and was now ruled by his brother Antiochos XII, who was surrounded by enemies, but who might well have inherited his brother's policy towards Judaea, and so could be hospitable to the exiles. Antiochos also faced enmity from the Ituraeans who had expanded their territory and were now organized as a kingdom. The Nabataean king – from about 85 this was Aretas III, Obodas' son and heir – was also ambitious for expansion and had his eye on Damascus. Antiochos' other brother, Philip I, had united much of North Syria once more, and had then tried to take Damascus as well. He had failed, but Antiochos XII must have felt thoroughly beleaguered.[2]

Alexander Iannai remained quiet in foreign affairs for several years after the end of the civil war, not surprisingly. In the midst of the competing states in Palestine and Syria, however, it was not possible to stay out of trouble. From 84 there developed a complex crisis in the region into which Judaea was inevitably drawn – not that Alexander showed any reluctance to be involved. Antiochos XII in Damascus had just survived the attack by his brother, and this success may have given him a measure of confidence. He was already at war with the Nabataeans, and now he attempted a new strategy. Rather than mounting a direct attack from Damascus southwards against the northernmost extension of the Nabataean lands, which was somewhere east of Gaulanitis, Antiochos brought his army across to the coastal plain and aimed to attack Nabataea by means of a march through Idumaea and south of the Dead Sea. His ultimate target was probably Petra.[3] (This was not a new approach; Antigonos I and Demetrios Poliorketes had tried it two centuries before, and it was a version of that used by Lysias to attack Judaea.)

This route took Antiochos and his army through some of Judaea's territory, along the road through the coastal plain and then through Idumaea. Josephus explains that Alexander prepared to deny him passage. He had developed a barrier at the narrowest point of the coastal plain, a little north of Joppa. It was a ditch stretching from Chabarsaba (Kefr Saba, the later Antipatris) to the sea, fortified with a wall and watchtowers and artillery.[4] The situation was well chosen, behind the Nahr el-Auja (the ancient Yarkon), which itself was an awkward obstacle, flanked by the sea on the west and the hills on the east – Kefr Saba is on the slopes of the plateau. A wall always seems a useful means of defence, but it is rarely successful. This wall was about twenty-seven kilometres long, and Alexander did not have the manpower to guard the whole thing. It was, in fact, not necessarily designed for warfare.

An attempt has been made to locate this system. As Josephus describes it – a ditch, towers, and so on – it would seem that archaeologically it should be discoverable. The remains found, however, are unconvincing. A 'fort' seems more likely to be a domestic dwelling or a farm. The 'watch towers' have been identified with some hexagonal stone buildings – two were found – and these are perhaps more likely to be military, but without more of them, in better positions, and without having located the ditch, they cannot be accepted as part of Alexander's defence line.

The dating of all these remains is vague – the late second or early first century BC is the closest date given. This may indicate another solution to the problem. It may be that the defence line was in fact something that was not built by Alexander for this particular purpose but something that had existed for some time. One suggestion might be that it was a fortified route linking Joppa with the hills, in which case it could be something instituted when Joppa was originally acquired by Simon Maccabee. If the watch towers, which are of stone construction, were really a part of the line organized by Alexander, they were not built quickly, or by him. So maybe only the ditch was new – but even that would have taken some time to construct, perhaps several months. There is clearly a need for a systematic archaeological investigation here, if anything can be found amid all the modern development and construction in the area.[5]

The choice of this position for a military obstacle is curious. On the one hand, it made sense to block the narrowest part of the coastal plain; on the other, it seems to have left unprotected a substantial part of the kingdom. Alexander ruled everything from northern Galilee south to the Sinai desert. The line he chose for the ditch effectively abandoned half of his lands to invasion – if Antiochos and his army were coming from Damascus, and if Alexander actually controlled all the coast, and if the system was actually intended for a military purpose. But it is known that Alexander did not control Ptolemais, and the date of the acquisition of the coastal towns of Dor and Strato's Tower and Apollonia is not known. It may be that Antiochos XII was in control of Ptolemais himself, as well as Damascus, and so he could commence his march from that city. So, assuming that Antiochos XII ruled both cities, it may well be that Dor and Strato's Tower and Apollonia were also at this time under his control, or perhaps independent. The fortified line that Alexander constructed would therefore be more or less at his boundary in the plain. It may be assumed that the passes leading up into Judaea proper were guarded, perhaps by a mobile army, as Simon had defended the plateau against Tryphon.

The ditch, the wall and the towers were, in fact, militarily useless. Alexander did not have sufficient armed forces to man the whole system. A huge force would be needed to occupy all the system, to guard the passes, and to place a substantial force in reserve with which to face Antiochos' army. Antiochos got through in the most obvious way. He concentrated his whole force at one point and ignored all the rest of the system. He set fire to the wooden towers, levelled part of the ditch and then simply marched through.[6]

The ease of the penetration of the line was such that its uselessness must have been obvious from the start. This might suggest that it was not a military construction in the first place, but more an imaginary construction in Josephus' mind. If the Greek cities from Ptolemais to Apollonia were not under Alexander's control, then the line was his boundary, and that may be what it actually was – a series of watch towers marking the border between Judaea and the independent cities to the north. (To call it the 'Yarkon Line', as some historians do, is a deliberate reminiscence of such modern constructions as the Maginot Line and the Siegfried Line, with the implication of strong military obstacles – though these were penetrated or bypassed just as easily. A better name should be found for it; even better still, it should actually be found.)

Alexander, in effect, let Antiochos through. Perhaps he thought the mere sight of the wall and ditch would deter Antiochos, whose army was only 8,000 infantry and 800 horse, figures that look more or less right when compared with those that had been commanded by Demetrios at Shechem. Perhaps, on the other hand, Alexander expected to be able to attack Antiochos' army from the rear while it was stuck attempting to get through the wall. Whatever his plan, if he had one, Alexander was foiled. He cannot have been unsympathetic towards Antiochos' purpose – the Nabataeans were a threat to Judaea as much as to Damascus.

Antiochos' campaign failed completely. He reached Nabataean territory in the south and was allowed to march on, into the desert. The Nabataeans retreated before him. His army was then surrounded by a mobile Nabataean force, larger than his own. His army was worn down, and when Antiochos himself was killed, the army collapsed. The remnants took refuge in a place called Kana, south of the Dead Sea, and were blockaded there until most had died of starvation.[7]

Damascus' army was thus destroyed and its king killed. The city was decisively weakened. The city council now had to make a choice of enemies to whom to submit. Philip was far off. The Ituraeans were close by but were detested by the Damascenes. The Damascene council, therefore, as much by process of elimination as with any particular pleasure, submitted to the Nabataeans. This makes some sense in that

Aretas was probably the strongest of the competitors and had, after all, won the war with Antiochos.[8]

The increase in Nabataean power that the annexation of Damascus represented made Aretas III an even greater threat to the Judaean state. Apart from the earlier enmity, Aretas was perhaps annoyed that Alexander had permitted Antiochos to march through Judaean territory to attack him. Despite his 'wall', Alexander had not seriously opposed Antiochos' march. Aretas found exiles from Judaea at Damascus, and no doubt listened to them. By taking over the city, Aretas had also taken over the policies towards Judaea that had been generated by Demetrios III in opposition to the current regime in Judaea.

Whatever his reasons, Aretas launched an attack on Judaea in 82, the year after his defeat of Antiochos XII and his annexation of Damascus. The connection between these events is never stated but the sequence is suggestive. The invasion reached as far as Adida, a little north-east of Lod, where Aretas was victorious. Josephus remarks that Aretas had begun at Damascus, but that may not be more than a casual literary link to his earlier sentence.[9] He gives no route for the invasion any more than he does for those of Demetrius III or Antiochos XII, but it would seem that the northern boundary of the Judaean kingdom was porous in the extreme. This was the third invasion in five years, and the third defeat: Aretas at Adida, Antiochos at the 'wall', Demetrios at Shechem.

Aretas and Alexander followed up the former's victory with a peace treaty. The terms are not listed by Josephus, which might suggest, as one would suppose in the circumstances, that they were a humiliation for Alexander. He was not compelled to receive back the exiles, nor does it seem that he was forced to surrender territory. Assuming that both kings accepted the conventions of Hellenistic royal diplomacy, the treaty will have established peace between the two men until the death of one of them. Alexander was thus prevented from attempting to recover his lost lands, but both kings were assured that they would not be attacked by the other for the foreseeable future. They were both therefore free to undertake adventures against third parties.

With peace established between the two kingdoms, the fate of the minor states of the region was effectively sealed. The Nabataean king, now that he had control of Damascus, found that he had problems with the Ituraeans, who felt deprived of Damascus, a prize they had hoped to acquire. They were now ruled by their most capable lord, Ptolemy son of Mennaeus, who had succeeded to power in 85. In such a situation Alexander, safe from Nabataean attack, and without any other neighbours strong enough to threaten him, was able to indulge in more aggression on his own part.

The invasions from the north, while not likely to be repeated while the treaty with Aretas held, made it necessary to push the Judaean boundary north. The 'Yarkon Line' was a failure, so it would be best to secure more territory. It was therefore probably at this time that the small Greek coastal cities – Apollonia, Strato's Tower, Dor – were taken. This pushed Judaea's border closer to Ptolemais, perhaps anchored on the much more defensible Carmel Mount. It also gave the kingdom a better link with Galilee. If Skythoplis had succumbed by now, Judaea's territory was a solid block from Idumaea to northern Galilee, from the edge of the trans-Jordan plateau to the coast from Carmel to Gaza. Once the coast was secured, the group of Greek cities across the Jordan was the only region into which Alexander could now expand.

The Nabataean king was unable to interfere in the area because of his preoccupation elsewhere and because he and Alexander had a binding peace agreement. Having recovered somewhat from the traumas of the civil war, and now free of the threat of attack by Aretas, a paradoxical result of the defeat at Adida, Judaea was now strong enough for Alexander to set about a series of campaigns to extend his kingdom eastwards.

Three campaigns in the east are noted by Josephus, but there was probably at least one more.[10] The places east of the Jordan fell into three groups. East the Dead Sea there was a series of small settlements strung along the old King's Highway, none of which seem to have been subject to any outside authority. To the north the second group comprised the small Greek cities east of the Sea of Galilee, which Alexander tried to protect against Arab raids several years earlier. They were probably independent, and may have been still allied with Alexander. The situation in the third group, the central region, east of the Jordan, was different again. Here there were four Greek cities, two independent, two under the rule of a 'tyrant'. The independent cities were Pella and Dion, both up on the plateau. The others formed the larger state of Philadelphia-plus-Gerasa.

Philadelphia had been the base for Zenon Kotylas, who had passed his power and position on to his son Theodoros. It is not clear in 83–80, when Alexander's wars were fought, whether Theodoros was still alive. Zenon had been in power before 134, and Theodoros by 103, so by 83 they had been in power between them for over half a century. In Alexander's war with Philadelphia, Josephus refers to 'Zenon' as ruling at Gerasa in *Antiquities*, and in *Jewish War* he says Alexander coveted the treasure of Theodoros there. This does not mean that Theodoros was still alive, only that the treasures that Alexander tried to steal when they were held at Amathos were known as those of Theodoros. The Zenon referred to in *Antiquities* can be taken as a mistake for 'Theodoros son of Zenon', but he may actually be the son of Theodoros, named for his grandfather. This would be a man who had inherited power from Theodoros, and so the third generation to rule. I would be inclined to assume this last, given the length of time involved. But whoever then ruled, Theodoros or his putative son, the two cities of Gerasa and Philadelphia was still under one ruler, as they had been twenty years before. (If Theodoros was dead, the peace treaty he had made with Alexander had also expired; Alexander was thus free to attack once more.)

There is a further puzzle in these events. Josephus provides two accounts. In *Antiquities* he says Alexander first took the city of Dion, then went on to attack Gerasa (though his manuscript has 'Essa'). In *Jewish War* he says Alexander first took Pella, then attacked Gerasa. Pella and Dion were two separate and distinct cities. Pella is the modern site of Tabakhat Fihl, on the edge of the plateau overlooking the Jordan. Dion is further east, probably at the village of Eidon, south of Irbid. It is natural to think that Josephus has made a mistake in summarizing his source, and has included one name instead of the other, though which of them is the error is not clear; it may be a mistake made by a copyist.

However, it is not reasonable to claim that only one city is meant. The two were quite distinct and they suffered different fates at Alexander's hands. Pella was destroyed because the citizens would not accept Jewish customs,[11] but Dion was only captured. There were thus two separate operations, with different results. Also implied are different time scales and different strategies by the conqueror.

Pella was fairly close to the Jordan, in much the same sort of geographical situation as Amathos and Medaba, on a spur of the plateau and with a good outlook west over the Jordan valley. Dion, on the other hand, is on the upper part of the plateau between Gerasa to the south, twenty-five kilometres away. Of the smaller cities east of the Sea of Galilee, the nearest was Capitolias (now Beit Ras),[12] ten kilometres from Dion, and Abila (Quweilbeh) in its well-watered valley, was another seven or eight kilometres to the north. The political situation of these northern cities is not known; they are not included in any list as being in Alexander's kingdom. They may well have been his already before 83, or taken in these later campaigns; some may equally have been subject to the Nabataeans. If they were independent, the third possibility, they might well have felt that they should assist other Greek cities when they were attacked by Alexander.

These cities formed a grouping referred to in the Roman period as the Decapolis, though the number seems to have varied over time. This organization did not yet exist, and the cities were subject to various powers – Judaea, Nabataea, or Theodoros/Zenon. The absence of a formal association, however, did not prevent the development of a common sentiment, which was clearly the basis for their later loose association as a Decapolis. In particular, the Judaean state was a serious enemy, politically, socially, and religiously, whereas the Nabataeans, who were less nationalistic, were more friendly and tolerant. Aretas III, the captor of Damascus, was called Phil-Hellene on his coins.[13]

The strategy chosen by Alexander in these campaigns in the east may be similar to that he deployed against Gaza and subsequent conquests. This was, of course, the same type of strategy as those employed by conquerors everywhere – a display of savagery (as in the destruction of Gaza) followed by an offer to other communities of lenient treatment if they would only surrender quickly. Alexander's problem in instituting this method of conquest was that he had inherited the old Maccabean policy of judaization and forcible conversion, even if it was not being imposed by him. Therefore his conquest path was the more difficult.

Pella, between Judaea and Dion, was resistant to the imposition of 'Jewish customs', even though that was no longer part of Alexander's policy. This means that the city was also resistant to conquest by Alexander and to incorporation into the Judaean state. The obviously increased threat of attack by Alexander is therefore the explanation for the fact that the city appears to have made serious preparations for defence. Two forts of the late Hellenistic period have been located on the outskirts of the city. One was apparently unfinished and is dated to the early first century BC; it was thus certainly built to defend the city against a threat at that time, and that threat can only have been from Judaea.[14]

The archaeological investigations have suggested, on the basis of greatly increased quantities of pottery, that the city experienced a sudden spurt of growth and expansion in the late second century, more or less at the time as the forts were being built. It then suffered extensive destruction. This destruction has been ascribed, inevitably and no doubt correctly, to Alexander. The earlier growth of the city, however, is just as interesting. It may well be the result of the arrival of evacuees fleeing from the Judaean conquest of other Greek cities – Samaria and Philotera, for example; even the more tolerant Judean policy of Alexander will have been too much for some people. This would help explain the strong resistance implied by the refusal to accept 'Jewish customs', the perceived need of Alexander to destroy the city physically once he had conquered it, and the unusual presence of major defensive fortifications.

The conquest of such a city, with its forts and a considerable population explicitly hostile to 'Jewish customs', would take time. The lack of siege expertise in the Judaean army means that a full campaigning season was probably needed for the siege and capture, which was then followed by the physical destruction of the city, and the killing or sale of the captives. This campaign must be seen as the first of those which Alexander directed at the Greek cities east of the Jordan, and it implies that the whole series was planned in advance. Pella blocked the direct route towards the cities on the higher plateau, particularly to Gerasa. Its population was apparently now substantial and its military forces could be expected to be active in opposing any Judaean aggression across the river. Its capture would clear the road to Gerasa and remove a potentially difficult enemy. Like Gaza, its destruction was a clear warning to other cities in the area of the consequences of opposing Alexander's enterprise too vigorously.

If this interpretation is correct, then the campaign described by Josephus in *Antiquities* against Dion and then Gerasa followed the conquest of Pella, and probably took place in the next campaigning season, that is, in 82. Alexander first captured Dion, thereby cutting the road leading along the top of the plateau. This was relatively easy to reach once Pella, due west of Dion, was in his hands, and by holding Dion he could now either move north against the minor cities there, or move south against the larger cities of Gerasa and Philadelphia. It was the latter alternative he chose, for the smaller cities could be secured without much difficulty later.

From Dion, therefore, he turned south against Gerasa. Josephus implies that the main reason for attacking the city was that it held 'the treasures of Theodoros', or alternatively 'Zenon's most valuable possessions'. This was perhaps one motive, but, after Pella and Dion, Gerasa and Philadelphia were also the last major Greek cities left unconquered in the region. To acquire the cities themselves was surely the main reason for the attack; the treasures would be a welcome supplement, but it is not reasonable to see treasure hunting as the main purpose for what turned out to be a major military enterprise.

Gerasa was blockaded, supposedly with a 'triple line of walls', or, more simply, 'three walls'. This seems extravagant. It was not unknown for a siege to be formed by a wall of circumvallation, and for the besieging army to be itself then protected by a second wall. But a third wall was scarcely needed for a normal siege; therefore this suggests the siege was exceptionally difficult. A second wall would protect the besiegers from attack by a relieving force, but what the third wall was for is unknown, possibly to block an approach route used by the enemy. Given that Gerasa was part of a state of which Philadelphia was the greater part, a relief attempt was certain. All this in turn makes it certain that, as one would expect with a siege by the Judaean army, the whole affair took a long time.

Gerasa's city wall was over four kilometres long, even longer than that round Samaria. A wall of circumvallation would be, given that it was at some distance from the city wall, even longer, and the other walls even longer again. This implies a large Judaean army – unless the wall building was designed also to economize on manpower. (The length of the city wall might also be too long for the city's military manpower.)

There is a further puzzle in this siege. Josephus seems to contradict himself as to the result of the fighting. In *Antiquities* he says that the siege ended with Alexander taking the city 'without a battle'; in *Jewish War* he says it was taken 'in battle'.[15] The difference in the Greek is only one or two letters, and this is a section of *Antiquities* that has suffered from bad copying – there are other mistakes in this paragraph. The wording in *Jewish War* is thus likely to be the more reliable, so long as it is not emended to make it fit with *Antiquities*.

So it is better to accept that the city was encircled by those walls, and then taken in battle, which must mean by assault. However, that was clearly not the end of the matter. Gerasa may have been captured and no doubt the treasure of Theodoros was swiftly appropriated by the conqueror, but the city was not held by Alexander for long. It is not included in any of the three lists of places he is said to have ruled at the end of his life, though Pella was, as was Dion.

These lists[16] are not necessarily accurate or comprehensive, of course. Dion is listed as Alexander's by Syncellus, but not by Josephus, and Syncellus includes several other places not listed by Josephus. Josephus lists a series of places with Aramaic names in his two lists, whereas Syncellus merely says Moabitis and Ammanitis, the regions where those places were. So the omission of a particular place from any list does not mean it was outside Alexander's kingdom; nor does the existence of the lists mean that we have a complete catalogue of the places he ruled – there is no mention of any place in Galilee, for example, which is known to have been, at least partly, within the kingdom. On the other hand, Gerasa had been a hard fight, and was a notable city. If it had still been Alexander's when he died it would have been included in the list. We must conclude that, if he captured the city in 82 or thereabouts, he lost it not long after. This conclusion is confirmed to some extent by the action he was taking when he died. He was attacking a place called Ragaba, which is stated to be in Gerasene territory.[17] This could have been held by Theodoros/Zenon even after the city had been captured, but it is more likely that the successful siege of the city carried with it all the city's territory. It seems that Gerasa, having been conquered, was then lost again.

Then there is the next move made by Alexander after Gerasa was taken. The next place to attack was surely Philadelphia, the capture of which would, in effect, bring all the cities east of the Jordan into his kingdom. Losing Gerasa significantly reduced Theodoros/Zenon's power. Alexander's army may well have suffered casualties in the siege, but the military force of Gerasa was now no longer Philadelphian to deploy. And Philadelphia was the main enemy. If it continued as an independent city, its ruler would make every attempt to recover his lost lands. By not capturing Philadelphia, Alexander would condemn the area to further warfare. Yet he turned away. No attack on Philadelphia is recorded, and at some time in the next four or five years, Philadelphia's ruler recovered Gerasa and its territory.

Alexander had spent a long time besieging Gerasa, and we may again assume that the siege had occupied most of another campaigning season, especially when it is recalled that he had begun the campaign by capturing Dion. His next campaign was in the north where he captured 'Gaulana and Seleukeia'.[18] The former is not a city but the region Gaulanitis, and Seleukeia was a small city in its eastern part. The city-lists also record that Alexander ruled the small city of Abila, north of Dion. This campaign was thus aimed to extend and consolidate his hold on this area. He had had to surrender some territory in this region to Obodas and Aretas in the past, which he was presumably carefully manoeuvring around. We may assume that all the small cities in the region had now been mopped up by either Judaea or Nabataea. The only independent place left was Philadelphia.

This northern campaign was probably not difficult, but one place had to be attacked. This was Gamla, a hill-top city where complaints had been made against the governor Demetrios. Details are absent, but Alexander was apparently responding to these complaints, received presumably from the inhabitants. Demetrios was the governor of 'these districts', which in the context must mean Gaulanitis. His name suggests that he was a Greek, and his appointment might have been a gesture to the Greek inhabitants. Gamla was his headquarters, it seems; no doubt with the assistance of the alienated inhabitants, Alexander captured it. Demetrios was then merely dismissed.[19]

This complaint against Demetrios may well have been the main reason for Alexander's turn to the north. If Demetrios was really causing trouble by misgovernment, this could have had serious repercussions throughout the region, and particularly on Greek cities within his kingdom. There was, surely, a strongly negative reaction in the region to Alexander's destruction of Pella, even among those Greeks who were content with Alexander's rule. But mere dismissal seems a mild punishment for a man whose misconduct may well have diverted the king from the final conquest of Philadelphia. There was clearly more involved than Josephus says.

The capture of Gamla should count as a notable military feat. It is a town spread along the spine of a hill, with steep slopes all round. It was a stronghold of the revolution in AD 67, and it took the Romans a month and heavy casualties to capture it.[20] But the Romans faced a united and hostile population; Alexander had the support of the inhabitants.

There was one other campaign, not mentioned by Josephus, but which must have taken place, judging by the list of places Alexander ruled when he died.[21] Combining the various lists shows that he controlled a series of villages and small towns along the King's Highway south of Medaba. At some point he had gained control of Heshbon, Medaba's neighbour to the north, which had been left isolated between Judaean territory and that of Philadelphia after Medaba's capture, and had fallen into Judaean control, though when is not known. South of Medaba the places Alexander held can be traced as far as the southern end of the Dead Sea where he also held Zoara and a couple of places south-west of the Sea, linking up with his lands in Idumaea. At some point therefore a Judaean army had marched along the King's Highway to establish control; probably there was no opposition, given the small size of the places involved. This late campaigning period, between 83 and 80, is the most likely time for this action, but it does presuppose that the region was not under the control of the Nabataeans or anyone else when Alexander secured it. Much of this area was not later retained.

These campaigns occupied a period of four years, according to Josephus. He implies that Alexander spent the whole of that time away from Jerusalem, so that on his return 'the Jews welcomed him eagerly because of his successes'.[22] It seems unlikely, however, that he was absent permanently. He was never very far from the city, and he could get there, even from his most distant conquests, in a few days at the most. It was always dangerous for a king to be away from his capital for very long, quite apart from the need for him to be administratively active. (It seems reasonable to assume that his wife, the capable Salome Alexandra, was in charge there in his absence.) On the other hand, it is certain that he had to spend much of his time in these years on these campaigns. The sieges of Pella and Gerasa were slow and difficult, and probably several months each. The campaign to the south, however, was probably easy, and may have taken only a month or so.

In these campaigns Alexander extended his kingdom considerably, but perhaps not by as much as he had originally hoped; Philadelphia was unconquered, and Gerasa was soon lost, though these were now the only places still independent between the two greater kingdoms of Judaea and Nabataea.

Alexander returned to his main kingdom, probably in 80, but fell ill, an illness made worse by heavy drinking (though this might be a deliberate attempt to link him with Alexander the Great, whose final illness was similarly aggravated). He was physically incapacitated for quite some time. This is the obvious time when the ruler of Philadelphia recovered Gerasa. Alexander replied by a new offensive, centring on an attack on the fort at Ragaba, but he died in the course of it.[23]

Alexander has a reputation as a great warrior and a great conqueror. Certainly the Judaean kingdom expanded considerably during his reign, but it was, even at the end, a small state, not much bigger than Cyprus or Crete, and smaller than most Roman provinces. And he is only a great conqueror in comparison with his predecessors; as a warrior he was defeated in every open battle he fought. Despite his distorted reputation and general military incompetence, he presided over a substantial extension of his kingdom, which grew from an inland and mainly highland state to one several times the size he inherited. The reason is not that Alexander was a great conqueror but that he faced, on the whole, surrounding territories very much fragmented, weak, and easy to capture.

When, however, he was faced by a serious opponent commanding a well-trained army, he was always beaten, by Ptolemy Lathyros, Theodoros of Philadelphia, Demetrios III, Antiochos XII, and Aretas III. The only victories he could claim were slow, grinding sieges – Gaza, Pella, Gerasa, or in civil conflicts – but in this work his army was no more proficient than that which his brothers had commanded at Samaria.

All this means that the enlarged Judaean kingdom, dominated by Jews from the original state, but including a large number of relatively small Greek cities, was a fragile thing. The army was barely competent at siege warfare and was repeatedly beaten in open battle. Against a determined enemy it was invariably beaten. That these enemies rapidly withdrew, or at least did not follow up their victories, was more to do with their preoccupations elsewhere than with Judaean strength. And that they did so implies their contemptuous assessment of Judaean military activity. The Judaean state was bound to crumble when confronted with an efficient military enemy who paid full and sustained attention to destroying it.

Furthermore, Alexander and his predecessors had left a powerful legacy of dislike among their subjects and neighbours. Destruction of cities, forced conversions, massacres, unprovoked aggression, exiles, not to mention serious political divisions within the Judaean population, all meant that there were plenty of subjects and enemies with grievances who were looking forward to co-operating with a determined enemy.

Chapter 15

A War for Damascus

Alexander Iannai had been made king by his wife Salome Alexandra, and so he necessarily left the choice of the next king and the next high priest to her. Josephus composed a speech for him on his deathbed, in which he is supposed to have addressed his wife on what policies she should adopt in the future.[1] Maybe she received this advice, but maybe Josephus simply took note of what she did and then attributed her deeds to following Alexander's advice. Josephus, like every ancient historian (and many modern ones), had major difficulties in coping with the notion of a woman ruler, even though many of those who came to rule were fully capable. Salome's early actions were to him necessarily dictated by her deceased husband; later he attributes her policies to her advisers.

Salome Alexandra knew exactly what she was doing. The siege of Ragaba that Alexander was engaged on when he died was completed and the fort captured,[2] and then the king's death was announced. Arrangements by then had been completed. She had two sons. The elder, Hyrkanos, became high priest. He was apparently unwilling to take much part in public affairs, rather taking after his retiring uncle Absalom, but as the eldest son of the previous high priest he had no choice but to succeed him. The second son, Aristoboulos, was left a private citizen, a condition not entirely to his liking.[3] Neither was made king; Salome kept that position for herself.

Salome made an attempt to heal the internal Judaean divisions. Alexander is said to have advised her to reinstate the Pharisees, though he had opposed them during his reign. Since Salome is also said to have been sympathetic to the Pharisees, this advice was perhaps superfluous, if it was ever given. She had opposed some of Alexander's internal measures, and this was apparently publicly known. Even though she is not mentioned at any point by Josephus in his account of Alexander's reign, it is evident that she had influence and was outspoken within the palace. As it happened, her attempt to reconcile opponents within Jewish society only made for an exacerbation of division, not a healing.

There were still plenty of Pharisees and their sympathizers in the kingdom; those who went into exile being only the most militant. Those present in the country were forthwith admitted to the court and consulted on affairs, presumably on a more or less equal basis with Alexander's own former Sadducee advisers. Since Salome was sympathetic to the Pharisee point of view, ultimately their influence rose.[4] Their recommendations included the return of at least some of those who went into exile, and when this was permitted some sought revenge for past wrongs, particularly the public execution of the rebels in 87. Alexander being dead, they turned on his advisers, and, once more claiming the right to interpret the law, began killing off those they held to be responsible for advising Alexander to execute the prisoners from the fighting at Bethoma. One man in particular was singled out as an example – Diogenes, 'a distinguished man who had been a friend of Alexander'. Having succeeded in his case, others were then killed. They clearly harked back to Judah Maccabee and his methods in their policies. As Josephus comments: 'if she ruled the nation, the Pharisees ruled her' in these matters, though in others she was clearly in control.[5]

The obvious result was that some of those former advisers became scared, and others appealed directly to the queen to protect them. Her son Aristoboulos put himself at their head, so Salome found herself faced with a major internal crisis. The Pharisee ideology was one that confided the administration of the law to themselves as its interpreters, which, as John Hyrkanos had seen, was bound to undermine royal power, even, eventually, to supplant it. It was perhaps with this in mind that Salome had been building up her armed forces, recruiting Jews and foreign mercenaries alike, in the process doubling the size of the Judaean army.[6] The immediate solution to the crisis provoked by the appeal of Aristoboulos and the persecuted former advisers of Alexander was to allow those threatened to go to several of the fortresses in the country, partly for refuge, and partly to be entrusted with the defence of the land.[7]

When these men went to the forts – twenty-two forts, Josephus says – Aristoboulos therefore could call on their loyalty, which gave him a substantial area of power. This, to those of a suspicious, conspiratorial turn of mind, would look dangerous, but there is no suggestion that Aristoboulos was at this time more than a player in the internal politics of the kingdom. Salome certainly trusted him, and anyway, reinforcing the defence of the kingdom was a sensible move at this time.

There was, however, clearly more to the situation than an internal crisis. Salome began recruiting troops as soon as she took power, probably a continuation of her husband's normal practice. The rebellion against Alexander had begun in the aftermath of the destruction of part of his army; he was presumably not going to be trapped in that way again. Salome had lived through all that, and no doubt was equally certain that she would not be trapped either. She will have known how the men around her felt about having a woman ruling them; it would be best for her to be well protected, and her control of the army would give her superior force with which to enforce any decisions she might make that might displease any of the quarrelling parties.

The internal Judaean situation was partly responsible for the only military exploit of Salome's reign. The control of Damascus remained a contentious issue. Aretas III of Nabataea held the city from 85 onwards, having been invited in by the citizens, but he appears to have lost control of it after about ten years, presumably by another citizen decision. Ptolemy son of Mennaeas of the Ituraeans was either threatening to take the city or had already done so.[8] In North Syria the situation was becoming more threatening as its cities were progressively taken over by the Armenian King Tigranes from the north.[9] The date of his invasion is less than clear, but by the late 70s he was threatening Ptolemy of the Ituraeans, and he took control of Damascus in 72 or thereabouts. The date (and indeed the event) is based on the coins issued by the city's mint; those of Tigranes cover the years 72/71 to 70/69.[10]

Damascus had therefore changed hands at least twice in the late 70s, from Aretas to Ptolemy (or into independence) and then to Tigranes. It was in the time of Ituraean control, or the threat of it, that Salome became involved. With Tigranes' power advancing southwards, Damascus became, for those in the south, a key strategic point. In the hands of a North Syrian power it was an open gateway to an invasion of the southern kingdoms. It had been the base for all three of the invasions of Judaea in the 80s as well as others earlier. In Aretas' hands its defence was secure, and constituted protection for lands to the south, but Aretas relinquished it and returned to his main political base at Petra. In Ptolemy's hands, or independent, the city would provide no defence for the south.

Ptolemy's principality was centred on Chalkis in the Bekaa Valley, and extended north to at least the site of the great Baal shrine at Baalbek. Like many Syrian kings, he had the title and position of high priest there. The valley provided an open route for an invader from the north. Ptolemy was therefore vulnerable to attack by Tigranes, who simply had to send an army southwards along the valley and he would be able to take Baalbek and Chalkis. Once he held that city he had control of the Barada River route leading to Damascus. This was undoubtedly clear to the rulers in the south, so if Aretas would not involve himself in the defence of Damascus, Salome would need to.

She gave Aristoboulos command of an army and sent him off to dispute control of Damascus with Ptolemy. There are no details of what transpired except that Aristoboulos had no success.[11] Presumably Ptolemy was well enough entrenched and had a big enough army to deter a serious attack, or the Damascenes were as determined not to be ruled by either Jews or Ituraeans. Rule by the more distant and explicitly 'phil-hellene' Nabataeans or Armenians was clearly preferable – and they did not resist either. Given the prominence of Pharisees and their murderous exploits, this is hardly surprising.

As a result Tigranes came through the pass and gained control of Damascus, apparently without fighting. His next priority was Ptolemais-Ake, which was under the control of Kleopatra Selene and her son Antiochos XIII, the last representatives of the Selekukid dynasty, and so the most potent forms of resistance to him. He began the siege of the city in 70.[12] The city was the most formidable fortified post in the south. Once Tigranes controlled it he would have a major base from which to extend his power throughout Palestine. Josephus suggests that he threatened Judaea, though this may only be what Judaeans apprehended.[13] Nevertheless, Salome made haste to placate him, as he laid siege to the city with a large army, said to be either 300,000 or 500,000 strong[14] – both impossible numbers, of course – but we may accept that his force was very large, and quite sufficient to overawe the small Judaean state. She sent envoys to him carrying gifts. This clear indication of subordination and submission was made explicit when the envoys asked for terms, as though Judaea had already been defeated in war. Tigranes graciously accepted both gifts and homage, 'and gave them reason to hope for the best'[15] – in other words, he would pronounce his terms later.

Judaea had several times in the past been saved from the threat of serious attack by external events that had distracted an enemy at the crucial moment – when Demetrios III was deserted by his allies; when Antiochos XII remained intent on attacking Petra; when Seleukid attacks were diverted by wars elsewhere; when Ptolemaic attacks were sidetracked – and now the presentation of Tigranes' terms was delayed, then abandoned. He was intent first on the conquest of Ptolemais, and perhaps was pleased to wait until this display of his power was accomplished before stating what he wanted from Judaea. Dismantling the Judaean kingdom was a clear possibility, for Tigranes' aim seemed to be to reunite all Syria under his rule as a successor to the Seleukids, though he also accepted subordinate kingdoms – Ptolemy son of Mennaeas was not removed, for example. He seems to have taken his surname of phil-hellene seriously, so the revived independence of Greek cities was quite likely to be one of his terms. But then a Roman army invaded his home kingdom and laid siege to his royal city. Soon after he captured Ptolemais he had to turn about and march away to the north, taking Kleopatra Selene with him, before executing her at Seleukeia-Zeugma.[16]

His withdrawal left confusion in North Syria, where Arab kings and the last of the Seleukid family fought each other over control of the cities, but in the south little had, in fact, changed, for neither Judaea nor Nabataea had been directly attacked. On the other hand, both Ptolemais and Damascus were now left without royal rulers. Both had their own councils and regularly elected magistrates, so they were able to go on functioning as political communities. (Kleopatra Selene had had to persuade the magistrates of Ptolemais to resist Tigranes; the Damascus council had invited Aretas in, and then perhaps expelled him; the city councils were capable and decisive.) But the world was no longer safe for individual and independent and relatively small cities, and both they and the cities of Phoenicia – and Philadelphia – surely feared attack by Ptolemy, Salome or Aretas. But nothing seems to have happened.

In Judaea, Salome, perhaps fixated on the internal problem, was never aggressive. Many of her forts were now occupied by the political and religious opponents of her principal advisers. Ptolemy son of Mennaeas was severely damaged by Tigranes' intrusion. Aretas of Nabataea, having tried once to gain control of Damascus, was apparently not willing to try again. That is to say, everyone was paralysed with indecision, waiting for the Romans.

Chapter 16

The Second Civil War

For much of her reign Salome Alexander was clearly in full control of her kingdom.[1] The resurgent Pharisees caused trouble by their presumption to be the exclusive interpreters of the law, but she managed to soothe everyone; her obvious partiality for the Pharisees helped keep them under control. It may also be that the contenders for power were willing to wait until she died before making overt moves: she was seventy-three when she died in 67 BC, according to Josephus;[2] she had been considerably older than her husband. This certainly appears to have been the attitude of Aristoboulos. His mother gave him command of her army and he brought it back from the unsuccessful Damascus expedition without, as he might have, using it to seize power.

And yet during her reign the divisions within Jewish society became even more serious. Aristoboulos had put himself at the head of the men who had been his father's advisers, a party that may be termed, for convenience, the Sadducees. The party with the ear of the queen, the Pharisees, would probably dominate Hyrkanos, the high priest, without difficulty when he was no longer dominated by his mother. In Josephus he emerges as a man without much force of character, and when he exercised his authority, he was liable to do so inappropriately. The two brothers were thus very different, just as the two parties in the state had serious differences over the type of society they wished Judaea to become. Some sort of conflict was inevitable, and Salome's solution to the earlier crisis had, probably inadvertently, signalled how it would begin. By exiling the Sadducees to forts in various parts of the kingdom, they and Aristoboulos were given a head start in any conflict. For, even if the argument had been about the interpretation of the Jewish religion, it inevitably emerged as a political matter, a dispute over the exercise of power.

Accounts of these events show that a considerable degree of fortification had been developed in Judaea in the previous fifty years or so. Jerusalem had been well fortified and the temple area was soon to show it could endure two sieges. Salome had reserved three fortresses for her own control when imposing internal exile on Aristoboulos' people, and these were where she stored her treasures, just as Theodoros of Philadelphia had kept his treasures at Amathos, and then at Gerasa – though clearly in his case he made the wrong choices. Salome distributed hers into three fortresses, at Hyrkania, Alexandreion, and Machaeros.[3] These and others were often in well-selected strategic locations, whose strength was primarily designed for defence – and they were thus also useful for holding portable wealth.[4]

Hyrkania (now Khirbet el-Mird) is assumed to have been built at the order of John Hyrkanos I, and so between 134 and 104.[5] It was a dozen kilometres east of Jerusalem, dominating a small plain, and looking down from the plateau towards the northern end of the Dead Sea. It was thus in a good position to block any invasion coming from the region of Philadelphia by way of the river crossings near Jericho. The Alexandreion (now Qarn Sabateh)[6] was similarly placed to block invasion from the east. It was west of the Jordan, on a hill looking east and overlooking the river crossing at Daliya, almost directly opposite the Philadelphia-Gerasa forts of Amathos and Ragaba. Presumably, from the name, it was constructed in Alexander's reign, no doubt one result of his conflicts with Theodoros, though one would suppose it originated earlier than the capture of Amathos; it was clearly sited for defence against attack from the east. In addition, it appears from a later comment by Josephus, that it was only three kilometres south of the border with the city territory of Skythopolis,[7] and so it was surely already fortified in Simon's and Hyrkanos I's time, and sited to block access to Judaean territory from the north. The third fortress, Machaeros (Khirbet Mukawir), was on the east side of the Dead Sea.[8] Its strategic function was presumably to dominate Judaean territory east of the Jordan; but it was a rather remote place in which to store one's treasures in safety. It also overlooked the small port that existed at Kallirhoe on the Dead Sea shore.

The location of the places to which those exiled from Jerusalem were sent is never stated, though one of them was probably Ragaba. They were all over the country, not just because that was where the forts were, but to separate the exiles from one another. Some such places have been found and excavated, as at Horvat Aleq,[9] above Dor and Strato's Tower on the Carmel Ridge, and at Jotapata in Galilee.[10] Apart from such places, most towns and cities were fortified in some way, garrisoned, and will have accommodated some of the internal exiles. Distributing them in this way, of course, was almost as dangerous as keeping them concentrated in Jerusalem. They could not be prevented from talking and persuading, and many of the soldiers in the garrisons had served under Alexander, with whose views the exiles were also associated.

Salome, in her seventies, became ill, and was clearly dying. This was the trigger for Aristoboulos to begin his *coup*. This time, unlike the *coup* attempted by Ptolemy in 134, there was no assassination of the incumbent, and the *coup* happened slowly and was ultimately successful. Aristoboulos did, however, begin in the same way, by the seizure of a fortress, and the events also included the captivity of dependants.

Aristoboulos was rightly fearful that if he was in Jerusalem when Salome died, her Pharisee advisers would dominate the weak-willed Hyrkanos and that he and his family would be eliminated. There is no reason to assume that the Pharisees' basically anti-monarchic tendency had changed. He left the city quietly and went to a fort to which one or more of the exiles had been sent, particularly where a trusted friend was living. He left his wife and children in the city. The fort he went to is named in Josephus' text severally as Agraba, Agrabra or Gabatha. It might well be Ragaba, the place taken by Salome at the start of her reign. Similarly, the name of the friend may be Galaistes or Palaistes.[11] These uncertainties, while exasperating, do not matter very much, though it would be good to know them accurately.

At first Salome did not believe he was beginning a *coup*, and, given that he had left his family in the city, she may well have been right. It is difficult at this remove to discern Aristoboulos' original intentions. His initial actions can be understood as the act of a man visiting a friend, and only later was this move taken to be the first part of his *coup*. Once he had made, or apparently made, this move he found that his supporters became involved. The fortresses in which his friends had been placed came over to him one at a time. He gained the support of twenty-two forts in the next fortnight, and in the process acquired an army and money. This could therefore be a spontaneous move, or a pre-concerted one, but once it began and spread Aristoboulos accepted it. The money was used to recruit more soldiers in Lebanon and Trachonitis and from 'the local princes', whoever they were. The named areas were those inhabited in part by Ituraeans, so perhaps one of these 'princes' was Ptolemy son of Mennaeas. In Jerusalem Salome took the precaution of bringing Aristoboulos' family into the Baris fortress (later called the 'Antonia') next to the temple, both as potential hostages and to protect them.[12] She no doubt recalled that her first husband had treated his mother and brothers in this way a third of the century before, but for a rather different purpose.

The sequence of events can be interpreted as a carefully planned *coup d'état*; it can also be seen as a sequence of events which only became a *coup* by accident. It all depends on the original intentions of Aristoboulos when he left Jerusalem. Salome clearly did not believe he was up to no good until several reports had arrived of the defection of the forts,[13] and it could be that those who rebelled pushed Aristoboulos into the *coup*. The men in the forts were surely primed to rebel, thanks to the presence in them of the exiles and of troops loyal to Alexander's memory and purposes. It would obviously not take much to set them off, perhaps simply a rumour that Aristoboulos intended a *coup*, for they apparently rose separately, as the news spread. Further, when he had twenty-two forts on his side, Aristoboulos spent more time recruiting extra troops, since the main Judaean army did not join him. If this was a planned *coup*, by not securing the army, it was unsuccessful. (Ptolemy had known better in 134; as had John Hyrkanos.) These events surrounding Aristoboulos look more like yet another move in the internal party contest to gain Salome's attention, and perhaps as protection for himself by Aristoboulos.

The reaction in Jerusalem was muted. Salome protected Aristoboulos' family, and when Hyrkanos and the Pharisee party came to consult her on the crisis, she decried the danger, pointing to the strength of her and their position, by which she presumably meant her control of the city and the army. Further, they were obviously unwilling to take any action while she lived, but when she died, soon after, the contest between Hyrkanos and Aristoboulos and their adherents inevitably came out into the open.

On the news of Salome's death, Hyrkanos assumed the title of king – 'John Hyrkanos II'; Aristoboulos then is said to have 'declared war' on him.[14] Josephus does not say what Aristoboulos wanted. We assume, of course, that he aimed to be king, but on what grounds did he do so? He did not have the hereditary right, for, unlike the succession in most ancient dynasties, that of the high priests always went to the eldest son; the rule is quite clear. Hyrkanos was already high priest, and he had been in that post for nine years; Salome may well have nominated him as king before she died, and this was the normal method of succession to the kingship. Aristoboulos clearly felt he would be a more capable king, but in his rebellion he did not, it seems, directly claim the title. It must be assumed therefore that his rebellion was directed at Hyrkanos' Pharisee supporters. The weakness of Hyrkanos was no doubt expected to allow the Pharisees to rule in his name, which would be an obvious threat to Aristoboulos and his Sadducee and exiled supporters. So the war that followed was only in part a fraternal war of succession, it was also a war between the rival parties in the state. When it was later seen that this conflict led to the destruction of the kingdom, it is easy to blame the brothers. But the basic cause of the collapse of the kingdom was its internal divisions, which stemmed from the very origins of the state in the Maccabean rebellion.

Hyrkanos is credited with a reign of three months by Josephus,[15] only an approximate figure, but longer than is implied by Josephus' minimal account of the war that followed.[16] Both men were already well armed, Hyrkanos with Salome's army, Aristoboulos with his friends and his mercenaries. There was no doubt a good deal of political manoeuvring as each side angled for support from the majority of the population which was neutral.

Hyrkanos had the larger force, which follows from the fight which took place. The site of the battle was 'near Jericho', so Hyrkanos brought his army down into the Jordan valley from Jerusalem. If Aristoboulos' headquarters were at Ragaba or in that area, Hyrkanos was attacking him, which suggests that he or his commanders had the larger army and were confident of victory. In the event they were mistaken. The two armies began to fight, but then many of Hyrkanos' soldiers changed sides. They were, like those in the forts, therefore, still loyal to Alexander's and Aristoboulos' ideas, and were perhaps commanded by officers whose sentiment were Sadducean rather than Pharisean.

It must be remembered that this was a civil war, and that the soldiers and commanders on both sides knew each other. There was surely a reluctance to fight, and an initial unwillingness to kill men on the other side, though this would change. It would not take much for Aristoboulos, the former commander of the whole army in the Damascus campaign, to persuade his brother's army to stop fighting – and Hyrkanos was no soldier. There is considerable evidence throughout this civil war of the existence of a strong body of opinion that deprecated the war and condemned both brothers. The army was clearly not immune from such sentiments.

Hyrkanos escaped back to Jerusalem. He still had control of the temple-and-citadel and Aristoboulos' family, yet it is unlikely that any threats he uttered would be taken seriously: not only were the children his nephews and nieces, but Aristoboulos' wife was Hyrkanos' first cousin, for she was the daughter of his uncle Absalom,[17] and Absalom was still in the city. Much of Hyrkanos' support in Jerusalem had disappeared. He drove out opponents from the temple, but when Aristoboulos came up, Hyrkanos at once offered to negotiate. He bargained for his life, his social position as the king's brother, and his possessions, all of which

Aristoboulos agreed to concede him. They went through a public parade of reconciliation and Aristoboulos became king – 'Judah Aristoboulos II' – and Hyrkanos took up residence in Aristoboulos' former house.[18]

The speed of Aristoboulos' victory unsettled his opponents, and they set about recovering from their defeat. The credit for their revival is given to Antipater, son of Antipas, from Idumaea, a man of great wealth and political acumen. He was opposed to Aristoboulos, though the source of his enmity is not known. His persuasiveness brought about an alliance of Aristoboulos' internal opponents, together with the Nabataean King Aretas III, and, eventually, Hyrkanos himself. Hyrkanos was the last to be involved, but once Antipater could show that he had gathered substantial support, Hyrkanos was persuaded.[19]

All this took some time to be organized. Salome died in 67, and the crisis over the succession lasted three months, by which time Aristoboulos was in power. The organization of Hyrkanos' return took over a year, so it was early in 65 when the plot came together. Hyrkanos left Jerusalem secretly and went to Petra with Antipater. (Antipater's wife was from a notable Nabataean family.) An alliance was negotiated with Aretas. He would bring his army to attack Aristoboulos; in return Hyrkanos agreed to cede to Aretas a large swathe of territory east and south of the Dead Sea, from Medaba round into the Negev. Aretas apparently claimed that Alexander had conquered it from him, but this cannot be verified,[20] though it was land that had probably been conquered by Judaea quite recently. It was, nevertheless, a heavy price to pay; it seems most unlikely that it was publicly announced.

It is noticeable that it was the Pharisees who were quite willing to call in Gentile help to enable them to gain power at home in this internal Jewish dispute, just as earlier they had called in Demetrios against Alexander. It is worth recalling also that the basic dispute between the Jewish parties was over their interpretation of their shared religion, and that the Pharisees were supposedly the more rigorous. Yet twice they had called in foreign armies. This rather suggests either a lack of confidence in their support or their cause; perhaps, more likely, they realized that Aristoboulos' control of the Judaean army precluded a successful internal rising.

No doubt anxious to claim his reward, Aretas quickly mustered a large cavalry army. Josephus claims it was a force of 50,000 horse plus infantry, which may perhaps be interpreted as meaning 'a large force'; alternatively, he says the army was 50,000 only, including all arms[21] – all obvious exaggerations. This was too much for Aristoboulos' forces, which were defeated. (The numerical exaggeration, of course, provided the excuse for the defeat.) Aristoboulos escaped to Jerusalem. Much of his surviving army was quickly recruited into Hyrkanos' force. On the other hand, Aristoboulos did retain a force large enough to allow him to go on fighting.[22]

The allies followed Aristoboulos up to Jerusalem. So far the return of Hyrkanos had copied that of Aristoboulos not long before. Aristoboulos was besieged in the temple-and-citadel, just as Hyrkanos had been. But now the sequence changed. This time the enemy was the Nabataean king, who was, it seems, the moving spirit in the siege, for though Josephus says he 'assisted' Hyrkanos in the siege, it was Aretas who sited the camps and commanded the fighting.[23] No doubt he was keen to be able to impose his own terms on the winner and to reap his reward – and perhaps to sack Jerusalem. It seems unlikely that he would be satisfied with the lands already promised. Once the Nabataean army was in Jerusalem, Aretas could well revise his agreement with Hyrkanos.

Not surprisingly, given that the king was besieged in the temple by the former high priest and an army of Arabs, stories clustered about the events. The population of Jerusalem appears to have changed sides again, as had part of the army, but the conflict also drove some people into exile in Egypt – suggesting that rather more violence was occurring than simply the siege of the temple at Jerusalem. There was presumably a purge in the country as a whole, with the Pharisees vengefully routing out Aristoboulos' supporters – Josephus says those who fled to Egypt were 'the Jews of the best repute', which might be code for the Sadducees.

For once the date of these events is reasonably clear. The fighting took place during the Passover of 65 (April, in that year), a circumstance that made the conflict even more disquieting to many Jews. One holy man publicly prayed that the besiegers be denied victory and was stoned to death; negotiations were conducted for the purchase by the besieged of animals for the Passover sacrifices in the temple, but having taken the money, the besiegers failed to deliver. The priests of the temple stayed there all through the siege, though it is unclear whether they did so because they were loyal to Aristoboulos, or were trapped there, or were unwilling to desert their posts. The conflict, presumably because of the place and the date, was obviously becoming more bitter. Outside the siege, bad weather began to cause a famine, attributed by the besieged to the bad faith of the besiegers over the matter of the Passover animals.[24]

Into this internal paralysis stepped a new actor: Rome, in the person of M. Aemilius Scaurus, a legate of Cn. Pompeius Magnus (Pompey), who was conducting a campaign to rid the Mediterranean of pirates and eliminate the threat of further wars with Mithradates of Pontos. He had accomplished these tasks and went on to find more work and pay for his forces. He pushed Tigranes of Armenia back into his original kingdom, and in the process acquired large new territories for the Roman people, including the Syrian territories that Tigranes had ruled briefly in the 70s. These were converted into a new Roman province.[25] Scaurus was sent by Pompey to scout the situation in southern Syria and presumably report back; the general purpose was to make sure everyone understood what was involved and to set out the boundaries of the new province. Scaurus had been preceded at Damascus by two earlier Roman officials, but it is evident that Scaurus had greater authority. He could make binding political decisions, and presumably had some Roman troops with him, at least as a bodyguard. He certainly showed good strategic understanding by moving directly to Damascus, and he quickly grasped the general political situation in the south. But it was not until he reached Damascus that he discovered that the two Judaeans were fighting each other and that Aretas was also involved.

On the other hand, neither Hyrkanos not Aristoboulos appears to have been at all surprised by Scaurus' arrival. Presumably they were kept informed of the Roman advances, and of the approach of Roman authority – the two earlier officials at

Damascus were a sign of things to come. The conversion of the Seleukid lands into a Roman province brought the Great Power of the Mediterranean very close; both brothers must have been expecting to be contacted soon, and both knew that Rome must be consulted over their dispute. Both sent envoys to meet Scaurus at the border (which must have been in Galilee or Golan) with rival requests for Roman assistance in their conflict. Aristoboulos was under siege and so was the more desperate; his envoy offered 300 or 400 talents to pay for that assistance. These sums are generally described as bribes, and Josephus claims that Scaurus was in search of 'a god-sent opportunity', supposedly for his own personal enrichment. The money, in fact, was required by the Roman forces to pay their soldiers and to purchase supplies, and such payments were a recognition of Roman supremacy. Hyrkanos' envoy came up with a similar offer. Salome's earlier submission to Tigranes in 70 could have been taken by the Romans as indicating that Judaea was already part of the new Roman province – if the Romans knew of it.

Scaurus came to a quick decision to support Aristoboulos. He was clearly in the weaker position and so could be expected to be more dependent on Rome than Hyrkanos, who had been reluctant to pay anything, and had more local support, together with the assistance of the Nabataeans. Hyrkanos also, with some justice, claimed to be the rightful king and that Aristoboulos was a usurper – but Hyrkanos had resigned that position, and Aristoboulos was the incumbent king. Since he did not meet either man in person it is unlikely that Scaurus was able to judge their personal qualities; his decision was therefore based on the politics of the situation, but mainly on Roman priorities and requirements. At this particular time it was more important to Rome that there should be a balance of power in the area; this meant the alliance of Judaea and Nabataea had to be broken, and the easiest way to do that was to recognize Aristoboulos as king in Judaea. It was only a short-term solution, subject to later alteration. No ruler in Syria was guaranteed his throne when Roman power approached. Scaurus also seems to have understood the strength of Jerusalem's fortifications – another short-term consideration. With a force perhaps no more than a personal bodyguard he could not contemplate joining in the siege.

He was as good as his word. He pronounced for Aristoboulos, and then threatened Aretas with being named a Roman enemy and so subject to attack when Pompey arrived with the main Roman forces. This ended the siege of Jerusalem. Aretas, with Hyrkanos (and presumably Antipater as well) took his army away. Scaurus returned to Damascus.[26]

Aristoboulos took the opportunity to attack Aretas and his forces as they withdrew towards Nabataea. The battle took place at an unknown place called Papyron, presumed to be somewhere near Jericho. Aretas was defeated and '6,000' of his soldiers killed.[27] Aristoboulos, until Scaurus arrived, had been besieged in the temple area of Jerusalem, and now suddenly had an army – 'a large force', according to Josephus – which was large and capable enough to defeat a Nabataean force of '50,000' men. This can only be Hyrkanos' army, the same Judaean army that had switched back and forth in allegiance during the past two years. Now that Hyrkanos had been defeated, the army had changed sides again.

The army was composed, as usual, of both mercenaries and Jewish levies. Salome had made an effort to recruit Jews, presumably so as to be less dependent on the mercenaries; Aristoboulos had recruited mercenaries from Lebanon and Trachonitis to increase the force that had come to him when the fort garrisons rebelled. Both elements were liable to change sides in a civil war. The mercenaries could change when their employer was beaten and so would be unable to pay them. The Jewish soldiers might change when to continue would lead to serious damage to their country, or when persuaded by the other side, or when a retreat to Arabia would take them out of Judaea. The battle between Hyrkanos and Aristoboulos in 67 near Jericho was hardly fought at all, but Aretas' invasion led to two serious fights. So it seems that the army was unwilling to fight in the civil war, but was not averse to fighting a foreign army. Notice also that the siege of Jerusalem was conducted by Aretas rather than the Jewish forces of Hyrkanos, who were presumably somewhat reluctant to attack their own city. Aristoboulos' army in 65 was therefore that which had been Hyrkanos' at the siege; it changed sides as soon as Aristoboulos had gained Roman support. The previous experience when it was an adjunct to the Nabataeans in the siege of Jerusalem temple surely soured the attitude of the Jewish soldiers, who cannot have been pleased at the prospect of the Nabataeans capturing their temple, while the mercenaries had either been recruited originally by Aristoboulos or by his mother, and owed no loyalty to Hyrkanos.

This demonstrates that Scaurus' decision in favour of Aristoboulos was a sensible one in terms of the ability of the ruler and of his military capacity. After the victory of Papyron, Aristoboulos ruled Judaea for over a year without Roman interference and without enmity from Aretas. It must be assumed that Aretas had secured his reward before invading Judaea with Hyrkanos, and that Aristoboulos let him keep it. It would not be sensible, with Pompey and his army on the way, to indulge in a new war.

Needless to say, however, Hyrkanos, backed and encouraged by Antipater, had not given up the struggle. Antipater's brother had been killed at the battle at Papyron, and this no doubt stoked his enmity towards Aristoboulos. The civil war was over for the time being, but Antipater dominated Hyrkanos, and the next stage in the process would not be merely a civil war.

Chapter 17

The First Roman War

Scaurus, though decisive, was a subordinate, and it is likely that he made it clear that his decisions were only tentative. So his chief could be persuaded to change the decision about who should be king in Judaea. As Pompey came south through Syria in the spring of 63 (having spent the winter of 64/63 in Antioch), he alternately suppressed and mulcted the several rulers he encountered. Silas the Jew was removed as tyrant of the town of Lysias in Syria; Dionysios was eliminated at Tripolis, and the tyranny he had built there and over the neighbouring Phoenician cities was removed. In the hills above Dionysios' kingdom, however, the small Ituraean principality centred on Arqa survived. Ptolemy son of Mennaeas kept his kingdom in the Bekaa and the nearby hills, but had to pay a thousand talents for the privilege.[1] Damascus remained a free city.

The general trend of Pompey's policy was to strengthen the independence of the cities, to cut down the petty tyrants who had emerged since the failure of the last Seleukids and the departure of Tigranes, but to confirm rulers in difficult country. This made the region easier for Rome to govern, since it was divided among many weak polities and those showing signs of strength were removed. A king who was submissive and in control of his territory, such as Ptolemy, was spared, especially if he controlled a wild mountain land.

Probably while Pompey was at Antioch finally disposing of the last of the Seleukids, he was contacted by envoys from both of the Judaean claimants, Antipater for Hyrkanos, and Nikodemos for Aristoboulos. Aristoboulos sent him a gift of a golden vine said to be worth 500 talents; Hyrkanos, out of power and now no longer allied to Aretas, could send nothing.[2] But to assume that a powerful Roman such as Pompey, who was probably also one of the richest men of his time, was amenable to bribery, is a mistake. When Aristoboulos accused Scaurus and A. Gabinius of taking money from him, he must have misunderstood where the money was going. These monies were being given to Rome, not to Pompey or Scaurus personally. They were regarded by the Romans as legitimate tribute, payments due from a subordinate ruler to the Roman Republic. Rome's conquests were always financed in this way, by the conquered.

Antipater, arriving necessarily without cash, was therefore accidentally showing up Aristoboulos as a boor and ignorant of proper diplomatic procedures, something Antipater was no doubt familiar with. By accusing Scaurus and Gabinius of being bribed Aristoboulos was insulting Rome itself. Pompey, however, ignored this *faux pas* and decided he needed to see the disputants themselves in person, in a meeting at Damascus in the spring.

His journey from Antioch to Damascus, removing tyrants, encouraging and freeing cities, and accepting tribute, should have given a powerful hint of Pompey's preferences and intentions. But Judaea was a different matter to these northern and middle Syrian polities. As a functioning state it was older than any of them except the Seleukid monarchy, though the fate of Antiochos XIII, dismissed with contempt, showed that the Roman was no respecter of historical priorities. Also Judaea included within its borders a number of Greek cities. Some of these were quite content with the protection this provided, but others had been destroyed politically and physically – Samaria, Pella, Gadara, Gaza – and this would not recommend Judaea to Roman benevolence. Then the central areas of the kingdom, the hill regions of Galilee and Judaea, were essentially without cities (except Jerusalem), and were populated by native Syrians, like the Ituraean kingdom. Judaea, therefore, could not be dealt with in a simplistic way; some care and finesse was needed.

Pompey had no prejudice one way or the other, for or against Syrians or Greeks. He was concerned particularly to sort out the region as a province. His political prejudice was generally in favour of cities, with which, as a Roman and a philhellene, he was familiar. In North Syria he announced that he did not wish to see the region fall under the rule of 'Jews and Arabs',[3] but there the Jews were men such as Silas the tyrant-bandit of Lysias, and the otherwise unknown Bacchias, and the Arabs were desert kings. Removing them meant freeing the cities; kings, on the other hand, like Ptolemy son of Mennaeas, usually survived. How much of the subtlety of Pompey's approach was understood in Judaea is unknown. If anyone did it was probably Antipater, who came out of the collision that now took place with an enhanced reputation among the Romans, the only man who did.

The meeting at Damascus was conducted in the midst of Pompey's Roman army, a clear indication that he intended to impose any settlement he reached, and that this time it would be permanent. The absence of any submission by Aretas of the Nabataeans was noted, and rectifying this error on Aretas' part was another item on Pompey's agenda. He first dealt with Damascus, which was established as what it already was, an independent city, though now subject to Rome. This protected it from the attentions of both Aretas and Ptolemy of the Ituraeans, though it was subject to Roman taxation. Then he turned to the Judaean delegations. Both Hyrkanos and Aristoboulos were present, but there was also a third group of envoys, claiming to represent 'the nation'.[4]

Just who this third group was is never stated, and there is no direct indication that Pompey paid them much heed. Their programme is said to have been a restoration of the ancient rule of the priests. No such rule, of course, had ever existed, but the suggestion implied the abolition of the monarchy, so it sounds very like a version of the programme of the Pharisees, in which the interpreters of the law would be in control. With Hyrkanos driven out of Judaea, Aristoboulos' Sadducees were dominant, so a Pharisee delegation was highly likely. They accused the rival kings of wanting to convert the country into a 'nation of slaves', though no king or queen had done so. (A Pharisee regime, however, would probably have produced it.)

The two kings spent much of their energy arguing with each other, so that Pompey, no doubt thoroughly exasperated, postponed his decision. Aristoboulos portrayed Hyrkanos as an ineffectual ruler and all-too subject to influence from others, so that his power would be dissipated. He may have been looking at Antipater when he said this, but he was also referring in an oblique way to Hyrkanos' Pharisee supporters. The third group, the self-styled representatives of 'the nation' who argued for a Pharisee settlement, may have actually been instigated by the intriguer Antipater. In such a settlement there would be room for a high priest, and since one was available in Hyrkanos, the coincidence of these two looks very likely, not to say suspicious.

Hyrkanos pointed to his status as the eldest son and rightful hereditary high priest, and the fact that Aristoboulos had usurped his position. He brought a great crowd of 'respectable' Jews to support him, and he denounced Aristoboulos as a promoter of violence. In a clear reference to Pompey's earlier anti-pirate work, he accused Aristoboulos of promoting piracy and of instigating raids on neighbouring peoples, though no precise evidence was produced. These are, in fact, just the sort of unsubstantiated allegations that were produced in a Roman courtroom; no doubt Pompey accordingly discounted them.[5]

Postponing his decision until he could visit Judaea in person, Pompey set off to deal with Aretas and the Nabataeans, marching due south from Damascus along the King's Highway. He was no doubt intending to go all the way to Petra, if necessary. He took Aristoboulos with him, partly to keep him under control, and because part of his march was through Aristoboulos' territory – that is, he was treating Aristoboulos, quite correctly, as the reigning king. Where Hyrkanos and Antipater were is not known. It is possible they had been left at Damascus, but they had been friendly with Aretas, and Antipater's wife was Nabataean, so Pompey is likely to have taken them along to smooth the diplomatic way. They were certainly present with Pompey later. It looks as though Pompey had tentatively decided for Aristoboulos. Their joint march may have been Pompey's way of testing Aristoboulos to see if he was likely to remain a good Roman client.

The marching force reached Dion. At this point Pompey was just a few kilometres north of the boundary between Aristoboulos' lands and the lands of Gerasa-with-Philadelphia. Nothing is known of these two cities since the recovery of Gerasa by Theodoros/Zenon in about 76, which was followed by Salome's reconquest of Ragaba, the Gerasan fort, after Alexander's death. There is no reason to suppose that the Zenon dynasty had expired, but even if it had, the two cities were independent, either separately or jointly. Having accompanied Pompey as far as Dion, Aristoboulos' task was now finished. He had taken the Roman forces as far as the boundary of his territory.[6] If he still ruled that part of the King's Highway from Medaba south, which Hyrkanos had presented to Aretas, he could resume his escort duties when Pompey reached it; more likely Aretas had now taken it over. If so, Aristoboulos' presence with Pompey would be a handicap in dealing with Aretas (and with whoever ruled in Philadelphia-Gerasa).

Aristoboulos therefore left the Roman force at Dion. Many interpret this as an anti-Roman action, though all Josephus says is that Aristoboulos left the Romans without waiting for Pompey's decision. Yet if Pompey, as he clearly intended at that point, was going on as far as Petra there was no point in Aristoboulos staying with him. He had a kingdom to govern. Pompey had been escorted through his lands to his border, and from now on the Roman army would be marching through lands not under Aristoboulos' rule. There seems nothing in all this which was underhand or going 'behind Pompey's back'.[7] Josephus claims that Aristoboulos was intent on raising Judaea 'in rebellion',[8] which makes no sense, since Aristoboulos was king, and had been treated as such by Pompey. And if Pompey was intent on fighting Aretas, he would not announce his final decision on Judaea until he finished. Aristoboulos left Dion and went to Alexandreion, the fortress across the River Jordan from Amathos. There he was in a good position to ensure that supplies were sent to the Roman army if that was what was required, though this is not suggested as his purpose.

Whatever Aristoboulos' own reasons, Pompey came to the conclusion that his purpose was to cause difficulties. He was influenced in this by the persuasiveness of Hyrkanos and Antipater, who must have been overjoyed to be free of Aristoboulos in what they could claim were suspicious circumstances. At the same time Pompey may have at last realized the difficulties he faced in attempting to reach Aretas at Petra. He had already marched 150 kilometres from Damascus, and had double that still to go; part of the march in front of him would be through desert, and the heat of summer was approaching. Making the assertion that Aristoboulos was trying to cause trouble would give Pompey a good excuse to break off the march before he became too deeply involved.

Pompey may have decided in favour of Aristoboulos, but he had not yet announced his decision, nor had he decided on the future of the kingdom itself. By now he must have realized the size of the Judaean kingdom, and the dislike – to put it no stronger – it had generated among its neighbours. He was presumably in contact with the ruler of Philadelphia; he had seen the ruins of Gadara and Pella; he may have received delegations from the conquered Greek cities. The turn aside he now took suggests that he had at last come to a decision on what to do with the Judaean kingdom, and that it was necessary to implement that decision at once. He would also postpone dealing with Aretas and so avoid a nasty desert campaign.

He followed Aristoboulos, by way of Pella (in ruins, of course) and crossed the Jordan to Skythopolis. There he discovered that Aristoboulos was in the Alexandreion fortress, and so he went south, camping at Koreai (Tell el-Mazar), which is three kilometres from Alexandreion.[9]

Koreai, as Josephus points out, was the 'beginning of Judaea'; that is, it was on the border of the kingdom with the lands of the city of Skythopolis. It is interesting that it was just at the border that Pompey stopped. It seems obvious that Pompey was uncertain as to Aristoboulos' intentions. By stopping at the border he was carefully not entering Judaea, and by stopping some distance from Alexandreion he was equally careful not to threaten Aristoboulos. Aristoboulos came out of his castle to meet with Hyrkanos for further negotiations, presumably at Koreai. These negotiations had thus become the main purpose of Pompey's change of direction. The talks went on for some time, with Aristoboulos each time coming out of his castle to attend. This was probably the last chance the two Hasmonaeans had to preserve their disputed kingdom in something like the size and configuration as it was at the time, in 63. During the talks Pompey finally made up his mind which of the two brothers he should support, and what to do with the kingdom. He had, however, first to ensure that his decisions could be implemented. The kingdom was well fortified and Aristoboulos had forces partly in Jerusalem and partly in his forts and castles, and these forces had to be neutralized. Aristoboulos had taken the precaution of ensuring that only an order in his own handwriting was to be obeyed by the garrison commanders – no doubt a precaution against Hyrkanos. Pompey persuaded him to issue an order to deliver up the forts.[10]

Aristoboulos was presumably doing this to prove his good faith. There is absolutely no indication that he was planning or instigating a 'rebellion' against Rome. Pompey in turn was securing control of the kingdom by means of these forts in preparation for announcing his decision, which neither brother had been told during the talks at Alexandreion – but he had presumably concluded that the kingdom was too big to be left as it was; whoever he adjudged to be king would not have the whole kingdom. Perhaps during the talks Pompey had appreciated at last the profound differences that separated the brothers. Hence his decision to gain control of the forts. But he also needed to gain control of the biggest and most powerful fortress of all in the kingdom: Jerusalem.

Aristoboulos now realized that he had been driven into a corner. If Pompey had already decided in his favour there was no point in his taking control of the forts; all Aristoboulos' displays of good faith – conducting the Roman army through his territory, negotiating with his brother, putting himself in Pompey's hands in those talks at Alexandreion, delivering up the forts – were to no avail. Aristoboulos left his castle and went up to Jerusalem. Pompey brought his army south along the Jordan to Jericho and climbed up to Jerusalem. Aristoboulos made one more attempt to save his throne. He came out of the city and promised to surrender it to the Romans. A. Gabinius was sent to take it over.[11]

At this point the Roman scheme went wrong. It turned out that Aristoboulos either did not control the city or perhaps had given orders that only he should be allowed to bring in the Romans. Gabinius was denied entry by Aristoboulos' supporters and soldiers. No doubt Aristoboulos intended to continue negotiations, aiming to hold Jerusalem as a final inducement to gain a concession, but Pompey had had enough. He put Aristoboulos under arrest, and prepared to attack the city.[12]

Aristoboulos' soldiers controlled the city, but the approach of the Roman forces, with Hyrkanos amongst them, encouraged those opposed to Aristoboulos to rise. Aristoboulos' men kept control of the temple area, as they had two years before, but the rest of the city was occupied by Hyrkanos and his Roman allies. The strength of the temple as a defensive position meant that the Romans and Hyrkanos' forces could do nothing but lay siege to it, after a first attempt to argue the defenders out had failed. The temple was cut off from the city, partly by the actions of the defenders who cut down a bridge, and partly by the attackers who blocked up the exits and fortified nearby buildings.[13]

The siege lasted into its third month, by which time the walls had been badly battered by the siege engines, some of which had been brought all the way from Tyre. It was the collapse of one of the towers under this battering that finally created a large enough breach for an assault to be successful. Many of the defenders continued fighting even then and were largely massacred. Others committed suicide. Josephus claims that 12,000 died, including the priests officiating at the altar. One of those captured alive was Absalom, the last surviving son of Hyrkanos I and father-in-law of Aristoboulos.[14]

Pompey had at last gained the position he required for imposing a settlement on the kingdom. He had control of Jerusalem and all the forts in the country. In effect, he could do what he wanted. Having seen the strength of the city, and the number of the forts, and having had to fight harder in this siege than anywhere else in his expedition through Syria, it made Roman sense to dismantle the state.

Hyrkanos was reinstated as high priest, but not as king. In this way Pompey satisfied both Hyrkanos and the anti-royalist faction. The state was reduced to its Jewish core of Judaea and Galilee plus part of Idumaea and the trans-Jordanian Peraia. These were the areas, inhabited by mainly Jewish populations, which just happened to be the regions without many cities. The rest of the kingdom was removed. Some sections went to the Nabataeans and the Ituraeans. The cities along the coast were made independent once more, and a group of those along the Jordan was formed into the Decapolis, which included Skythopolis, Philadelphia and Gerasa.[15] (Philadelphia had therefore submitted to Pompey and the Zenon dynasty had been removed.) The cities that had suffered destruction at Jewish hands were ordered to be re-established, a most pointed gesture. A year later Aretas of the Nabataeans, threatened once more by a Roman invasion, commanded by Scaurus, handed over tribute and this was accepted; the invasion was cancelled and the parts of Judaea he had been awarded by Pompey were now no doubt delivered,[16] though this may, in fact, have been only a confirmation of the cession of the lands passed to him by Hyrkanos. This brought the last of the Syrian states into a formal and subordinate relationship with Rome.

Josephus blamed the brothers for the destruction of the kingdom,[17] and, of course, he was in a way correct. But they were only bickering over the crown. The kingdom itself was far too heterogeneous and fragile to survive a serious attack. It was only within the last decade and a half that it had swelled to the size it was in 63, and the last annexations were Greek cities, by no means integrated with the older, basic, kingdom. Pompey was the first invader to make both a successful attack and then to follow through with a detailed political settlement – or perhaps amputation. It might have happened with any of several similar external interventions in the past – Demetrius III, Antiochos XII, Aretas – all of whom had been called in by a Jewish faction as part of the ongoing internal dispute, just as had the Romans, in the end. Yet the Jews, though they had lost their little empire, had retained the basis of their kingdom, and their religion, and their legitimate and hereditary high priest. They still, however, hankered after the freedom to attack those neighbours once more.

Chapter 18

The Second Roman War

The process of slow defeat during the conflicts of 67 to 63 and the treatment meted out to Judaea in Pompey's settlement was costly, unpleasant, and very damaging, but the Jews did not see it as the last word. They had an ideology of independence, empire, and distinctiveness, centred on their religion, and this prevented them from accepting the finality of Pompey's settlement. For the next two centuries they held to that ideology until the Jewish community in Judaea (and in other areas) was destroyed. For the Hasmonaeans, however, who had originated, and then benefited most from, that set of beliefs, the end was not far off.

Aristoboulos and his family were taken off to Rome by Pompey,[1] a sensible move that left Hyrkanos without a rival, and Antipater was able to govern through him. The Roman governors of Syria were also close by and very willing to intervene and supervise. The Syrian province included the cities of the Decapolis on the eastern borders of Judaea and Galilee, and the cities of the Mediterranean coast from Ptolemais to Gaza, as well as north Syria, together with the several kingdoms Pompey had permitted to live on. Several of the cities destroyed in the wars were re-established, a deliberate gesture to emphasize Roman preferences and Judaean defeat. Rebuilding and re-population would clearly take time, but the more they developed and recovered the more obvious the Judaean defeat and isolation would become, and the more constricted the state would be.

The precise political situation in Judaea/Galilee may not have been all that clear to the surviving population after Pompey's decisions. Clearly Aristoboulos had been removed, but Hyrkanos was still in office, so many might console themselves with the view that the kingdom had lost territory but had retained its autonomy and its hereditary high priest. In this view Pompey's intervention was assistance provided to Hyrkanos to return to his rightful position, just as Aretas had intervened to help him earlier. After all both had been paid, and both had supported the man who was high priest by hereditary right. For many, such as the third party at the Damascus meeting, the loss of the kingship was perhaps no loss; they had retained their religious system, and had got rid of the contaminating gentile cities. It could be claimed that Judaea was still independent. In the process, of course, the Saducean supporters of Aristoboulos lost their position of influence, a change that at least one author of a scroll found at Qumran rejoiced in.[2]

So long as Roman authority was not exerted and governors refrained from any intervention, it remained possible to see Pompey's intervention as, in a way, benign. The first three governors were either uninterested or were unable to achieve much. Scaurus, in office after Pompey until 61, was mainly concerned with his Nabataean war, in which he was assisted by Antipater, who organized supplies for the struggling Roman forces. No doubt this was a generally popular move in Judaea, for the Nabataeans had been seen as an enemy for several decades. Antipater exerted himself to bring about an agreement by which Aretas paid 300 talents in tribute. But Aretas died in 62, and it seems that his successor, Obodas II, was less than impressed by the Roman agreement.[3]

Scaurus' successors, L. Marcius Philippus and Cn. Cornelius Lentulus Marcellinus each held office for two years (61–57), and both had trouble with the Nabataeans, which prevented them from paying much heed to Judaea. (They also, of course, had responsibilities in the rest of Syria – one must not get too engrossed in Judaean affairs. Philippus did restore the ruined town of Gabai north of Mount Carmel, which had probably been destroyed by Alexander Iannai.[4] Their restraint may also be because they understood the dangers of stirring up the Jews, but they were also assisted by the continuing internal disputes within Judaea.

Aristoboulos had been taken to Rome along with his sons, Alexander and Antigonos, his two daughters, and his father-in-law Absalom. But Aristoboulos' wife (Absalom's daughter) had been left in Judaea. At some point, perhaps during the journey to Rome, the boy Alexander escaped.[5] (Aristoboulos was featured in Pompey's triumph, but not apparently the other members of the family, though the children of other kings were displayed; Plutarch says Aristoboulos was executed after the triumph,[6] but this is wrong and he turns up again later.)

Josephus says that Alexander's escape happened during the journey to Rome, at the same time as Scaurus' expedition against the Nabataeans, which was in 62. He returned to Palestine and gathered a number of followers, despite the fact that a considerable number of Aristoboulos' supporters had been carried off to Rome by Pompey along with Aristoboulos himself. Alexander's purpose was presumably to reclaim the kingship and high priesthood for his branch of the family (he was Aristoboulos' eldest son and so had a claim himself if Aristoboulos remained a prisoner), but he seems to have made little or no progress for several years. By 58/57, however, he had gathered sufficient support to seize control of Jerusalem.[7]

None of the Roman governors interfered in this fight between Alexander and Hyrkanos, but when Alexander began to rebuild the wall of the city, which had been overthrown by Pompey, Romans in the city stopped him.[8] The presence of these Romans is curious but enlightening. It seems unlikely that there were enough Romans in Jerusalem to fight Alexander's forces, so the halt must have been caused by a threat made by individual Romans. These Romans had clearly not disputed Alexander's capture of the city, nor had there been any Roman assistance for the evicted Hyrkanos.

The governors of Syria were certainly very involved in other problems, including fighting the Nabataeans, but the overthrow of Pompey's Judaean settlement would surely qualify as a major problem fully meriting the involvement of the Roman governor. The Roman concern, therefore, did not extend to the person of the high priest, but was confined to the maintenance of the territorial settlement and to the confinement of Judaea within its new boundaries. The defortification of Jerusalem was part of that settlement. The conclusion must be that the internal independence of Judaea was intended; the governors therefore allowed the internal conflict to continue. Of course, it was also the case that an internal conflict in Judaea meant that the country was not able to cause much trouble outside its borders, for which the governors, with plenty of other problems to concern them, may well have been thankful.

The arrival of A. Gabinius as governor in 57 brought to the east a man familiar with the country. He found that the situation in Judaea had developed rapidly from an internal conflict to one he considered to be a serious threat. Alexander interpreted the Roman interference with his plans for Jerusalem as a Roman threat. He recruited an army, both to enforce his own authority over Hyrkanos (wherever he was), and to defend his conquest against the Roman forces – but a Judaean army of '10,000 hoplites and 1,500 cavalry',[9] the equivalent of two Roman legions, was also a threat to all Judaea's neighbours.

Gabinius had ambitions to invade Parthia,[10] but this would be impossible with a well-armed and hostile Judaea behind him. He collected a variety of forces, including his own legions, a Jewish force commanded by Peitholaos and Malichos – described by Josephus as 'submissive' Jews, by which he must mean supporters of Hyrkanos – Antipater's personal guard, and some Romans who were gathered up and armed by Gabinius' lieutenant Mark Antony. Antony went on ahead, perhaps to test the temper of Alexander's forces, and Gabinius probably came in from the coastal area, though we have no details of their precise movements. Alexander, presumably outnumbered, and wishing to fight in Judaean territory and among a population favourable to him, retired towards Jerusalem before Antony's force. He stood to fight, but when Gabinius brought up his legionary force, was beaten, losing half his army. He retired again with the survivors to the three Hasmonaean fortresses, Hyrkania, Alexandreion, and Machaeros, which he had earlier seized.[11]

The battle near Jerusalem gave Gabinius control of the Judaean hill region, but the three forts had to be taken to deprive Alexander of these bases. (Galilee does not figure in this war; its loyalties are unknown.) Gabinius attacked Alexandreion first, which is where Alexander himself had taken refuge. Much of Alexander's army was camped outside the fort – there was only a relatively small area within the fortifications – and was defeated again. The fort itself held out, and the garrison was reinforced by some of the fugitives and survivors.[12]

Gabinius left Alexandreion under siege and toured the surrounding lands, where he organized the restoration of ruined cities and strengthened the walls of existing ones. Josephus gives us two overlapping lists of these restored cities. Most of them were in the coastlands – Apollonia, Ashdod, Gaza, Anthedon, Raphia, and Iamnia; two were in the land between Judaea and Galilee, Samaria and Skythopolis. But two were the main cities of Idumaea, Marisa and Adora, which suggests that this area had remained under Hyrkanos' control, or perhaps Antipater's.[13] These cities had not all been physically destroyed during the Judaean wars of conquest, but it is possible that their walls had been breached, and, of course, 'restoration' of a city could also mean its reconstitution as an independent city. These places were strengthened, so Judaea was now ringed by a string of well-fortified cities. Having once been subjected to Jewish rule, they could be expected to be especially hostile to the revival of Jewish military power. Gabinius, more definitely than Pompey, was undoing all the work of Hasmonaean conquerors back to the time of John Hyrkanos.

When Gabinius returned to the Alexandreion, the siege was continuing. Josephus says that Gabinius pressed the siege 'strongly', and Alexander now decided that he was beaten. He tried to bargain, hoping to keep the Alexandreion fort, but give up Hyrkania and Machaeros, though Gabinius would not agree. Alexander's mother intervened, and arranged that Alexander would surrender if Gabinius arranged the return of her husband and other children from Rome. Gabinius agreed; Alexander surrendered, and the three fortresses were then demolished.[14]

Geopolitically the result of this campaign was that Judaea was de-fortified while the lands around had their fortifications strengthened. Further, Gabinius now weakened Judaea still more. Hyrkanos returned to Jerusalem as high priest, but his authority was clearly weakened by recent events. Gabinius now further reduced it by introducing a new scheme. The Jewish lands were subdivided into five smaller sections, each with its own priestly council (*sanhedrin*). This might provide a useful alternative to Hyrkanos' feeble rule, giving the men of these *sanhedrin*s a personal and political stake in the new settlement.[15] Hyrkanos was deprived of much of what authority he retained. Since Antipater's authority derived from Hyrkanos', the effect was to marginalize him as well. Religious and secular authority were thus separated, unless Hyrkanos could influence the political *sanhedrin*s. This was a promising scheme, but it did not have a chance to work.

Before the return of Aristoboulos from Rome could be arranged – the Senate would need to approve, and Gabinius would want to see that Alexander behaved himself first – Aristoboulos escaped, along with his other son Antigonos. They returned to Palestine.[16] At least that is how Josephus puts it. Possibly Gabinius arranged their release, but it is more likely that it was news of Alexander's early successes that galvanized Aristoboulos into escaping.

Aristoboulos' re-appearance in Judaea revived the war that Gabinius had hoped was finished. He attracted a considerable crowd of supporters, including Peitholaos, who had fought against Alexander, and who now deserted Hyrkanos with a thousand men. This may indicate a division between Aristoboulos and Alexander. Peitholaos clearly disapproved of Alexander's campaign, and possibly his intentions, while he quickly accepted Aristoboulos. The quick response of many Jews to Aristoboulos' return also suggests that he was more acceptable than his son. (Alexander cannot therefore have been campaigning on his father's behalf, or with his blessing.)

The de-fortification of Judaea prevented Aristoboulos from making much progress. He tried to retake Alexandreion, which was perhaps the least damaged of the fortresses Gabinius had pulled down, but quickly decided it was indefensible. He selected an army of 8,000 men from among his followers – many of those who had joined him were unarmed, perhaps the result of another of Gabinius' measures, though it could also be that the arms were held under strict guard, possibly in Jerusalem. He retired across the river to Machaeros, but his army was caught on the way by a Roman force and defeated with heavy losses. Aristoboulos and a small surviving force reached Machaeros, but taking refuge in yet another dismantled fortress was a hopeless gesture. After a siege of just two days he gave in, and was shipped back to Rome.[17]

Aristoboulos was kept at Rome, though his children were allowed to return to Palestine, in accordance with Gabinius' agreement and with the Senate's permission. It seems that Antigonos was sent back to Rome with his father, but Alexander was clearly still in Palestine, rather surprisingly; their mother and sisters were later living in Ashkelon, which was always an independent city free of Judaean control.[18] It may be that they (and perhaps Alexander) remained there as part of the agreement for the girls' release. It was, as Alexander and Aristoboulos had shown, too dangerous for members of this branch of the Hasmonaean family to live in Judaea.

Gabinius, at last free of the Judaean problem, turned to attack Parthia, his main objective. But then trouble developed in Egypt and he was ordered by Pompey to go there to restore Ptolemy XII Auletes to power. This was not an expedition authorized by the Senate, but Ptolemy was a generous man who was accustomed to spread plenty of Egyptian wealth through the upper ranks of Roman society; it was clearly payback time, and an upheaval in Egypt was even less to be tolerated than one in Judaea. Gabinius had a contingent of Jewish soldiers to accompany his legions into Egypt, commanded by Antipater. Antipater also provided decisive assistance when he persuaded the partly-Jewish garrison at Pelusion to let Gabinius through. Supplies of food, cash, and arms were also provided on Hyrkanos' instructions. No doubt both men were keen to demonstrate their usefulness to Gabinius, and Antipater in particular will have wished to regain credit lost as a result of Gabinius' reorganization of Judaea.[19] Yet the absence of the Roman and the Jewish garrisons, of Gabinius' army, and of Antipater's forces, left Judaea open for the return of Alexander.

Gabinius and Antipater were away in Egypt for some time, but this was long enough for the new insurrection to affect a large part of Judaea. A new dimension to the fighting was that the insurgents deliberately sought out and killed Romans; also the fighting spread into the non-Judaean area between Judaea and Galilee, the areas of Samaria and Skythopolis. The surviving Romans took refuge on Mount Gerizim beside Shechem, where they were besieged. On his return form Egypt Antipater persuaded as many as possible of the insurgents to go home; no doubt his persuasiveness was much reinforced by the approach of Gabinius' legionaries. The hard core of rebels, however, could not be persuaded. They retreated northwards. Gabinius caught up with them at Mount Tabor, sixty kilometres north of Shechem. This campaign was thus very wide-ranging, and took place largely outside Judaea/Galilee. Alexander also had a considerably greater army at his command than his or his father's risings. Josephus claims that 30,000 men were following him, whereas he did not claim any more than a third of that for earlier Jewish forces. The usual problem resulted, however, for they were faced with tough Roman legionaries. Supposedly 10,000 of the Jewish insurgents died in the battle.[20]

The rebellion convinced Gabinius that more changes were needed in the Judaean governing scheme. The *sanhedrin*s disappeared, and Antipater returned to the centre of affairs. The usefulness he had displayed at Pelusion and in the suppression of this latest rising, and the supineness of Hyrkanos in the face of all the activity by the rival family, seems to have convinced Gabinius to adopt Antipater's ideas. As Josephus reports, 'Gabinius then proceeded to Jerusalem, where he reorganized the government in accordance with Antipater's wishes'.[21] We can be quite certain that such a reorganization resulted in Antipater being at the centre of affairs and having a clearly established position of power.

Alexander had not died in the fighting, unlike so many of his men. Despite his repeated rebellions, neither was he executed, nor even dispatched to join his father in Roman exile. The reason must be his mother, and in this case Hyrkanos as well. By this time Alexander was married to Hyrkanos' daughter Alexandra. Their eldest daughter Mariamme was born in 55 or 54, which puts the marriage perhaps as early as 56. It gave Hyrkanos a strong incentive to intervene on Alexander's behalf. This time, however, Alexander's defeat was definitive, and he was persuaded to stay quiet for the next several years.

Gabinius' term of office as governor was extended once, but his Egyptian expedition ensured that it would not be extended again. One of Pompey's partners in the triumvirate that now dominated Roman politics wanted the post. M. Licinius Crassus came out to Syria in the spring of 54 intent on an invasion of Parthia, taking up the task Gabinius had failed to undertake. As part of his preparations he came to Jerusalem and appropriated a large treasure from the temple. (After all the attacks that the temple had undergone in the past few years, it is surprising that there was much left.) Some 8,000 talents, in gold, was taken,[22] so Josephus says, a sum that can perhaps for once be taken as accurate, given the propensity of temple guardians to strict accountancy.

Crassus' invasion of Parthia next year failed, and his quaestor, C. Cassius Longinus, found himself the ranking officer and governor of Syria for the next two years. Crassus' defeat, the loss of a large number of Roman soldiers, and the rising anti-Roman sentiments in Judaea, which Alexander's latest revolt had demonstrated, inevitably produced a Judaean revolt. This time it was led by Peitholaos, the commander who had survived all of the fighting so far, first on Hyrkanos' side, then on Aristoboulos'. But the rebels now faced a Roman commander who was in desperate straits, with a Parthian invasion threatening from beyond the Euphrates. Cassius was not inclined to leniency in any way.

Having repelled one Parthian attack, Cassius marched south, by way of Tyre, and so came towards Judaea by the coast road. The subsequent campaign is wholly unknown in detail but he ended at Tarichaeai on the southern shore of the Sea of Galilee, more or less at the site of the destroyed city of Philoteria. Presumably, he had campaigned through the Vale of Jezreel, the same area that had been fought over in the last rising. In the fighting the Jewish insurgent army was wholly destroyed and 30,000 captives were sold into slavery. Peitholaos was executed, not surprisingly. Before hurriedly returning to the north, Cassius contacted Alexander, who agreed by a solemn treaty that he would keep the peace. Alexander had evidently taken no part in this rebellion, but Cassius equally clearly knew who were the most influential men in the area. Josephus says he was called in to help suppress the rising by Antipater, though this may be Josephus' own agenda in operation, for he was not fond of the Herodian house. With Alexander neutralized, Antipater on his side, and the rebel army dead or enslaved, Cassius was safe from further trouble in the south, at least for the time being.[23]

Bundling together the several risings and campaign as a 'Roman War', is perhaps lending the period between 57 and 54 a spurious military unity. There were four distinct Jewish risings, two led by Alexander, one by his father Aristoboulos, and the fourth by Peitholaos, who was explicitly fighting on behalf of Aristoboulos.[24] Uniting them was the fact that they were all attempts to overthrow the settlement imposed by Pompey, and their increasingly anti-Roman sentiment. The ferocity of the fighting steadily increased, each Jewish defeat leading to great casualties and to a greater effort. It is notable that the reactions of Gabinius were much less brutal than those of Cassius, which might be a matter of temperament. Gabinius in his last battle at Mount Tabor did inflict heavy casualties, but in all cases Gabinius spared the leaders and the commanders. Cassius, whose general situation was a good deal more desperate than that of Gabinius, was much more ferocious. Similarly, the Jewish attitude hardened perceptibly, so that during Alexander's second rising the Romans in the area were explicitly targeted and killed. But then in his first rising they had been recruited as an auxiliary force by Mark Antony: we may say, anachronistically, that they were thus a legitimate military target.

The repeated Jewish risings also developed a pattern by which any Roman setback or distraction – Egypt, Parthia, a defeat anywhere – would be seized on as a signal to attempt a new rising. Gabinius' original intention had been to invade Parthia, but he had to conduct three Judaean campaigns, as well as the Egyptian one that is always blamed for stopping his plan. Cassius' brutality – he had totally destroyed his Jewish enemy by killing or enslaving all of the army – and his insistence that Peitholaos be executed and Alexander be muffled, are reactions to the distraction from the main problem he faced, which was the threat of a new Parthian invasion. Furthermore, his policy worked, at least when it was combined with Gabinius' repeated defeats of earlier risings. It seems likely that the key element, however, was the exile and silencing of the family of Aristoboulos. With those three pretenders out of the way there was less incentive to rebel, and the failure of Alexander to join the fourth rising must have dented his prestige seriously. That is to say, the purpose of the risings had been not just to rid Judaea of the Romans, but it had been aimed at restoring full Judaean independence.

Chapter 19

The Parthian War – and Herod

The marriage of Alexander the son of Aristoboulos II with Alexandra the daughter of Hyrkanos II was presumably intended to reunite the two branches of the Hasmonaean family, and so bring an end to the fighting between them that had gone on since the death of Salome Alexandra. If so, it did not work. Aristoboulos and his second son Antigonos were in exile in Rome, but they had not given up hope of returning to power in Palestine.

The family was inevitably caught up in the Roman civil wars that began in 49. Josephus has a strange tale of their involvement. Since Hyrkanos and Antipater supported Pompey (who put them in power, after all), he claims that Caesar sent Aristoboulos to Syria, supposedly with two legions. There he was murdered by poison by Pompey's partisans. His son Alexander also turned up in Antioch, where he was captured by the governor Q. Caecilius Metellus Scipio and, charged with his 'original offences against Romans', was executed.[1]

Considerable doubt must surround much of this. Where, for a start, did Caesar get two spare legions in 49? How did Aristoboulos get these legions to Syria when Pompey's ships controlled the Mediterranean as far as Italy, indeed to the very harbour mouth of Brundisium? It would need a substantial fleet of ships to move 10,000 men, and these Caesar did not have. And then death by poison is always a suspicious matter. Given the general ignorance of disease in the ancient world, any mysterious death was likely to be labelled as by poison, especially if the accuser was a political enemy of the supposed murderer.

Josephus has probably condensed the sources he was using too drastically. Bits and pieces of the story are accurate: it is the way Josephus puts it all together that is wrong. The normal Roman garrison of Syria was two legions, for instance. One interpretation would be that Caesar intended that Aristoboulos should take command of these legions away from the new governor, Metellus Scipio. But why he would expect him to be able to do so is difficult to understand. Another reference to this matter is in Dio Cassius, where Aristoboulos was sent to Palestine,[2] not Syria, and where there were no legions. This destination, of course, is likely to be an assumption by Dio, since Palestine was where Aristoboulos had performed before, but sending him to Palestine would surely stir up trouble for Scipio in North Syria. Perhaps we may presume that Aristoboulos really went to Syria, and died (or was poisoned – but why do so?) before he could get to Palestine.

I conclude that Aristoboulos had no legions and no chance of getting any, and that his death in Syria was probably by illness. Whether Caesar sent him is also not clear. Caesar himself does not mention it in his *Commentaries* on the civil war, and neither Josephus nor Dio Cassius are all that reliable in this matter. Nonetheless, sending Aristoboulos to Syria, where he was to be joined by Alexander, might have seemed a useful ploy, though the aim would be to stir up trouble in Judaea, not seize command of the Roman legions.

The presence and execution of Alexander is a different matter. He may have gone to Antioch to meet his father, or he may have been taken there under arrest. Josephus says his trial and execution was ordered by Pompey, who may well have been angered by Alexander's past conduct, and fearful (after Aristoboulos' appearance in Syria) that he would break his bond with Cassius (who was on Caesar's side in the war) and begin a new rebellion. It was Alexander's conduct in 55 of seeking out and killing Romans that now rebounded on him, and from Scipio's point of view he was fully justified in trying and executing Alexander.

The result of all this was that Alexander's family, who were living in Ashkelon, were collected by the son of Ptolemy son of Mennaeus and given refuge at Chalkis, Ptolemy's capital. There was a subsequent family crisis over this, for Ptolemy's son proposed to marry one of the girls, but Ptolemy prevented him, had him executed, and then married the girl himself.[3] It is not clear who threatened the family at Ashkelon. Pompey secured Alexander's death, but Antipater and Hyrkanos must also have been uncomfortable at the presence so close to Judaea of the surviving boy Antigonos. They were clearly safer in Chalkis with Ptolemy than in the free city of Ashkelon – safer from their own point of view, and safer from Hyrkanos', for Ptolemy could both protect and control them.

This removed a good deal of pressure from Hyrkanos and Antipater. Both of the dead men had been constant threats to their positions in Judaea and their removal made Hyrkanos and Antipater's positions more secure. They now successfully navigated the difficulties of the Roman civil wars, deftly accommodating themselves to the changes brought by the successive victories of Pompey, Caesar, the Liberators, and then Antony and Octavian. In the process Judaea even gained some territory, for Caesar returned Joppa and the Great Plain of Esdraelon to Hyrkanos' rule.[4] This was by way of thanks to Antipater who brought a Jewish force of 3,000 men to his assistance in the Alexandrian War.[5]

Antigonos, the second son of Aristoboulos II, chose the moment when Caesar was handing out rewards to Hyrkanos to put forward his own claims.[6] Caesar ignored him, but he was no doubt pleased that Hyrkanos and Antipater could see the threat he posed; it would help keep them in line.

Two of the concessions Caesar provided were that Hyrkanos should be entitled ethnarch (a title the Jews simply translated as king) as well as being high priest, and have the right to rebuild the walls of Jerusalem. He also gave Antipater a formal Roman title, possibly procurator, as governor under Hyrkanos (and Roman citizenship as well).[7] Antipater then appointed two of his sons to govern parts of the Judaean kingdom: Phasael was governor of Jerusalem (and presumably of the country round about), and Herod was given charge of Galilee.[8]

This growth in the power of what now had become an Idumaean dynasty troubled many in Judaea, including Hyrkanos himself. Herod put down a bandit called Ezekias who had been troubling Galilee, but he was then accused, by Hyrkanos and others, of killing the bandits without them first having been legally condemned. The internal disputes within Jewish society in Judaea were clearly as common as ever, and just as likely to be lethal to their victims. Herod was sent out of the kingdom to save his life. He gained the support of the governor of Syria, however, and was then appointed to govern Koele Syria, which here meant the Decapolis cities and Samaria, as a subordinate of the governor.[9]

In the same vein a feud developed between Antipater and the Jewish noble called Malichos, who had been a commander of forces against Alexander alongside Peitholaos back in 57. In 42 Malichos was accused of poisoning Antipater, who had died at a feast. Malichos denied it, of course, but Herod organized his death at another feast, at Tyre. The killing was carried out by Roman soldiers sent by the governor, and in front of Hyrkanos, who, not surprisingly, fainted.[10] Such doings were the surface manifestations of continuing internal divisions within Judaea.

The political changes in Rome had as much influence on these matters as the upheavals in Judaea. Herod's various appointments to rule Galilee or the Samaria area came from the governor in Antioch, either directly or through Antipater, and Syria itself was constantly disturbed between 50 and 30. It was also threatened by the Parthians, who had not forgotten the Roman invasions of their empire by Crassus. Syria underwent a series of wars and sieges throughout Caesar's dictatorship (48–44).

Judaea was disturbed in another way. On his appointment as procurator in 47 Antipater spent some time quieting disorders that were basically anti-Roman and anti-Hyrkanos, continuations of the risings that had disturbed the 50s. Antipater's method was persuasive, partly, it is clear, due to his own personality.[11] Herod and Phasael faced rather more violent problems: Herod with the bandit Ezekias; Phasael a popular rising led by Helix, the commander of Hyrkanos' forces. Phasael blamed Hyrkanos.[12] The extent of the violence had pushed the region close to a civil war.

After the defeat of the Liberators in 42, Mark Antony, another Roman who was already familiar with Judaea, took charge in the eastern Roman provinces. Herod persuaded him to grant some favours, including the return of some territory taken by Tyre and the release of Jewish slaves sold by Cassius during his second governorship in 44–42. He also three times denied the request of Herod's enemies to remove the family from power.[13] Then the Parthians invaded Syria.

Mark Antony was in Rome at the time. The Parthian army, commanded by the king's son Pakoros and a commander, Bazarphranes, swiftly conquered North Syria, and there Pakoros was contacted by Antigonos. Ptolemy son of Mennaeas of the Ituraeans died in 40, about the time of the Parthian invasion, and was succeeded by his son Lysanias. He and Antigonos, who had been living at Ptolemy's court since 49, favoured the Parthian invaders and were accepted as Parthian allies.[14] No doubt Lysanias expected an expansion of his kingdom, and Antigonos would expect to be installed in Judaea. To the Parthians it was a good bargain, for the two men would now be indissolubly linked to Parthia and, if in power, would be able to control all the southern and central parts of Syria between them.

Two detachments of the Parthian army marched south. Pakoros moved his force along the coast road, and Bazarphranes his along the interior route, by way of the Bekaa valley. Tyre resisted Pakoros, but Sidon and Ptolemais welcomed him.[15] Barzaphranes made contact with Lysanias. Presumably, one of Lysanias' targets was Damascus, an old Ituraean desire. A Roman soldier called Fabius had been there a year or so before,[16] but we hear nothing of any fighting, or of any Ituraean expansion. Barzaphranes went on to operate among the coastal cities. Presumably, Lysanias had been satisfied – he was later executed by Antony, so his actions were very obviously anti-Roman.

Pakoros sent a Parthian detachment to raid in the Carmel area, where they were welcomed. Pakoros seized the moment and sent a mounted detachment into the Judaean kingdom. A great rising in favour of Antigonos followed, and carried the invaders along. At Jerusalem Herod and Phasael and Hyrkanos, now allied, resisted this popular rising, and fought their opponents; a civil war raged through the city.[17]

The fighting in Jerusalem caused many casualties. Control of the city passed back and forth between Antigonos' and Hyrkanos' partisans. Antigonos arrived and proposed that the commander of the Parthian detachment – another Pakoros, called 'the cupbearer' – be called in as a mediator. This was as cunning a move as anything Herod could have contrived. The connection between Antigonos and the Parthians seems not to have been realized in Judaea. Nevertheless, Herod appreciated that it was a trap, but Hyrkanos and Phasael were more trusting, or perhaps only more hopeful that a truce might help their people recover. They went out to negotiate, eventually meeting Barzaphranes, but when they discovered that the Parthians were really present as allies of Antigonos, Phasael complained at the deception; Barzaphranes had both men arrested.[18]

It is evident that the rule of the Idumaeans Phasael and Herod, in the name of, and at times despite, Hyrkanos, was desperately unpopular. Antipater's sons did not have his emollient ways, and being young, inexperienced, and probably lacking in confidence, were too violent. They were also burdened by Roman support and exploitation. C. Cassius Longinus, in particular, twice intervened in Judaea with great brutality: the first time at Tarichaeai in 52; the second time as governor of Syria in 43 when he impatiently carried off as slaves the people of four townships when his monetary demands were not instantly complied with. When Herod and his family did supply his demands, they were marked as Roman lackeys.[19] Hyrkanos by this time was regarded as their tool. The rising led by Helix and Malichos' brother may well have been Hyrkanos' attempt to rid himself of Phasael and Herod, but its failure put him even more decisively into their hands. So when Antigonos arrived, with the support of a Parthian army that had driven the Romans from the rest of Syria, it is hardly surprising that there was a popular uprising in his favour.

The removal of Hyrkanos and Phasael into Parthian captivity put most of Jerusalem into the hands of the Parthians, despite Herod's resistance. Herod finally decided that he had to get out of Jerusalem, which had become a trap. He took his family and his followers and escaped by night, escorted by his remaining forces. They were in sufficient strength – several thousands – to hold off and defeat the pursuit that followed, and they seized the fortress at Masada. This was a secure refuge, but it hardly helped him to return to power. He dismissed most of his followers, left his family in the fort guarded by 800 soldiers, and fled to Nabataea.[20]

This left Judaea to Antigonos. The Parthians plundered Jerusalem, and then helped to clear Herod's supporters from Idumaea, a task that required the destruction of Marisa – Antipater's Idumaean origins thus came back to haunt his people. Some of the victims will have been Herod's men, no doubt. Bazarphranes handed his prisoners over to Antigonos. He mutilated Hyrkanos, so making him theoretically ineligible to be high priest, and he was sent off to exile in Babylonia. Phasael killed himself to avoid being tortured and killed. Antigonos was installed as king and high priest.[21]

The Parthians got the credit for much of the fighting, but it is clear that they were only the catalyst for the change of regime. Antigonos was welcomed by a large proportion of the Jewish population, though not all – Herod had considerable support. Yet this local support was not a sign of Antigonos' own popularity, for he was unknown to anyone in Judaea. The land had been hard hit (like all the eastern provinces) by the exactions of the competing Roman warlords. Hyrkanos, Antipater, Herod and Phasael had been the Romans' agents in this, and had been all too eager to oblige. The welcome for Antigonos, therefore, was a sign of the unpopularity of Roman domination and of its local agents rather than pleasure at Antigonos' arrival. There were plenty of people who took the side of Herod and Hyrkanos – Herod is said to have been followed in his flight from Jerusalem by 9,000 people. Some of these were certainly Idumaeans, but not all of them, and some must have understood that the Parthian presence might well be only brief and fleeting.

Herod had a clearer idea of where real power lay than Antigonos. He was rebuffed by the Nabataean king, then went to Egypt and on to Rhodes. The situation in Italy was not clear, but from Rhodes Herod corresponded with Antony, who needed local support in Syria against the Parthians. Antony had Herod appointed king of the Jews by a decree of the Senate. This was necessary, for Antigonos was already using that title, and Herod would need to have equal status to combat him effectively. His appointment by the Senate made it clear that he had Roman support beyond the warlord. He went to Italy for his formal appointment at Rome, and then headed back to Palestine to make his kingship good.[22] Whether Antony expected Herod to succeed is not known; for his purposes a disturbance in the Parthians' rear would suffice. Herod's support was pure Roman opportunism.

Herod was not appointed high priest. His ancestry – his mother was Nabataean, his father Idumaean – barred him from the post. For the present no other high priest could be appointed (Antigonos held the post in the city), but with Herod as king, the two positions would clearly have to be formally separated. This, in fact, only laid out in formal terms a situation that had informally existed for almost twenty years. His father Antipater's political ascendancy had effectively made him the secular governor while Hyrkanos was ethnarch and high priest, but with little secular authority. This was the situation that had been attempted by Gabinius some fifteen years and more earlier with his five *sanhedrin*s. But even earlier the dispute between Hyrkanos II and Aristoboulos II in the 60s had tended at times towards Hyrkanos being high priest while Aristoboulos took over as war leader.

Herod may have had the title of king, courtesy of Rome, but Antigonos still had the kingdom, as well as the title. In North Syria the Roman forces commanded by P. Ventidius Bassus drove out the Parthians, and then came south into Judaea, though no attempt was made to remove Antigonos; instead, Ventidius collected money from him for his expenses.[23] Removing Antigonos would require a siege of Jerusalem at the very least, and Ventidius knew that the Parthians would return to invade Syria again, especially if he was tied down to a siege hundreds of kilometres to the south. It was the same dilemma that had faced C. Cassius Longinus nearly fifteen years before: the Parthians were the main danger; the Judaean crisis had to be put off until later. So Ventidius left a force under Poppaedius Silo to mark Roman interest and returned to the north. What strength Silo had is not known, but from later events it seems it was not great. Part of Antigonos' forces, meanwhile, were besieging Masada, but making no progress.[24]

Herod had landed at Ptolemais, which had returned to Roman control, in the spring or early summer of 39. He set about recruiting an army, the usual mixture of Jews and foreign mercenaries, though this took time, during which Ventidius came and went. Herod began active operations with a raid into Galilee, where he found some support. He then marched south, aiming to relieve the siege of Masada. On the way he captured Joppa, so as not to have a hostile force behind him on his march, and to cut the main kingdom off from the sea. It also gave him a base within the Judaean state, independent of Roman territory. He was not opposed on the march except by a force of Antigonos' troops, which was chasing Silo from Jerusalem, and which Herod's army defeated. Silo's conduct in all this was clearly aimed at avoiding all fighting.[25] Josephus claims that Silo had been bribed not to fight, but it is more likely he simply did not have a large enough army to achieve anything, except to maintain a Roman presence.

Herod's route to Masada lay through the coastal lowlands and Idumaea, much as had that of Lysias over a century before. Antigonos' forces laid ambushes for him, so the march was slow and careful, with a good deal of fighting. He was welcomed in Idumaea – the Parthian sack of Marisa had that effect. Also, he was a local boy made good and it was to this area he had sent his surplus followers from Masada. Masada itself was easily relieved and his family rescued, but he had seen that, apart from in Idumaea, he had little support among much of the Jewish population.[26]

The key to everything was Jerusalem. The lesson of the past century of warfare was that whoever held Jerusalem controlled Judaea. Herod brought his army up to the city, together with Silo's force. The Romans complained of a lack of supplies, but when Herod organized food convoys, Antigonos was able to get them ambushed and intercepted, choosing the points where the convoys reached the plateau after the steep climb up from the lowlands. Herod pulled his forces away from the city, defeated by logistics.[27]

Herod resorted to Pompey's method, which was also that of most other soldiers who conquered Judaea. He seized control of Jericho, sent a detachment under his brother Joseph to secure Idumaea, and put his family into Samaria with a strong garrison. Controlling these places and Joppa, he held all the approaches to Judaea. He took a part of his force into Galilee, and secured control of Sepphoris, the main urban centre of the region. Then he attacked the 'bandits' who were based in the caves of Arbela overlooking the Sea of Galilee, defeated them and drove the survivors out. This secured Galilee for him for a time. He gave his brother Pheroras the job of refortifying Alexandreion.[28]

Judaea was now encircled by Herod's forces. The problem of the cave-dwelling 'bandits' recurred – the term is typically one used to describe guerrilla-type opponents – and Herod had to spend the rest of the winter of 39/38 smoking them out. None of them surrendered – they were clearly not merely 'bandits'.[29] By the spring of 38 he had isolated Antigonos' base and eliminated the parties that had been harassing and distracting his own forces. But all this was labour- (or rather soldier-) intensive in the sense that, given the basic unpopularity of Herod and his family, occupying all this territory used up most of his army. Joseph needed 2,000 infantry and 400 cavalry to control Idumaea, and that was friendly territory. By the time he occupied the coastal areas, the Jordan Valley, Galilee, and Samaria, as well as Idumaea, Herod was short of troops for his field army. He needed more manpower and only the Romans could supply it. He also needed siege expertise, and again only the Romans could provide this.

Herod went off to assist Antony in the siege of Samosata in the north, leaving Joseph in charge in Judaea. But Joseph was defeated and killed by a detachment of Antigonos' forces, and all Galilee reverted to Antigonos' control. Joseph had been commanding a unit of five 'cohorts' – a few hundred men.[30] Mark Antony, however, finally free of trouble in the north, sent the new governor of Syria, Q. Sosius, with a substantial force to finish off the fighting in the south. Like Gabinius and Crassus and Cassius, he was aiming to invade Parthia and required a quiet Palestine behind him. Herod followed and took part of the Roman forces directly into Galilee. He was held up by the defence of a strong position (not named by Josephus), but the arrival of a second legion caused the opposition to collapse.[31] Galilee was thus conquered for the third time.

Judaea, however, on the plateau, proved more difficult to reach. Herod and Sosius had the same problem as all the other Judaean enemies who controlled the lowlands and tried to reach the plateau: there were few routes, all easily blocked. One attempt was repelled, but then Antigonos sent an army north towards Samaria under a commander called Pappas, who had commanded the force by which Joseph was killed. Both sides were now using terror methods, burning villages and towns and massacring their opponents.[32] But Pappas and his army stood to fight, and were beaten. Antigonos' army was then trapped in the streets of the village of Isana and suffered heavy casualties.[33] The way up to the plateau was opened, and Herod was able, in the spring of 37, to advance again to attack Jerusalem. Yet another siege of the city began.

Herod's army was joined by that of Sosius. Josephus gives a rather confusing set of figures for the besieging army – eleven units and 6,000 cavalry for Sosius' force, or 30,000 men in another place. Neither of these can be in easily fitted to the problem. 'Eleven units' cannot mean eleven legions, but neither can it mean cohorts, for Josephus would have said so. Sosius' force, in fact, consisted of several forces: a number of legions, cavalry, and Syrian auxiliaries. This last group was made up of men recruited from the cities under Roman control in north and central Syria, but there is no indication of how many there were. Nor is there any direct clue as to the size of Herod's own army. The best calculation is that between them Herod and Sosius brought between 30,000 and 50,000 men to the siege, and of these less than half were Herod's – though the organization of supplies fell to him, and many more of his men were employed as occupation forces in other areas of Palestine. The siege, as Sosius claimed at his triumph, was mainly a Roman fight,[34] but it was given necessary support by Herod's forces.

The assault on the city had to be made from the same direction as Pompey's attack (and that of Herod himself earlier). The re-fortification authorized by Caesar had left the city well defended, an ironic tribute to the work of Hyrkanos and Antipater. Herod was now joined by plenty of Jewish volunteers, for he was at last seen to be winning; the arrival of Sosius and his army must also have been persuasive to those sitting on the fence, showing determined Roman commitment to Herod. Antigonos had made good preparations and had collected plenty of provisions from the nearby land – which were thereby not available to the besiegers, so it took time before the city was properly isolated, and strictly besieged.

Once the city was sealed off by a surrounding wall and ditch and a firm grip had been established on the country districts, it was only a matter of time before the attackers broke in. The attack was directed at the city wall rather the temple. The two successive walls were breached, giving Herod and the Romans access to the city. If it was hoped to avoid an attack on the temple area itself this failed, for, as they had to, Antigonos' men took refuge in that well-fortified area. Herod held off an assault for a time, hoping for a surrender to avoid polluting the temple, and even allowed in animals for the sacrifices, but this had no softening effect on Antigonos' people. An assault was made. Once the attackers were within the temple precinct the defenders were massacred, though Herod did manage to prevent any looting of the temple itself. As usual the inanimate offerings were preserved, but the humans were killed, and this was counted a success and a mercy. Antigonos survived, to be captured by giving himself up to Sosius,[35] who handed him over to Antony, who had him executed, reportedly at Herod's urging, though that was hardly necessary.[36]

The Hasmonaean family was not yet quite finished. Herod had married Mariamme, daughter of Alexander, just before the siege of Jerusalem began, and there were other children, including Aristoboulos, a younger brother of Mariamme, whom Herod made high priest briefly in the next year, and the daughter of Antigonos who was later married to Herod's son Antipater. These people were moved into Herod's family in order to deny them any independent life. Herod was determined not to allow any claims to the kingship by members of the house he had replaced.

Chapter 20

Conclusion: a Belligerent Dynasty

The Maccabees, or Hasmonaeans, began as the leaders of a terrorist group, venting their religious righteousness on their own people, until they were defeated and their land of Judaea occupied militarily by their rulers. Judah, revered as a freedom fighter though he may be, was essentially a failure, and his methods caused much misery among his people. They also provided a precedent that was all too readily followed by his successors, and was too quickly taken as a pattern for others to follow.

The more devious Jonathan and Simon, Judah's brothers and successors, were able to use Judah's reputation, which was enhanced by distorted propaganda that converted his defeats into victories and hid the essential brutality of his policies. There developed a new state, Judaea, under Jonathan's rule, but Judah's inheritance made it necessary for him and his successors to be warriors. They had to legitimize their accession by military victory. For fifty years they built fear and enmity among their neighbours by such obnoxious practices as the destruction of cities, massacres, and – a peculiar twist all their own – forced conversion to Judaism.

As in most dynasties, the succession of a new ruler was a time of instability and every succession amongst the Maccabees was a crisis. The accessions of Simon, of Hyrkanos I, and of Alexander Iannai, all of whom faced opposition, indicate the particular difficulty for a dynasty that was founded originally on insurrection. Further, the fact that it was a religiously based dynasty left it open to challenge at its most vulnerable point. Early wars were thus often directed at religious dissidents or competitors, and when Alexander Iannai adopted a conquest policy that was not based on the expansion of Judaism, but simply on expanding his kingdom, he was more successful but was opposed by his internal critics, to the extent of civil war.

The contradictions within the Judaean polity were such that it was bound to fail sooner or later. Those contradictions were present from the very beginning, in the conflict between Maccabees and hellenizers, and they re-emerged regularly in other guises. It did not help that the only political model for a new kingdom at the time was Hellenistic monarchies, all essentially with a military basis. It was thus necessary to use Hellenic methods to produce a viable state that was theoretically anti-Greek. The end result was first the dismemberment of the kingdom by Pompey, and then the forcible conquest of Judah by Herod using Roman force. The period between the death of Salome Alexander and Herod's conquest (67–37) was essentially one of almost continuous civil war. The only way of stopping that was by a brutal conquest, which convinced the bickering parties that they would be beaten. Herod therefore ruled, in effect, as a military dictator, employing terror methods against those who opposed him. Ironically, more than any other Judaean ruler, he was captivated by Hellenic culture, so he used Maccabean terrorism against the internal heirs of the Maccabees, both family members and the rigorous Jews, while at the same time building new Greek cities, and paying generous sums to develop other Greek cities.

Herod's rule was personal and it ended as soon as he died in 4 BC. For the next two generations the Romans wrestled with a variety of attempts to rule Judaea, until the explosion of 66–73 showed the impossibility of any success. Judaea's internal conflict again resulted in a brutal and destructive conquest. Even after that disaster, Jewish religious exclusivity brought about other explosions in 115–117 and 132–135. The only way to control Judaea was to destroy the Jewish community. This is the final lesson of the career of Judah Maccabee, whose methods were used eventually by the Romans against his people to destroy them.

Notes

Introduction
1. Schürer 1.158, n. 49.
2. See Eshel on this.

Chapter 1
1. Hengel 1.24–25, referring to the Ptolemaic period.
2. Livy 35.13.4.
3. Jos. *AJ* 12.132–146.
4. See the brief accounts of the towns and cities in Schürer 2.85–178, and the previous section on 'The Spread of Hellenism', 29–80. The issue is discussed in every general book on the Hellenistic period.
5. II Mac. 4.2.
6. II Mac. 4.7–10; Daniel 9.26 and 11.22.
7. E. J. Bickerman, *The God of the Maccabees*, tr. H.R. Mohring, Leiden 1979, 38–42.
8. E.S. Gruen, *Heritage of Hellenism*, California 1998, 3–7, argues that the term does not appear in the sources, but it is convenient nonetheless.
9. II Mac. 4.23–25.
10. II Mac. 4.33.
11. II Mac. 4.26.
12. Hengel 1.267–277; Menelaos himself is discussed by H. H. Rowley, 'Menelaos and the Abomination of Desolation', *Studia Orientalem J. Pedersen*, Copenhagen 1955, 303–315.
13. II Mac. 4.30–34.
14. II Mac. 4.39.
15. II Mac. 4.40–42.
16. II Mac. 5.4–5.
17. For this war see Grainger, *Syrian Wars*, ch. 13.
18. II Mac. 4.21–22.
19. I Mac. 1.20–28; Jos *AJ* 12.246.
20. I Mac. 1.20–24; II Mac. 5.11–16; for the sequence of events cf Eshel 14–17.
21. Hengel 275, 276.
22. II Mac. 5.7–10.
23. II Mac. 5.22.
24. Polybius 9.27.5; Grainger, *Syrian Wars*, 306–308.
25. I Mac. 1.29; II Mac. 5.24.
26. I Mac. 1.30–36; the location of this fortress is not certain; the suggestions are summarized by L.I. Levine, *Jerusalem, Portrait of the City in the Second Temple Period*, 95–98.
27. I Mac. 1.29–30.
28. I Mac. 1.42–50; II Mac. 6.1–2.
29. Discussed by Rowley (note 12).

Chapter 2
1. I Mac. 1.51.
2. I Mac. 1.52.
3. I Mac. 1.42.
4. II Mac. 5.27.
5. I Mac. 1.54.
6. I Mac. 2.15–25.
7. I Mac. 2.27–28.
8. I Mac. 2.29–38.
9. I Mac. 2.39–41; Bar-Kochva, *Judas*, 481–484.
10. II Mac. 2.6, 10–11, 18–31, 7.1–42; these stories are described as 'wonderful' in Schürer 1.155; in fact, they are deeply unpleasant, and related with the most unseemly relish.
11. I Mac. 2.42; the Hasidim have drawn considerable interest, though given that there are only three references to them, most of the work on this is speculative: cf P. Davies, 'Hasidim in the Maccabean Period', *JJS* 28, 1977, 127–140.
12. I Mac. 2.44.
13. II Mac. 8.6.
14. I Mac. 3.10.
15. Shatzman, *Armies*, ch 1, discusses the weapons and composition of the Jewish army, but assumes it faced a 'Hellenistic army', and suffered from a determination to establish a wide contrast between the two armies. There is, as always, considerable disagreement over all this, personified by Shatzman and Bar-Kochva, *Judas* .
16. I Mac. 3.11; Jos. *AJ* 12.287 adds nothing. Modern accounts include Avi-Yonah in A. Schalit (ed.), *The World History of the Jewish People*, vol 6, *The Hellenistic Age*, London 1976, 153–155; the best consideration of the battle is Bar-Kochva, *Judas*, 199–206 cf also cf. Plöger, 159–162.
17. Avi-Yonah (previous note), 155.
18. I Mac. 3.13; Jos. *AJ* 12.288.
19. I Mac. 3.25; Jos. *AJ* 12.289; an alternative translation would be 'renegades', but 'sinners' best indicates the general approach of the author of I Maccabees .
20. I Mac. 3.15.
21. II Mac. 8.1 and 16.
22. I Mac. 3.13–24; Jos. *AJ* 12. 289 – 292; Avi-Yonah (note 14) 155–157; Bar-Kochva, *Judas*, 207–218 (the best discussion); Polger 162–163.

Chapter 3
1. Polybios 30.27.1–4.
2. I Mac. 3.32–35; Jos. AJ 12.295–297.
3. O. Morkholm, *Antiochos IV of Syria*, Copenhagen 1966, ch. IX.
4. I Mac. 3.46, 55.
5. II Mac. 8.1.
6. I Mac. 3.31–37.
7. For the best examination of the Seleikid army cf. B. Bar-Kochva, *The Seleukid Army*, Cambridge 1977.
8. I Mac. 3.28.
9. I Mac. 3.39–41.
10. I Mac. 3.56.
11. I Mac. 3.47–54.
12. I Mac. 4.1–2.
13. I Mac. 4.3 – 4; Jos. *AJ* 12.300 puts Judah's up at Ammaus; cf. Plöger 163–166.
14. I Mac. 4.5–7; Jos. *AJ* 12.305– 06.
15. I Mac. 4.12–14.

16. I Mac. 4.4–16.
17. I Mac. 4.7–22; Jos. *AJ* 12.310–311.
18. I Mac. 4.23; for the battle see Avi-Yonah, 158–162; Bar-Kochva, *Judas*, 219–274.
19. II Mac. 10.12–13; T.R. Mitford, 'Ptolemy Macron', *Studi in onore de A. Calderini e M. Paribeni*, Milan 1957, 163–187; Bar-Kochva, *Judas*, 534–538.
20. Mitford (previous note).
21. II Mac. 11.16–21.
22. II Mac. 11.34–38.
23. II Mac. 10.12–13.
24. II Mac. 11.27–33; on the order in which these letters are to be understood see the discussion in Bar-Kockva, *Judas*, 516–533.
25. I Mac. 4.28; II Mac. 11.2–4 gives him 80,000 foot and 'thousands' of cavalry, plus eighty elephants, a larger force than any Seleukid king ever fielded.
26. I Mac. 4.29; cf. Plöger 166–169.
27. I Mac. 4.34; II Mac. 11.11; Jos. *AJ* 12.314.
28. I Mac. 4.35.
29. Bar-Kochva, *Judas*, 279–281, 289–290; Avi-Yonah ignores the political context and insists that the fight at Beth Zur was significant in persuading Lysias to negotiate (163).
30. I Mac. 4.35.
31. II Mac. 9.

Chapter 4
1. I Mac. 3.24, 41, 4.22, for example.
2. I Mac. 3.13.
3. I Mac. 4.1.
4. I Mac. 4.9.
5. I Mac. 4.30–31.
6. I Mac. 4.60.
7. I Mac. 4.61.
8. Judges 20.1.
9. I Mac. 5.10–13.
10. I Mac. 5.14–15.
11. II Mac. 10.15; they were refugees from Jerusalem, expelled by the Maccabees themselves.
12. I Mac. 5.3.
13. I Mac. 5.4–5.
14. II Mac. 10.14–15.
15. II Mac. 10.16–23.
16. II Mac. 12.2.
17. II Mac. 10.24; on the chronology of these campaigns see Bar-Kochva, *Judas*, 508–515.
18. Confusion exists over Jazera, which is at times confused with Gezer in Palestine, but the story locates it firmly to the east of the river.
19. I Mac. 5.6–8; II Mac. 10.27 – 37; Jos. *AJ* 12.319.
20. Jos. *AJ* 12.229–236.
21. For Iraq el-Amir see Arav, 106 – 110; at least one 'Tobiad', Dositheos – note the Greek name – joined the Maccabees, commanding a unit in Idumaea (II Mac. 12.35).
22. I Mac. 5.9 – 17.
23. J. Sievers, *The Hasmonaeans and their Supporters*, Athens GA, 1990, 49–57.
24. F.M. Abel, 'Topographie des campaignes Machabèennes', *Revue Biblique* 32, 1923, at 512–521. These identifications are not always convincing, nor wholly accepted.
25. I Mac. 5.24 – 51; II Mac. 12.10–28; Jos. *AJ* 12.335–347.
26. I Mac. 5.21 – 23.
27. I Mac. 5.18–19, 56–62.

170 The Wars of the Maccabees

28. I Mac. 5.65–68; II Mac. 12.32–37; Jos. *AJ* 12.350–353.
29. *New EAEHL*, 2.609.
30. Ibid. 3.48 – 957.
31. II Mac. 12.3–9.

Chapter 5
1. Bar-Kochva, *Judas*, 343; the number is not known, but that men returned suggests that Philippos' claim to the regency was not articulated for some time after Antiochos IV's death.
2. II Mac. 10.11–13.
3. J.D. Grainger, *The Cities of Seleukid Syria*, Oxford 1990.
4. I Mac. 6.18.
5. I Mac. 6.20.
6. I Mac. 6.21; II Mac. 13.3.
7. I Mac. 6.28–31.
8. I Mac. 6.30; Jos. *AJ* 12.366; Jos. *BJ* 1.41; II Mac. 13.2; clearly nobody knew the correct number.
9. Bar-Kochva, *Judas*, 307.
10. I Mac. 6.49–50 (misplaced); Jos. *BJ* 1.41; II Mac. 13.22; new fortifications at the site have been assigned to this period, though the argument is circular, depending on the written sources for the history; see the comments by Shatzman, *Armies*.
11. II Mac. 13.21.
12. I Mac. 6.35 – 38; Bar-Kochva, *Judas*, 312–325.
13. I Mac. 6.42; Jos. *AJ* 12.372.
14. I Mac. 6.43 – 46.
15. I Mac. 6.47; Jos. *BJ* 1.45 – both euphemistically; II Mac. 13.22 claims a Maccabean victory; Plöger 169–176.
16. Jos. *BJ* 1.45.
17. I Mac. 6.48, 51–54.
18. I Mac. 6.55–59.
19. II Mac. 11.3–15, 22–28; Judah is said to have agreed to this.
20. I Mac. 6.60–62; Jos. *AJ* 12.382.
21. I Mac. 6.63; Jos. *AJ* 12.383.
22. II Mac. 11.34–38.
23. G.S. Gruen, *The Hellenistic World and the Coming of Rome*, California 1984, 745–747, with a brief bibliography.
24. As is concluded by O. Morkholm, *Antiochos IV of Syria*, 162–165.
25. II Mac. 13.5– ; Jos. *AJ* 12.384–385.
26. I Mac. 7.6; II Mac. 14.3; Jos. *AJ* 12.387.
27. Jos. *AJ* 12.387–388.
28. I Mac. 7.12–14.
29. Diodoros 31.27a; App., *Syrian Wars* 47.
30. I Mac. 7.5–7.
31. I Mac. 7.5.
32. I Mac. 7.8 – 11; Bakchides had been mentioned as a colleague of Timotheos in Ammanitis (II Mac. 8.30); this may or may not be correct.
33. I Mac. 7.16.
34. I Mac. 7.17–18; II Mac. 14.6.
35. I Mac. 7.19–20.
36. I Mac. 7.21–25.
37. I Mac. 7.26; II Mac. 14.12.
38. II Mac. 15.3; Jos. *AJ* 12.402; (Polybios 31.14.4).
39. I Mac. 7.26–28; II Mac. 14.12–13.

40. II Mac. 14.15–17.
41. I Mac. 7.31–32.
42. II Mac. 14.19.
43. II Mac. 14.19–25.
44. I Mac. 7.27–30.
45. II Mac. 14.26–30.
46. I Mac. 7.33–35; II Mac. 14.31–34; Bar-Kochva, *Judas*, 347–358.
47. II Mac. 15.1.
48. I Mac. 7.31–32.
49. I Mac. 7.27 ('a large army'), 32; Plöger 176–177.
50. I Mac. 7.39–50; II Mac. 15.20–37; Jos. *AJ* 12. 408–412; Bar-Kochva, *Judas*, 359–373; Ploger 177–178.
51. Jos. *AJ* 12.415–419; I Mac. 8.17–32; W. Wirgin, 'Judah Maccabee's Embassy to Rome and the Jewish-Roman Treaty', *PEQ* 101, 1969, 15– 20; Th. Liebemann-Frankfort, 'Rome et le Conflit Judéo-Syrien (164–161 avant notre ère)', *Antiquité Classique* 38, 969, 101–120.
52. I Mac. 9.4–6.
53. I Mac. 9.2–4; Bar-Kochva, *Judas*, 382–388.
54. I Mac. 9.11–18; Bar-Kochva, *Judas* 390–399; Plöger 182–185.
55. I Mac. 9.23–26.
56. I Mac. 9.28–35.
57. I Mac. 9.50–53.
58. I Mac. 9.55–57.
59. I Mac. 9.58–72. It has been suggested that a man referred to by his followers as the 'Teacher of Righteousness' acted as high priest without a formal appointment between 159 and 152, when Jonathan was appointed. The evidence is poor and subject to heavy interpretation. Josephus, who should have known, repeated the statement from I Maccabees (*AJ* 13.210–237) and this seems good evidence.
60. I Mac. 9.73.

Chapter 6
1. I Samuel 13–14; I Mac. 9.3; Jos. *AJ* 13.34; cf. G. A. Smith, *The Historical Geography of the Holy Land*, 25th ed., London 1931, 150, 172–173, 198–199.
2. I Mac. 9.73; Jos. *AJ* 13.34.
3. Now argued to be a genuine son of Antiochos, by *Polygamy, Prostitutes and Death*, 143–146.
4. Diod. 31.32a; Appian, *Syrian Wars* 67.
5. Jos. *AJ* 13.35.
6. I Mac. 10.3 – 9; Jos. *AJ* 13.37.
7. I Mac. 10.6–11.
8. I Mac. 10.13.
9. Jos. *AJ* 13.42.
10. L. I. Levine, *Jerusalem, Portrait of the City in the Second Temple Period*.
11. I Mac. 10.11; Jos. *AJ* 13.41–42.
12. I Mac. 10.15–20; Jos. *AJ* 13.44–45.
13. I Mac. 10.25–45; Jos. *AJ* 13.47–57.
14. I Mac. 10.44.
15. Much of this is disputed, though the identification of Jonathan as the 'Wicked Priest' is largely accepted; cf Eshel, ch 2.
16. Justin 35.1.8–9; Jos. *AJ* 13.48–50, 58–61.
17. I Mac. 10.59–60; Jos. *AJ* 13.83–85.
18. Justin 35.2.1.
19. Livy, *Epit* 50.
20. I Mac. 10.67; Jos. *AJ* 13.86.

172   The Wars of the Maccabees

21. I Mac. 10.69; Jos. *AJ* 13.88.
22. I Mac. 10.74–75; Jos. *AJ* 13.91.
23. I Mac. 10.77; Jos. *AJ* 13.92.
24. I Mac. 10.75–77; Jos. *AJ* 13.91–92.
25. I Mac. 10.77–83; Jos. *AJ* 13.92– 8; B. Bar-Kochva, 'Hellenistic Warfare in Jonathan's Campaign near Azotos', *Scripta Classica Israelica*, 2, 1975, 83–96.
26. I Mac. 10.88–89; Jos. *AJ* 13.102.
27. I Mac. 11.1–7; Jos. *AJ* 13.103–105.
28. I Mac. 11.9–12; Jos. *AJ* 13.109–111; for all this cf. Grainger, *Syrian Wars*, 337–350.
29. I Mac. 11.13; Jos. *AJ* 13.113.
30. I Mac. 11.14– 8; Jos. *AJ* 13.116–119.
31. I Mac. 11.19; Jos. *AJ* 13.120.
32. I Mac. 11.20–37; Jos. *AJ* 13.121–128.
33. I Mac. 11.41–53; Jos. *AJ* 13.133–142.
34. I Mac. 11.39–40; Jos. *AJ* 13.131–132.
35. I Mac. 11.57–59; Jos. *AJ* 13.145–146.
36. I Mac. 11.60; Jos. *AJ* 13.148.
37. I Mac. 11.60–62; Jos. *AJ* 13.149–153.
38. Jos. *AJ* 13.153.
39. I Mac. 11.63–64; Jos. *AJ* 13.154.
40. I Mac. 11.64–65; Jos. *AJ* 13.154–156.
41. I Mac. 11.67–74; Jos. *AJ* 13.158–163.
42. I Mac. 11.74, 12.24–25; Jos. *AJ* 13.163, 174.
43. The extant remains date from the first century BC onwards: *New EAEHL*, 2.573–577.
44. I Mac. 12.26–30; Jos. *AJ* 13.174–179.
45. I Mac. 12.31–33; Jos. *AJ* 13.179.
46. I Mac. 11.66; Jos. *AJ* 13.156–157.
47. I Mac. 12.33–34; Jos. *AJ* 13.180.
48. I Mac. 12.1–4; Jos. *AJ* 13.164–165.
49. I Mac. 12.5–23; Jos. *AJ* 13.165–170.
50. I Mac. 12.35–38; Jos. *AJ* 13.181–183.
51. Jos. *AJ* 13.184–186; Justin 36.1.2–6.
52. I Mac. 12.41–47; Jos. *AJ* 13.188–191.
53. I Mac. 12.48; Jos. *AJ* 13.192.
54. I Mac. 12.50–53; Jos. *AJ* 13.192–196.
55. I Mac. 13.1–10; Jos. *AJ* 13.197–200.
56. I Mac. 13.11; Jos. *AJ* 13.202.
57. I Mac. 13.12–19; Jos. *AJ* 13.203–207.
58. I Mac. 13.20; Jos. *AJ* 13.207.
59. I Mac. 13.21–22; Jos. *AJ* 13.208.
60. I Mac. 13.24–24; Jos. *AJ* 13.209.
61. Eshel 44, quoting 1QpHab, a *pesher* on Hebakkuk.
62. I Mac. 13.33–42; Jos. *AJ* 13.213.

Chapter 7
1. I Mac. 13.42.
2. J. Murphy-O'Connor, *The Holy Land, an Oxford Archaeological Guide*, 5th ed., Oxford, 2008; Smith, *Historical Geography*, 153–154.
3. I Mac. 13.43–48.
4. Shatzman, *Armies*, 40–41; Murphy-O'Connor, *Holy Land*, 292; B.-Z. Rosenfeld, 'The 'Boundary of Gezer' Inscriptions and the History of Gezer at the End of the Second Temple Period', *IEJ* 38, 1987, 235–245.

5. Arav, 43.
6. I Mac. 13.49–52; Jos. *AJ* 13.215.
7. I Mac. 13.25–30; Jos. *AJ* 13.210–212.
8. I Mac 14.16–24 and 15.15–24; cf. W. Wirgin, 'Simon Maccabaeus' embassy to Rome – its purpose and outcome', *PEQ* 1974, 141–146, is concerned to elucidate possible economic content in this exchange. It may be noted that this document is the first primary source for Maccabean history so far.
9. I Mac. 14.27–49.
10. I Mac. 15.10–11; Jos. *AJ* 13.222–223.
11. I Mac. 15.1–9.
12. I Mac. 15.25; Jos. *AJ* 13.224.
13. I Mac. 15.31.
14. I Mac. 15.15, 32–35.
15. I Mac. 15.37–38; Jos. *AJ* 13.224.
16. I Mac. 15.39–41.
17. I Mac. 16.1 and 4–5.
18. I Mac. 16.2; Jos. *AJ* 13.226–227.
19. Jos. *AJ* 13.227.
20. I Mac. 16.4 and 10.
21. I Mac. 16.5–10.
22. I Mac. 16.11–16; Jos. *AJ* 13.228.
23. I Mac. 16.18–20.
24. I Mac. 16.21–22; Jos. *AJ* 13.229.
25. Jos. *AJ* 13.230.
26. Jos. *AJ* 13.230–233; for the archaeological reports see Z. Meskel, 'The Siege Systems during the Hasmonaean Period', in Zev Vilmay's Jubilee volume, vol. 1, Jerusalem 1984, 256–258 (in Hebrew); Eshel 74, gives this reference.
27. Jos. *AJ* 13.234.
28. Jos. *AJ* 13.236 for the confused chronology; see the discussion, inevitably inconclusive, in Schürer 1.202, note 5.
29. Jos. *AJ* 13.235.
30. Jos. *AJ* 13.236–241.
31. Jos. *AJ* 13.242243.
32. Diod. 34/35.1.
33. Jos. *AJ* 13.246–247; Diod. 34/35.5; T. Rajak, 'Roman Intervention in a Seleukid siege of Jerusalem?', *GRBS* 22, 1981, 65–81, cannot produce any clear evidence for her proposal.
34. Jos. *AJ* 13.249.
35. Jos. *AJ* 13.249.
36. Jos. *AJ* 13.250–251.
37. Jos. *AJ* 13.254.
38. I Mac. 16.23.

Chapter 8
1. Jos. *AJ* 13.267.
2. Jos. *AJ* 13.254–258.
3. B. Bar-Kochva, 'The Chronology of John Hyrcanos' first Conquests', Excursus 1 in *Judas*, 560–562.
4. *New EAEHL* interprets this as indicating a transition from nomadic to 'semisedentary' occupation (whatever that is), though the dating of the fort would more suggest Seleukid work.
5. G. E. Wright, 'The Samaritans at Shechem', *HTR* 55, 1962, 357–366, and G. E. Wright and R. J. Bull, 'Newly Discovered Temples at Mount Gerizim in Jordan', *HTR* 58, 1965, 234–237.

6. F. M. Cross, 'Aspects of Samaritan and Jewish history in Late Persian and Hellenistic Times', *HTR* 59, 1966, 201–211.
7. Jos. AJ 13.257.
8. Jos. *AJ* 15.255–256.
9. The Samaritans still exist, or did in 1959 when I visited them at Nablus; I bought a pamphlet, by Priest Amran Ishak, *The History and Religion of the Samaritans*, setting out their case.
10. Jos. *BJ* 1.31–33; R. Hayward, 'The Jewish Temple at Leontopolis: a Reconsideration', *JJS* 33. 1982, 429–433.

Chapter 9
1. App. *Syrian Wars.*, 69; Justin 39.2.
2. Jos. *AJ* 13.270.
3. Diod. 24/25.34.
4. Jos. *AJ* 13.273.
5. App. *Syrian Wars.* 68; Justin 39.3; the evidence of the changes of fortune is very largely numismatic: A. R. Bellinger, 'The End of the Seleucids', *Transactions of the Connecticut Academy of Arts and Sciences*, 1949, and now Oliver Hoover, 'A Revised Chronology for the Late Seleucids at Antioch (121/0–64 BC), *Historia* 56, 2007, 280–301. The research continues.
6. Jos. *AJ* 13.327.
7. Jos. *AJ* 13.275.
8. 'Marisa' is universally assumed to be a corrupt name, but 'Samaria' is only one correction; 'Marrous' is another, a place north of Samaria. The consensus is somewhere in the Samaria region, and probably in that city's territory; Shimon Applebaum et al., 'The Towers of Samaria', *PEQ* 10, 1978, 99.
9. Bellinger, 'End'.
10. Cf. Schürer, vol. 1, 210, note 22.
11. Jos. *AJ* 13.276; *BJ* 1.64.
12. J. W. Crowfoot *et al.*, *The Buildings at Samaria*, London 1942; cf. Arav, 88–91.
13. Jos. *AJ* 13.276.
14. Assuming a population density of 200 per hectare, the city's population would be about 4,400, to which must be added an unknown number of refugees driven into the city by the outbreak of war. A population of, say, 8,000 would produce a military-age male population of 2,000 to 3,000. See G.G. Aperghis, *The Seleukid Royal Economy*, Cambridge 2004, 35 –36 for the basis of this calculation.
15. Jos. *BJ* 1.65–66.
16. Jos. *AJ* 13.276 – 279.
17. Jos. *AJ* 13.278.
18. Jos. *AJ*. 13.279 – 280.
19. Jos. *AJ* 13.278.
20. Jos. *AJ* 13.280.
21. Jos. *AJ* 13.281; *BJ* 1.65.
22. Crowfoot *et al.*, and Arav (note 12).
23. Jos. *AJ* 13.277.
24. Jos. *AJ* 13.280.
25. Jos. *BJ* 1.66.

Chapter 10
1. Jos. *AJ* 13.297–298.
2. Jos. *BJ* 1.67.
3. Jos. *AJ* 13.290–295.
4. Jos. *AJ* 13.302.
5. Ibid.

6. Discussed by B. E. Scolnic, *Thy Brother's Blood, the Maccabees and Dynastic Morality in the Hellenistic World*, Latham MD 2008.
7. Jos. *AJ* 13.301.
8. Forty years before, Jonathan had been referred to as king in a bulla (a seal for document): N. Avigad, 'A Bulla for King Jonathan', *IEJ* 25, 1975, 245–247. This may refer alternatively to Alexander Iannai, but it does suggest that the Hasmonaeans were regarded as a royal family from the time of Jonathan's rule. The hereditary succession would also assert that.
9. Jos. *AJ* 13.303–309.
10. Jos. *AJ* 13.302.
11. It has been suggested that the mother was in fact Hyrkanos' second wife, and that Antigonos and Aristoboulos were her stepsons; there is no evidence, but she is always referred to as their mother: J. Wellhausen, *Israelitische und Judäische Geschichte*, Berlin 1895, 264; the notion is not generally accepted.
12. Jos. *AJv* 13.314–318.
13. Jos. *AJ* 13.304; BJ 1.76.
14. Jos. *AJ* 13.318.
15. See also E.A. Myers, *The Ituraeans and the Roman Near East, Reassessing the Sources*, Cambridge 2010, 24–30; in keeping with the sub-title no conclusions are drawn.
16. Jos. *AJ* 13.39; M. Stern, *Greek and Latin Authors on Jews and Judaism*, vol. 1, Jerusalem 1976, s.v. Timagenes.
17. Jos. *BJ* 1.76; in *AJ* he simply says 'with glory' (13.304).
18. Jos. *AJ* 13.337–338.
19. I Mac. 5.6–54.
20. Schürer, vol 3, 181.
21. I Mac. 15.15–24.
22. Jos. *AJ* 13. 319 and 318.
23. S. Freyne, *Galilee from Alexander the Great to Hadrian*, Edinburgh 1998, dismisses this episode in a paragraph (42–43) and ignores the Ituraeans.
24. Jos. *AJ* 13.320; *BJ* 1.85.
25. Jos. *AJ* 13.323.
26. Jos. *AJ* 13.322.
27. Jos. *AJ* 13.324, 328.
28. Jos. *AJ* 13.326.
29. Jos. *AJ* 13.328; G. Hölbl, *A History of the Ptolemaic Empire*, London 2001, 207–208.
30. Jos. *AJ* 13.329.
31. Jos. *AJ* 13.333–334; the war which followed is discussed, and the varied evidence listed, in E. van 't Dack *et al.*, *The Judaean-Syrian-Egyptian conflict of 103–101 B.C., a Multilingual Dossier concerning a 'War of Scepters'*, Brussels 1969. The main discussion there is of Ptolemaic involvement, but here the Judaean viewpoint is paramount. See also Grainger, *Syrian Wars*, ch. 18.
32. Jos. *AJ* 13.335–336.
33. Jos. *AJ* 13.337–338.
34. Jos. *AJ* 3.337; as to these numbers, even Josephus seems doubtful.
35. Jos. *AJ* 13.338–344; the casualties are put at 20,000, or 50,000; which seems to be an attempt to bring the size of the army down to a more reasonable number.
36. Jos. *AJ* 13.347.
37. Jos. *AJ* 345–347.
38. Eshel, chs 4 and 5.
39. Jos. *AJ* 13.348–352 and 358.
40. Jos. *AJ* 13.352.
41. Jos. *AJ* 13.353–355.
42. Jos. *AJ* 13.285, 351.

Chapter 11
1. Jos. *BJ* 1.86.
2. Jos. *AJ* 13.356.
3. Arav, 113–114.
4. L.I. Levine, 'The Hasmonaean Conquest of Strato's Tower', *IEJ* 24, 1974, asserts that Alexander did take the town, but his argument is no more than assertion; no evidence is produced beyond that of Josephus.
5. A.B. Brett, 'The mint of Ascalon under the Seleucids', *ANSMN* 4, 1950, 43–54; A. Spaer, 'Ascalon from Royal mint to Autonomy, in *Festschrift for Leo Mildenburg*, Wetteren, Belgium 1984, 229–240.
6. Jos. *AJ* 13.365.
7. Jos. *AJ* 13.357.
8. Jos. *AJ* 13.358–360.
9. Jos. *AJ* 13.360–361.
10. Jos. *AJ* 13.362–364.

Chapter 12
1. Jos. *AJ* 13.372–374; *BJ* 1.88.
2. G.W. Bowersock, *Roman Arabia*, Cambridge MS 1983, 22–23.
3. Jos. *AJ* 13.374; BJ 1.89.
4. This is a much studied problem, of course. The following are worth consulting (listed in order of publication): Schürer 2.381–414; C. Rabin, 'Alexander Jannaeus and the Pharisees', *JJS* 7, 1956, 3–11; W.W. Buchler, *The Pre-Herodian Civil War and Social Debate*, Basel 1974, ch. 4; M.J. Geller, 'Alexander Jannaeus and the Pharisee Rift', *JJS* 30, 1979, 202–211; A.J. Saldarini, *Pharisees, Scribes and Sadducees in Palestinian Society*, Edinburgh 1989; J. Sievers, *The Hasmonaeans and their Supporters*, Athns GA 1990; H. Newman, *Proximity to Power and Jewish Sectarian Groups of the Ancient Period*, Leiden 2006. There are innumerable others.
5. Jos. *AJ* 13.395–398; George Syncellus, *Chronicle*, ed. G. Dindorf, Bonn 1829, vol. 1, 558–559.
6. Jos. *AJ* 13.374; BJ 1.89.
7. Syncellus, p. 558.
8. Jos. *AJ* 13.398.
9. Jos. *AJ* 13.375; *BJ* 1.90.
10. Ibid.

Chapter 13
1. This is a misnomer in the sense that Judah's insurrection was in part a civil war, as well as being a terrorist campaign; also a brief note in Josephus (BJ 1.67) indicates a rebellion against Hyrkanos, while the attempted coup by Ptolemaios son of Abubos led to a conflict between him and Hyrkonos. Nevertheless, Alexander Iannai's civil war is the first lengthy internal conflict of the established Judaean state – hence my title.
2. Jos. *AJ* 13.376.
3. Tessa Rajak, *Josephus, the Historian and his Society*, London 1983, 29–34.
4. See the items listed in note 4 in the previous chapter.
5. Eshel, ch 6; the scroll is 4Q169.
6. Jos. *AJ* 13.376; *BJ* 1.90–92.
7. Ibid.
8. Jos. *AJ* 13.376–377; *BJ* 1.92.
9. Jos. *AJ* 13.377; *BJ* 1.93.
10. Jos. *AJ* 13.378; *BJ* 1.93.
11. Jos. *AJ* 13.378; *BJ* 1.95.
12. Jos. *BJ* 1.95.
13. Jos. *AJ* 13.379; *BJ* 1.95.

14. Jos. *BJ* 1.95.
15. Jos. *AJ* 13.382; G. W. Bowersock, *Roman Arabia*, Cambridge MA 1983, 24.
16. Jos. *AJ* 13.379–380; *BJ* 1.96.
17. Eshel, ch 6, for a summary of these arguments.
18. Jos. *AJ* 13.380 and 383; *BJ* 1.97.
19. Jos. *AJ* 13.383; *BJ* 1.98.

Chapter 14
1. In the Loeb edition of Jos. *AJ*, vol. 7, p. 419, note 4; this appears to be the occasion for the composition of the 'Damascus Document', parts of which have been found in the Cairo Geniza and at Qumran as one of the 'Dead Sea Scrolls'.
2. See Bellinger 'End', on all this.
3. Jos. *AJ* 13.389; *BJ* 1.99.
4. Jos. *AJ* 13.390; *BJ* 1.99.
5. Arav, 48 and figs 31 and 32, citing unpublished work by J. Kaplan.
6. Jos. *AJ* 13.390–391; *BJ* 1.100.
7. Jos. *AJ* 13.391; *BJ* 1.101–102.
8. Jos. *AJ* 13.392; *BJ* 1.107.
9. Ibid.
10. Jos. *AJ* 13.393–394; *BJ* 1.104–105.
11. Jos. *AJ* 13.397.
12. It is not certain that a city actually existed at this place at this time: its name suggests a Roman foundation, and the visible and dated remains are Roman; on the other hand, any site of a Roman city was very likely already inhabited.
13. G.W. Bowersock, *Roman Arabia*, Cambridge MA 1983, 25–26.
14. Description of the site: S. Rollin and J. Streetly, *Jordan* (Blue Guide), London 1998, 132–136; *New EAEHL*, 3.1174–1180; for reports on the excavations: A.H. McNicoll *et al.*, *Pella of Jordan*, Sydney, 1992.
15. Jos. *AJ* 13.393; *BJ* 1.104; see also in the Loeb edition, *AJ*, vol. 7, pp 424–425 *BJ* vol. 1 pp 50–51, notes.
16. Jos. *AJ* 13.395–397 and 14.18; Syncellus (ed. Dindorf), 558–559.
17. Jos. *AJ* 13.398.
18. Jos. *AJ* 13.393; *BJ* 1.105.
19. Jos. *AJ* 13.394.
20. Jos. *BJ* 4.–83.
21. Note 16.
22. Jos. *AJ* 13.394.
23. Jos. *AJ* 13.398; *BJ* 1.106.

Chapter 15
1. Jos. *AJ* 13.399–404.
2. Jos. *AJ* 13.405.
3. Jos. *AJ* 13.407–408; *BJ* 1.109.
4. Jos. *AJ* 13.408.
5. Jos. *AJ* 13.410–411; *BJ* 1.112–113.
6. Jos. *AJ* 13.409; *BJ* 1.112.
7. Jos. *AJ* 13.415, 417.
8. Neither Bowersock, *Roman Arabia*, nor Myers, *Ituraeans*, admits Ptolemy to power in Damascus, but Jos. *AJ* 13.418 and *BJ* 1.115 seem to imply his control, or at least his imminent threat of control, which further implies that Aretas had lost the city.
9. App., *Syrian Wars* 65.
10. E. J. Newell, *Late Seleukid Mints in Ake-Ptolemais and Damascus*, New York 1939, 78–100.

178   The Wars of the Maccabees

11. Jos. *AJ* 13.418; *BJ* 1.115.
12. Jos. *AJ* 13.419–420.
13. Jos. *AJ* 13.419.
14. Ibid.
15. Jos. *AJ* 13.420; *BJ* 1.116.
16. Jos. *AJ* 13.421; *BJ* 1.116; Strabo 16.2.3.

Chapter 16
1. James S. McLaren, *Power and Politics in Palestine, the Jews and the Governing of their Land 100 BC–AD 70*, Sheffield 1991, 60–67.
2. Jos. *AJ* 13.430.
3. Jos. *AJ* 13.417.
4. For fortification in general in Judaea see Shatzman, *Armies*, ch 2.
5. Khirbet el-Mird: G.R.W. Wright, 'The Archaeological Remains at el-Mird in the Wilderness of Judaea', *Biblica* 42, 1961, 1–21. The Hasmonean remains are largely covered by later buildings; cf. Jerome Murphy–O'Connor, *The Holy Land, an Oxford Archaeological Guide*, 2nd ed., Oxford 2007, 345–348.
6. Qarn Sartabeh: Samuel Rocca, *The Forts of Judaea 168 BC–AD 73*, Oxford 2008, 30–32; Y. Tsafrir and Y. Magen, 'Two Seasons of Excavation at the Sartaba-Alexandreion Fortress', *Qadmoniot* 17, 1984, 26–32.
7. Jos. *AJ* 14.49.
8. Khirbet Mukawir: Rocca, *Forts of Judaea*, 33; V. Corbo, 'Maceronte, la Regia fortezza erodiana', *Liber Annus* 29, 1979, 315–326; Sue Rollin and Jane Streetly, *Jordan* (Blue Guide), 2nd ed., 1998, 175–178.
9. Rocca, *Forts of Judaea*, 37–39; Y. Hirschfeld, *Ramat Hanadiv Excavations, Final Report of the 1984–1998 Seasons*, Jerusalem 2000.
10. M. Aviam, 'Yodefat/Jotapata: The Archaeology of the First Revolt', in A. M. Berlin and J. A. Overman (eds), *The First Jewish Revolt, Archaeology, History and Ideology*, London 2002, 121–133.
11. Jos. *AJ* 13.422–424.
12. Jos. *AJ* 13.425–427; *BJ* 1.118.
13. Jos. *AJ* 13.425.
14. Jos. *AJ* 13.430, 14.4; *BJ* 1.119–120.
15. Jos. *AJ* 15.180.
16. Jos. *AJ* 14.4–5; *BJ* 1.120–121.
17. Jos. *AJ* 14.71.
18. Jos. *AJ* 14.5–7; *BJ* 1.121–122.
19. Jos. *AJ* 14.8–15; *BJ* 1.123–124.
20. Jos. *AJ* 14.16–18; *BJ* 1.15–126.
21. Jos. *AJ* 14.19; *BJ* 1.126.
22. Ibid.
23. Jos. *AJ* 14.20–21.
24. Jos. *AJ* 14.21–28; the famine is referred to in several of the Qumran documents, cf Eshel, ch 7.
25. Dio Cassius 37.7a; Plutarch, *Pompey* 39; App., *Mithradatic Wars* 106, *Syrian Wars* 49.
26. Jos. *AJ* 14.29–33; *BJ* 1.127–129.
27. Jos. *AJ* 14.33; *BJ* 1.130.

Chapter 17
1. Jos. *AJ* 14.38–39.
2. Jos. *AJ* 14.34–37; *BJ* 1.131 – 132; Josephus' account is somewhat confused here; there were two meetings, one in the winter of 64/63 and therefore at Antioch, and a second at Damascus, with the rivals themselves present.

Notes 179

3. Justin 40.2.2–5.
4. Jos. *AJ* 14.40.
5. Jos. *AJ* 14.42–45.
6. Jos. *AJ* 14.46; modern accounts wholly ignore the geographical aspect of all this, following Josephus' interpretation without question – but Josephus' account is all too clearly his interpretation (or his source's) and it is necessary to weed out that interpretation and isolate the facts.
7. E. Mary Smallwood, *The Jews under Roman Rule*, 2nd ed., Leiden 1981, 23.
8. Jos. *AJ* 14.47.
9. Jos. *AJ* 14.48–49; *BJ* 1.133–134.
10. Jos. *AJ* 14.50–52; *BJ* 1.135–137.
11. Jos. *AJ* 14.52–56; *BJ* 1.137–140.
12. Jos. *AJ* 14.56–57; *BJ* 1.140–141.
13. Jos. *AJ* 14.58–60; *BJ* 1.142–144.
14. Jos. *AJ* 14.61–71; *BJ* 1.145–151; Samuel Rocca, *The Forts of Judaea, 168 BC–AD 73*, Oxford 2008, 44–46.
15. Jos. *AJ* 14.74–76; *BJ* 1.153–156; A.H.M. Jones, *The Cities of the Eastern Roman Empire*, 2nd ed, Oxford 1971, 258–259.
16. Jos. *AJ* 14.80–81.
17. Jos. *AJ* 14.77.

Chapter 18
1. Jos. *AJ* 14.79; *BJ* 1.157–158.
2. Eshel 134–135, referring to 4Q471a.
3. Bowersock, *Roman Arabia*, 32–34.
4. Schürer 1.244–245; A. H. M. Jones, *The Cities of the Eastern Roman Provinces*, 2nd ed., Oxford 1971, 259.
5. Jos. *AJ* 14.79; *BJ* 1.158.
6. Plutarch, *Pompey*, 47.
7. Jos. *AJ* 14.82; *BJ* 1.160.
8. Jos. *AJ* 14.83; *BJ* 1.160.
9. Jos. *AJ* 14.83; *BJ* 1.161.
10. Schürer 1.245 – 246.
11. Jos. *AJ* 14.83–85; *BJ* 1.161–163.
12. Jos. *AJ* 14.86; *BJ* 1.164–165; see also Rocca, *Forts*. 31–33.
13. Jos. *AJ* 14.87–88; *BJ* 1.165–166.
14. Jos. *AJ* 14.89–90; *BJ* 1.167–168.
15. Jos. *AJ* 14.91; *BJ* 1.170; Schürer 1.268–269; Smallwood 31–33.
16. Jos. *AJ* 14.92.
17. Jos. *AJ* 14.92–96; *BJ* 1.171–176.
18. Jos. *AJ* 14.97; *BJ* 1.168; for Ashkelon: *BJ* 14.126.
19. Jos. *AJ* 14.98–99; *BJ* 1.175.
20. Jos. *AJ* 14.100–102; *BJ* 1.176–177.
21. Jos. *AJ* 14.103; *BJ* 1.178.
22. Jos. *AJ* 14.105–109; *BJ* 1.180–182.
23. Jos. *AJ* 14.119–121; *BJ* 1.180–182.
24. Jos. *AJ* 14.120; *BJ* 1.180.

Chapter 19
1. Jos. *AJ* 14.123–125; *BJ* 1.183–185.
2. Dio Cassius 41.18.1.
3. Jos. *AJ* 14.126; *BJ* 1.185–186.

4. Jos. *AJ* 14.202–211.
5. Jos. *AJ* 14.127–136; *BJ* 1.187–193; [Caesar] *Alexandrian War* 26–32; App., *Civil Wars* 2.378.
6. Jos. *AJ* 14.140–142; *BJ* 1.195–199.
7. Jos. *AJ* 14.137, 143–144; *BJ* 1.195–199.
8. Jos. *AJ* 14.158; *BJ* 1.203; for Josephus' treatment of the contest between Antipater and Hyrkanos, see D.R. Schwartz, 'Josephus on Hyrkanos II', in F. Parente and J. Sievers (eds), *Josephus and the History of the Greco-Roman Period*, Leiden 1994, 210–232, and P. Richardson, Herod, *King of the Jews and Friend of the Romans*, Columbia SC, 1996, 105–108.
9. Jos. *AJ* 14.159–180; *BJ* 1.04–213.
10. Jos. *AJ* 14.281–282, 291–293; *BJ* 1.226–227, 233–235.
11. Jos. *AJ* 14.156–157; *BJ* 1.201–202.
12. Jos. *AJ* 14.294–296; *BJ* 1.236–238.
13. Jos. *AJ* 14.301–329; *BJ* 1.242–247; Smallwood, *Jews*, 49–51.
14. Jos. *AJ* 14.30–331; *BJ* 1.248.
15. Jos. *AJ* 14.332–333; *BJ* 1.249.
16. Jos. *AJ* 14.295; *BJ* 1.236.
17. Jos. *AJ* 14.333–339; *BJ* 1.250–253.
18. Jos. *AJ* 14.340–348; *BJ* 1.254–261.
19. Jos. *AJ* 14.272–276; *BJ* 1.220–222.
20. Jos. *AJ* 14.352–362; *BJ* 1.263–267.
21. Jos. *AJ* 14.365–369; *BJ* 1.268–269; he was treated as high priest by the Jews in Babylonia despite the mutilation.
22. Jos. *AJ* 14.370–389; *BJ* 1.274–275; Richardson, *Herod*, 127–130.
23. Jos. *AJ* 14.392; *BJ* 1.288.
24. Jos. *AJ* 14.390–391; *BJ* 1.286–287.
25. Jos. *AJ* 14.394–397; *BJ* 1.290–293.
26. Jos. *AJ* 14.398–400; *BJ* 1.293–294.
27. Jos. *AJ* 14.400–412; *BJ* 1.294–301.
28. Jos. *AJ* 14.413–419; *BJ* 1.302–308; S. Freyne, *Galilee from Alexander the Great to Hadrian*, Edinburgh 1980, 66–67.
29. Jos. *AJ* 14.420–430; *BJ* 1.309–314.
30. Jos. *AJ* 14.448–449; *BJ* 1.323–325.
31. Jos. *AJ* 14.452–453; *BJ* 1.329–330.
32. Jos. *AJ* 14.456–457; *BJ* 1.333–334.
33. Jos. *AJ* 14.456–461; *BJ* 1.335–339.
34. Jos. *AJ* 14.468–469; *BJ* 1.346; Shatzman, *Armies*, 157–166.
35. Jos. *AJ* 14.470–486; *BJ* 1.347–356.
36. Jos. *AJ* 14.489–490; *BJ* 1.357.

Bibliography

(This list includes books not referred to in the notes, but that provide other ways of interpreting the events recounted here; see also Abbreviations.)

F.M. Abel, 'Topographie des campaignes Machabèennes', *Revue Biblique* 32, 1923,
G.G. Aperghis, *The Seleukid Royal Economy*, Cambridge 2004.
S. Applebaum et al., 'The Towers of Samaria', *PEQ* 10, 1978.
S. Applebaum, 'Jewish Urban Communities and Greek Influence', *SCI* 5, 1979/1980, 158–177.
S. Applebaum, *Judaea in Hellenistic and Roman Times, Historical and Archaeological Essays*, Leiden 1989.
N. Avigad, 'A Bulla for King Jonathan', *IEJ* 25, 1975, 245–247.
M. Avi-Yonah, 'The War of the Sons of Light and the Sons of Darkness' and 'Maccabean Warfare', *IEJ* 2, 1952, 1–5.
M. Avi-Yonah, *The Holy Land from the Persian to the Arab Conquests (536 BC–AD 640), A Historical Geography*, London 1966.
M. Avi-Yonah, *Hellenism and the East*, Jerusalem 1978.
B. Bar-Kochva, 'Hellenistic Warfare in Jonathan's Campaign near Azotos', *SCI*, 2, 1975, 83–96.
B. Bar-Kochva, 'Manpower, Economics, and Internal Strife in the Hasmonean State', in H. Van Effenterre (ed.), *Armées et Fiscalité dans la Monde Antique,* Paris 1977, 167–194.
B. Bar-Kochva, *The Seleukid Army*, Cambridge 1977.
J.R. Bartlett (ed), *Jews in Hellenistic and Roman Cities*, London 2002.
A.R. Bellinger, 'The End of the Seleucids', *Transactions of the Connecticut Academy of Arts and Sciences*, 1949.
A. Ben-David, 'When did the Maccabees began to Strike their First Coins?', *PEQ* 1972, 93–103.
A.M. Berlin and J. A. Overman (eds), *The First Jewish Revolt, Archaeology, History and Ideology*, London 2002.
E.J. Bickerman, *The God of the Maccabees*, trans. H.R. Mohring, Leiden 1979.
G.W. Bowersock, *Roman Arabia*, Cambridge MS 1983.
A.B. Brett, 'The Mint of Ascalon under the Seleucids', *American Numismatic Society Museum Notes* 4, 1950, 43–54.
W.W. Buchler, *The Pre-Herodian Civil War and Social Debate*, Basel 1974.
J.J. Collins and G.E. Sterling (eds), *Hellenism in the Land of Israel*, Notre Dame, Indiana, 2001.
C.R. Conder, *Judas Maccabeus and the Jewish war of Independence*, New York 1879.
V. Corbo, 'Maceronte, la Regia fortezza erodiana', *Liber Annus* 29, 1979, 315–326.
F.M. Cross, 'Aspects of Samaritan and Jewish history in Late Persian and Hellenistic Times', *HTR* 59, 1966, 201–211.
J.W. Crowfoot *et al.*, *The Buildings at Samaria*, London 1942.
P. Davies, 'Hasidim in the Maccabean Period', *JJS* 28, 1977.
J. Efron, *Studies in the Hasmonean Period*, Leiden 1987.
S. Freyne, *Galilee from Alexander the Great to Hadrian*, Edinburgh 1998.

M.J. Geller, 'Alexander Jannaeus and the Pharisee Rift', *JJS* 30, 1979, 202–211;
M. Gelzer, *Caesar, Politician and Statesman*, trans. P. Needham, Oxford 1969.
D. Gera, *Judaea and Mediterranean Politics, 219 to 161 BC*, Leiden 1998.
J.D. Grainger, *The Cities of Seleukid Syria*, Oxford 1990.
E.S. Gruen, *The Hellenistic World and the Coming of Rome*, California 1984.
E.S. Gruen, *Heritage and Hellenism, The Reinvention of Jewish Tradition*, California 1998.
C. Habicht, 'Royal Documents in Maccabees II', *Harvard Studies in Classical Philology 80*, 1976, 1–17.
R. Hayward, 'The Jewish Temple at Leontopolis: a Reconsideration', *JJS* 33, 1982, 429–433.
C. Herzog and M. Gichon, *Battles of the Bible*, London 2002.
Y. Hirschfeld, *Ramat Hanadiv Excavations, Final Report of the 1984 – 1998 Seasons*, Jerusalem 2000.
G. Holbl, *A History of the Ptolemaic Empire*, London 2001.
M. Holleaux, 'Le Mort d'Antiochos IV Epiphanes', *Revue des Etudes Anciennes* 18, 1916, 77–102.
M. Holleaux, 'Sur un Passage de Flavius Josèphe', *REJ* 39, 1899, 161–176.
R.A. Horsley with J.S. Hanson, *Bandits, Prophets, and Messiahs: Popular Movements at the Time of Jesus*, San Francisco 1988.
Oliver Hoover, 'A Revised Chronology for the Late Seleucids at Antioch (121/0–64 BC)', *Historia* 56, 2007, 280–301.
Priest Amran Ishak, *The History and Religion of the Samaritans*, Jerusalem, n.d.
A.H.M. Jones, *The Cities of the Eastern Roman Empire*, 2nd ed, Oxford 1971.
A. Kasher, *Jews and Hellenistic Cities in Eretz-Israel*, Tubingen 1990.
U. Leibner, *Settlement and History in Hellenistic, Roman and Byzantine Galilee*, Tubingen 2009.
L.I. Levine, 'The Hasmonaean Conquest of Strato's Tower', *IEJ* 24, 1974.
L.I. Levine, *Caesarea under Roman Rule*, Leiden 1975.
L.I. Levine, *Jerusalem, Portrait of the City in the Second Temple Period*, Philadlephia 2002
L.I. Levine, *Judaism and Hellenism in Antiquity: Conflict or Confluence?*, Peabody, MA, 1998.
Th. Liebemann-Frankfort, 'Rome et le Conflit Judéo-Syrien (164–161 avant notre ère)', *Antiquité Classique* 38, 969, 101–120.
W.S. McCulloogh, *The History and Literature of the Palestinian Jews from Cyrus to Herod*, Toronto 1975.
J.S. McLaren, *Power and Politics in Palestine, the Jews and the Governing of their Land 100 BC–AD 70*, Sheffield 1991.
A.H. McNicoll et al, *Pella of Jordan*, Sydney, 1992.
D. Mendels, *The Rise and Fall of Jewish Nationalism, Jewish and Christian Ethnicity in Ancient Palestine*, New York 1992.
Y. Meshorer, 'The Beginning of the Hasmonean coinage', *IEJ* 24, 1974, 59–61.
Y. Meshorer, *Ancient Jewish Coinage*, vol. 1, Dix Hills, NY, 1982.
Z. Meskel, 'The Siege Systems during the Hasmonaean Period', in *Zev Vilmay's Jubilee volume*, vol. 1, Jerusalem 1984, 256–258 (in Hebrew).
F. Millar, *The Roman Near East, 31 BC–AD 337*, Cambridge MA, 1993.
T.R. Mitford, 'Ptolemy Macron', *Studi in onore de A. Calderini e M. Paribeni*, Milan 1957, 163–187.
O. Mørkholm, *Antiochos IV of Syria*, Copenhagen 1966.
J. Murphy-O'Connor, *The Holy Land, an Oxford Archaeological Guide*, 5th ed., Oxford, 2008.
E.A. Myers, *The Ituraeans and the Roman Near East, Reassessing the Sources*, Cambridge 2010.
E.J. Newell, *Late Seleucid Mints in Ake-Ptolemais and Damascus*, New York 1939.
H. Newman, *Proximity to Power and Jewish Sectarian Groups of the Ancient Period*, Leiden 2006.
D. Ogden, *Polygamy, Prostitutes and Death*, London 1999.
M. Pearlman, *The Maccabees*, London 1973.
S. Perowne, *The Life and Times of Herod the Great*, London 1956.
K. Prag, *Israel and the Palestinian Territories* (Blue Guide), London 2002.

A. Raban, 'The City Walls of Strato's Tower: some new Archaeological Data', *Bulletin of the American School of Oriental Research*, 268, 1987, 71–88.
C. Rabin, 'Alexander Jannaeus and the Pharisees', *JJS* 7, 1956, 3–11.
T. Rajak, 'Roman Intervention in a Seleukid siege of Jerusalem?', *Greek, Roman and Byzantine Studies* 22, 1981, 65–81.
Tessa Rajak, *Josephus, the Historian and his Society*, London 1983.
U. Rappaport, 'La Judée et Rome pendant le Regne d'Alexandre Jannée', *REJ*, 128, 1979, 329–345.
P. Richardson, Herod, *King of the Jews and Friend of the Romans*, Columbia SC, 1996.
S. Rocca, *The Forts of Judaea 168 BC–AD 3*, Oxford 2008.
S. Rollin and J. Streetly, *Jordan* (Blue Guide), London 1998.
B-Z. Rosenfeld, 'The 'Boundary of Gezer' Inscriptions and the History of Gezer at the End of the Second Temple Period', *IEJ* 38, 1987, 235–245.
H. H. Rowley, 'Menelaos and the Abomination of Desolation', *Studia Orientalem J. Pedersen*, Copenhagen 1955, 303–315.
D.S. Russell, *The Jews from Alexander to Herod*, Oxford 1967.
A.J. Saldarini, *Pharisees, Scribes and Sadducees in Palestinian Society*, Edinburgh 1989.
D.R. Schwartz, 'Josephus on Hyrkanos II', in F. Parente and J. Sievers (eds), *Josephus and the History of the Greco-Roman Period*, Leiden 1994.
S. Schwartz, *Imperialism and Jewish Society, 200 BCE to 640 CE*, Princeton NJ 2001.
B. E. Scolnic, *Thy Brother's Blood, the Maccabees and Dynastic Morality in the Hellenistic World*, Latham MD 2008.
A. Schalit (ed.), *The World History of the Jewish People*, vol. 6, *The Hellenistic Age*, London 1976.
R. Seager, *Pompey, a Political Biography*, Oxford 1979.
J. Sievers, *The Hasmonaeans and their Supporters*, Athens GA, 1990.
E. Mary Smallwood, *The Jews under Roman Rule*, 2nd ed., Leiden 1981.
G. A. Smith, *The Historical Geography of the Holy Land*, 25th ed., London 1931.
A. Spaer, 'Ascalon from Royal mint to Autonomy', in *Festschrift for Leo Mildenburg*, Wetteren, Belgium 1984, 229–240.
E. Stern, *Dor, Ruler of the Seas*, Jerusalem 1994.
M. Stern, *Greek and Latin Authors on Jews and Judaism*, vol. 1, Jerusalem 1976.
A.M. Streane, *The Age of the Maccabees*, London 1898.
V. Tcherikcover, *Hellenistic Civilization and the Jews*, trans. S. Applebaum, New York 1985.
Y. Tsafrir and Y. Magen, 'Two Seasons of Excavation at the Sartaba-Alexandreion Fortress', *Qadmoniot* 17, 1984, 26–32.
E. van 't Dack *et al*, *The Judaean-Syrian-Egyptian conflict of 103–101 BC, a Multilingual Dossier concerning a 'War of Scepters'*, Brussels 1969.
J. Wellhausen, *Israelitische und Judäische Geschichte*, Berlin 1895.
J. Whitehorne, *Cleopatras*, London 1994.
J.E.G. Whitehorne, 'A Reassessment of Cleopatra III's Syrian Campaign', *Chronique d'Egypt*, 70, 1996, 197–205.
W. Wirgin, 'Judah Maccabee's Embassy to Rome and the Jewish-Roman Treaty', *PEQ* 101, 1969, 15–20.
W. Wirgin, 'Simon Maccabaeus' embassy to Rome – its purpose and outcome', *PEQ* 1974, 141–146.
M. Wise, M Abegg, E, Cook, *The Dead Sea Scrolls, a New Translation*, London 1996.
G. E. Wright, 'The Samaritans at Shechem', *HTR* 55, 1962, 357–366.
G. E. Wright and R. J. Bull, 'Newly Discovered Temples at Mount Gerizim in Jordan', *HTR* 58, 1965, 234–237.
G.R.W. Wright, 'The Archaeological Remains at el-Mird in the Wilderness of Judaea', *Biblica* 42, 1961, 1–21.

Index

Abila 103, 111, 124, 127
Absalom, Maccabean envoy 22
Absalom, Maccabee 94, 98, 138, 148, 150
Accaron - see Ekron
Adasa 46, 48
Adida 62, 64–65, 122, 123
Adora 65, 81, 83, 110, 151
Adullam 35
Aemilius Scaurus, M., Roman commander 140–143, 148, 150
Akrabattene 28
Alexander the Great 1, 81, 87, 105, 128
Alexander I Balas, Seleukid king 52, 53–57, 85
Alexander II Zabeinas, Seleukid king 77
Alexander Iannai, Maccabean king 94, 98–107, 108–117, 119–129, 131, 139, 150, 165
Alexander, son of Aristoboulos II 150–155, 157–158
Alexandra, daughter of Hyrkanos II 154, 157
Alexandreion 135–136, 146–147, 151–153, 163
Alexandria 158
Alkimos, high priest 43–45, 49
Amanaias, Ptolemaic commander 100
Amathos 102–104, 107, 109, 111–112, 124, 136, 146
Ammanitis 3, 4, 29, 31, 32, 34, 126
Ammaus 18–20, 22, 27, 29
Ammonios, Ptolemaic official 55
Anthedon 105–107, 110, 151
Antigonos I, king 129
Antigonos, Maccabee 87, 90, 94–96, 97
Antigonos, son o aristoboulos II 150, 152, 153, 158–163
Antigonos, Seleukid prince 55
Antioch 3, 4, 14, 18, 22, 23, 24, 27, 39–40, 41, 44 55, 57–58, 86, 143, 144, 157
Antiochos III, Seleukid king 1, 57, 59
Antiochos IV, Seleukid king 2–6, 9, 14, 22, 30, 39, 42, 44, 45, 51, 55, 85, 110

Antiochos V, Seleukid king 17, 24, 40, 42, 43
Antiochos VI, Seleukid king 58, 62, 63
Antiochos VII, Seleukid king 58, 64, 75, 77–78, 85
Antiochos VIII, Seleukid king 85–87, 88
Antiochos IX, Seleukid king 85–87, 88, 99
Antiochos XII, Seleukid king 117, 119–121, 129, 134, 148
Antiochos XIII, Seleukid king 133, 144
'Antiochenes in Jerusalem' 2, 6, 7, 9, 18
Antipater, son of Antipas 139, 142–145, 149–155, 157–159, 161
Antipater, son of Herod 164
Antipater son of Jason, Maccabean envoy 63
Antony, Mark, Roman commander 151, 155, 158–161, 163
Apamea 39, 71
Apharaema 54, 58, 77
Apollo 3, 4
Apollodotos, Gazan commander 106–107
Apollonia 105, 120–121, 122, 151
Apollonios, Seleucid official 6, 7, 8, 11–15, 17, 18, 29, 54, 87
Apollonios son of Genaios, Seleukid commander 29
Apollonios Taos, Seleukid official 55–57, 60, 63
Apollophanes, Seleukid commander 30
Arabia 61
Arabs 109–111, 112, 144
Arbela 163
Aretas I, Nabataean king 5
Aretas II, Nabataean king 107, 109
Aretas III, Nabataean king 119,122–124, 127, 129, 131–134, 139–141, 144–146, 148, 150
Arqa 143
Arimatheia 54, 58, 77
Aristoboulos I, Maccabean king 87–90, 94–98, 110
Aristoboulos II, Maccabean king 131–150, 152, 154, 157–158, 162

Aristoboulos 'III', Maccabean 164
Ashdod 20, 29, 34–35, 36, 105, 151
Ashkelon 57, 59, 60, 67, 105, 153, 158
Asia Minor 17
Asochis 97, 99
Asophon 99, 100, 109
Aspendos 87
Assyrians 80, 100
Athenobios, Seleukid envoy 70
Attalid kingdom 51, 55
Azarias, Maccabean commander 34 35

Baalbek 133
Babylonia 17, 65, 80, 85, 161
Bacchias 144
Bacsama 65
Baianites 28–29
Bakchides, Seleukid commander 44, 45, 48–50, 51, 52, 56, 63, 67, 71
Barada, river 133
Barzaphranes, Parthian commander 159–161
Bathbasi 49
Beit-Guvrin 35, 83
Bekaa valley 133, 143, 160
Bethel 49
Beth Horon 15–19, 47, 62, 64–65
Bethoma/Bemeselis 117, 132
Beth Zakaria 41, 42, 47
Beth Zur 23–24, 25, 27, 29, 32, 34, 38, 40–41, 42, 49, 52, 60, 62, 64, 77, 80, 82, 101
Brundisium 157

Caecilius Metellus Scipio, Q., Roman commander 157
Capitolias (Beit Ras) 124
Carthage 63
Cassius Longinus, C., Roman commander 154–155, 158–160, 162
Chabarsaba (Kafr Saba) 120
Chaereas, Seleukid commander 29–30
Chalkis 133, 158
Chelkias, Ptolemaic commander 100
Cornelius Lentulus Marcellinus, Cn., Roman governor 150
Crete 55
Cuthaeans 80
Cyprus 22, 51, 52, 100

Daliya 136
Damascus 33, 39, 54, 59, 98, 102, 103, 106, 114, 115, 117, 119–121, 124, 132–134, 135, 140, 143, 144, 146, 149, 160

Daphne, near Antioch 3, 14, 18
Dead Sea 28, 65, 77, 78, 82, 121, 123, 128, 136, 139
Dead Sea Scrolls xviii, 100, 113
Decapolis 124, 148, 149, 159
Demainetos 99
Demetrios Poliorketes, king 120
Demetrios I, Seleukid king 43–46, 48, 51–55, 85
Demetrios II, Seleukid king 54–58, 60–63, 65, 69, 77, 85, 115
Demetrios III, Seleukid king 114–116, 117, 119, 122, 129, 134, 139, 148
Demetrios, governor of Gamla 127
Demophon, Seleukid commander 29
Diathema 28, 31, 33–34, 36
Diodotos of Kasiana – see Tryphon
Diogenes 132
Dion 32, 102, 110, 123–127, 145–146
Dionysios, tyrant 143
Dok 72–74
Dor 69–70, 98–99, 105, 120–122, 136
Dositheos, Maccabean commander 34

Egypt 1, 4, 5, 43, 52, 93, 98–99, 101, 105, 119, 140, 153, 155, 161
Ekron (Accaron) 57, 58, 67, 77
Elasa 48
Eleazar, Maccabee 41
Eleutheros river 57, 61
Ephron 32
Epikrates, Seleukid commander 89–90
Epiphaneia 61
Esdraelon, plain of 158
Essenes 93–94
Euphrates, river 154
Ezekias, bandit 159

Fabius, Roman commander 160

Gabai 150
Gabinius, A., Roman governor 143, 147, 151–155, 162, 163
Gadara 32, 33, 101–103, 110–112, 144, 146
Gadora (es-Salt) 103–104, 107, 109, 110
Galaaditis 28, 29, 31–32, 34, 36, 41, 65
Galaistes 136
Galilee 28, 31, 33–34, 35, 41, 63, 65, 94–97, 99, 103, 111, 120, 141, 144, 148, 149, 151, 158, 159, 162
    Sea of 29, 60, 65, 90, 102, 103, 109, 111, 112, 123, 154, 163

Gamla 127
Garada 112
Gaulanitis (Golan) 112, 114, 120, 127, 141
Gaza 18, 23, 59, 60, 78, 98–100, 104–107, 109–110, 123, 124, 129, 144, 149
Gerasa 32, 102, 111, 112, 123–129, 136, 145, 148
Gezer 20, 21, 47, 49, 53, 67–69, 70, 72, 77, 80
Gibeon 46
Gilgal 48
Gophna Hills 13–15, 17, 19, 41, 44, 46, 77
Gorgias, Seleukid commander 18, 19–21, 23, 27, 29, 34–35, 39, 81
Greece 63

Haifa Bay 99
Hamath (Hama) 60
Hammath Tiberias 61
Hasidim 12, 43, 44
Hasmonaeans xvii, 86, 114, 164
Hebron 23, 34–35
Helix, Maccabean commander 159, 160
Herakleides, Seleukid official 44, 52
Herod, Judaean king xvii, 158–166
Heshbon 78–79, 104, 128
Hieronymos, Seleukid commander 29
Hippos 32, 33, 102, 103, 110, 111
Horvat Aleq 136
Huleh, lake 60
Hyrkania 135–136, 151–152
Hyrkanos, Tobiad 3–6, 30, 33, 79
Hyrkanos I (John), Maccabean ruler 70–73, 75, 77–8, 85–91, 93–95, 97, 98
Hyrkanos II, Maccabean king 131, 135, 137–153, 157–162

Iamnia 20, 34–36, 57, 62, 70, 71, 151
Idumaea 18, 23, 27, 29, 33–35, 65, 81–82, 86, 87, 101, 120, 148, 151, 161
Iran 22, 69
Iraq el-Amir 3, 30, 79, 80, 93, 103
Isana 163
Italy 44–45, 157
Ituraeans 52, 96, 122, 132–133, 137, 144, 148, 160

Jabbok, river (Nahr el-Auja) 102, 104, 112
Jazera 29–31, 33
Jericho 49, 51, 52, 136, 138, 141, 160
Jerusalem xvii, 2–6, 9, 15, 17, 19, 23, 25, 27, 29, 41, 48, 51, 60–61, 64, 68, 72, 96, 135–137, 147, 150–151, 154, 160–161

Index   187

Akra 6, 11, 19, 25, 27, 32, 36, 37, 39–41, 47, 49, 53, 58, 63, 67–69, 70, 72, 75
Sieges 74–75, 80, 140–141, 147–148, 162–164
Temple 2, 4–7, 10, 23, 39, 41, 42, 46, 81–82, 147, 154, 164
Jesus/Jason, high priest 2–4, 5, 6, 43
Jezreel, Vale of 52, 59, 60, 76, 80, 90, 154
Jisr bint Yaqub 103
Johanan, Maccabean envoy 22
Jonathan, Maccabean ruler 49, 51–65, 67, 93, 115, 165
Joppa 35, 37, 55–57, 62, 64–65, 67, 70, 72, 75, 77, 105, 110, 120, 162, 163
Jordan, river 3, 4, 5, 28, 48, 49, 52, 60, 65, 72, 77–78, 90, 101, 123, 146
expeditions across 28–35, 62, 78, 82, 97, 101–102, 105, 109, 123–124
Joseph, son of Antipater 163
Josephus son of Zacharias, Maccabean commander 28, 34
Jotapata 136
Judaean army 13–14, 16, 19, 21, 23–25, 27, 40–41, 46–49, 55, 67, 70, 75, 80, 83, 88, 104, 106, 109, 113, 115, 137, 139, 151, 155
Judaean government (see also under individual Maccabees) 63, 64, 67, 69
Judah Maccabeus xvii, 12–14, 15–16, 17–20, 23–24, 25, 27, 29–37, 39–40, 42, 44–46, 48–50, 67, 74, 93, 97, 110, 132, 165
Judah, son of Simon 70, 71
Julius Caesar, C., Roman commander 157–159, 163, 164

Kallirhoe 136
Kallimandos, Seleukid commander 89
Kana 121
Karnaim 32
Kedesh 59
Kedron 70, 71
Kefar Salama 45, 48
Kendebaios, Seleukid official 70–72
Kidron, river 70–71
Kilikia, Kilikians 55, 112, 115
Kleopatra Selene, Seleukid queen 133–134
Kleopatra Syra, Ptolemaic queen 1
Kleopatra Thea, Seleukid queen 55, 57, 69, 85
Kleopatra III, Ptolemaic queen 89, 99–101, 105
Koele Syria 11, 12, 14, 18, 22, 29, 159
Korai (Tell el-Mazar) 146

Laodike, Seleukid princess 52
Latrun 18
Lebanon 96, 142
Leontopolis 82, 100
Licinius Crassus, M., Roman commander 154, 163
Lydda (Lod) 15, 54, 58, 62, 67, 77
Lysanias, Ituraean ruler 159–160
Lysias, Seleukid regent 17, 18, 22, 23–25, 27, 29, 32, 39–42, 43, 45, 52, 56, 65, 81, 120, 172
Lysias 143, 144
Lysimachos, Gazan commander 107

Maccabees xvii, 9, 12
  Methods 11, 12, 36–37, 44, 51, 82, 107, 124–125, 165
  Army – see Judaean army
Macedon 12, 63
Machaeros 135–136, 151–153
Malichos, Maccabean commander 151, 159, 160
Marcius Philippos, L., Roman governor 150
Mariamme, daughter of Alexander 164
Marisa 34–35, 81–83, 98, 101, 110, 151, 161, 162
Masada 161, 162
Mattathias, Maccabee xvii, 9–12, 49
Mattathias, envoy 45
Medaba (Madaba) 78–80, 82, 83, 86, 88, 102–104, 109–110, 116, 128, 139
Mediterranean Sea 28, 47, 69, 77, 104, 140, 149, 157
Menelaos, high priest 3, 4–7, 9–11, 13, 22–25, 39, 40, 42–44
Mesopotamia 44
Michmash 51, 52, 72
Mithradates VI, king of Pontus 140
Mizpah, Judaea 17–18, 19–21
Moab 109–110, 112, 116, 126
Modiin, xvii, 9–10, 13, 15, 49, 62, 68, 70
Moses 78
Mount Carmel 90, 91, 97, 99, 122, 136, 150, 160
Mount Gerizim 80–83, 87, 153
Mount Nebo 78
Mount Tabor 153–154, 155
Mysians 6, 13

Na'aman, river 99
Nabataeans 32, 52, 61, 79, 81, 107, 109, 112, 119, 121, 123, 132, 141, 148, 150, 161

Negev 139
Nikanor, Seleukid commander 44–47
Nikanor son of Patroklos, Seleukid commander 18–20, 23, 32, 44
Nikodemos, Maccabean envoy 143
Numenios son of Antiochos, Maccabean envoy 63, 69

Obodas I, Nabataean king 109–110, 112, 114, 116, 117, 119, 127
Obodas II, Nabataean king 150
Octavian, Roman commander 158
Octavius, C., Roman envoy 43, 45
Onias III, high priest 2–4, 6, 24, 43, 82
Onias 'IV' 43, 82, 100
Ophel, Jerusalem 6

Pakoros, Parthian prince 159–160
Pakoros the cupbearer, Parthian officer 160
Pamphras 68
Panion 59
Pappas, Maccabean officer 163
Papyron 142
Parthia, Parthians 52, 63, 75, 80, 86, 95
Peitholaos, Maccabean commander 151–152, 154–155, 159
Pella 32, 102, 103, 111, 123–125, 128, 129, 144, 146
Pelusion, Egypt 5, 105
Peraia 79, 82, 102, 103, 148
Persia, Persians 1, 17
Petra 79, 133, 134, 139, 145, 146
Pharisees 93–95, 107, 110–111, 113–114, 131–132, 135–139, 144–145
Phasael, son of Antipater 158–161
Pheroras, son of Antipater 163
Philadelphia (Amman) 29, 33, 74, 78–79, 81, 98, 102–104, 109–112, 123, 125–128, 134, 136, 145, 148
Philip I, Seleukid king 119, 121
Philip the Phrygian, Seleukid officer 5, 6
Philippos, Seleukid regent 24–25, 39–42
Philoteria 111–112, 125, 154
Phoenicia 6, 57, 119, 134
Pisidians 112, 115
Pompeius Magnus, Cn. (Pompey), Roman commander 140, 143–152, 157–158, 163–165
Popillius Laenas, C., Roman envoy 5, 6
Poppaedius silo, Roman commander 162–163
Poseidonios, Seleukid envoy 45
Ptolemaic kings 1, 17, 86

Index

Ptolemaios Makron, Seleukid official 22, 29, 39
Ptolemaios son of Abubos 72–74,77, 78, 95, 98
Ptolemaios son of Dorymenes, Seleukid official 18, 22
Ptolemais-Ake 14, 22, 23, 28, 31, 33–34, 39, 52, 54, 63–64, 97, 98–102, 105, 114, 120–134, 149, 160, 162
Ptolemy V, Ptolemaic king 1, 22
Ptolemy VI, Ptolemaic king 4, 5, 48, 51, 55, 57–58
Ptolemy IX Alexander, Ptolemaic king 99–101, 102, 106
Ptolemy XII Auletes, Ptolemaic king 153
Ptolemy Lathyros, Ptolemaic king 87–89, 98–101, 103–106, 129
Ptolemy son of Menneas, Ituraean ruler 122, 132–137, 143, 144, 158, 159

Qumran 54, 113, 149

Ragaba (Rajib) 112, 126, 131, 136, 145, 151
Ramallah 15
Raphanea 32
Raphia 105–107, 110
Raphon/Romphon 31, 32
Rhodes 161
Rome, Romans xvii, 5–6, 17, 22, 43–44, 47–48, 51, 61–63, 69, 82, 95, 97, 127, 134, 140–143, 150–153, 155, 157–61, 166

Sadducees 93–94, 107, 110–111, 113, 131, 135, 138, 140, 144, 149
Salome Alexandra, Maccabean queen 98, 128, 131–135, 137–139, 141, 157
Samaria, 12–13, 15, 29, 44, 46, 59, 65, 80, 82, 86–91, 94, 96–98, 101, 104, 110, 125, 144, 151, 153, 159, 163
Samaritans 80, 81, 86, 91, 93
Samoga (Samak) 78, 79, 83
Samosata 163
Seleukeia-in-Pieria 39, 57, 69, 70
Seleukeia-Zeugma 134
Seleukid army 12, 15, 18–20, 23, 27–28, 33, 40, 47–49, 56, 71, 115
  government 12, 14, 79
  kings xvii, 1
Seleukos IV, Seleukid king 1, 2
Seleukid V, Seleukid king 85
Sempronius Gracchus, T., Roman envoy 17
Sepphoris 97, 99, 163
Seron, Seleukid commander 14–15, 17, 18, 19, 23, 32

Shechem 80, 81, 83, 86, 115, 121, 153
Sidon 28, 31, 33–34, 160
Silas, tyrant 143, 144
Simon, Maccabean ruler 29, 31, 33–34, 35, 37, 45, 51, 59, 60, 62, 64–65, 67–73, 75, 93, 95, 98, 110, 120, 121, 136, 165
Sinai 5, 105, 120
Skythopolis 33, 59, 65, 80, 88–91, 97, 100, 102, 103, 111–112, 136, 146, 148, 151, 153
Sosius, Q., Roman commander 163–164
Sparta 5, 63
Strato's Tower 98–99, 105, 120–122, 136
Sykamenos (Shikmona) 99
Syria 4, 5, 15, 47; Roman province 149
Syrian War, Sixth 4, 22

Tarichiae 154, 160
Taurus mountains 52
'Teacher of Righteousness' 93
Tekoa 49
Tell el-Rumeideh 35
Tell es-Saidiyeh 99
Tell Hazor 60–62
Theodoros, lord of Philadelphia 78–79, 102–104, 111–112, 123, 126, 129, 136
Theodotos, Seleukid envoy 45
Tigranes, Armenian king 133–134, 140, 143
Timarchos, Seleukid king 44, 47, 49, 52
Timotheos, Seleukid governor 29–32, 33, 35, 39, 74
Tobiads of Ammanitis 3, 4, 5, 29–30, 93
Trachonitis 142
Tripolis 88
Tryphon, Seleukid king 58–59, 63–65, 67, 69–72, 81, 93, 121
Tyre 28, 31, 33–34, 148, 154, 159

Umm Qais (Gadara) 103

Ventidius Bassus, P., Roman commander 162

Wadi Ali 18–19

Yarkon, river (Nahr el-Auja) 120
Yarmuk river 33, 111, 112

Zacharias, Maccabean commander 29
Zenon Kotylas, lord of Philadelphia 73–74, 78–79, 102, 123, 126, 145, 148
Zeus Olympios 6
Zoara 128
Zoilos, lord of Dor 98–99